DEVELOPING PUBLIC

FINANCE IN EMERGING

MARKET ECONOMIES

DEVELOPING PUBLIC

FINANCE IN EMERGING

MARKET ECONOMIES

EDITED BY
KÁLMÁN MIZSEI

© 1994 by the Institute for EastWest Studies

Printed in the United States of America.

The Institute for EastWest Studies does not take or encourage specific policy positions. It is committed to encouraging and facilitating the discussion of important issues of concern to East and West. The views expressed in this report do not necessarily reflect the opinion of the Board of Directors, the officers, or the staff of the Institute.

Distributed by:
    Westview Press
    5500 Central Ave.
    Boulder, Colorado 80301
    (800) 456-1995

Library of Congress Cataloguing-in-Publication data

Developing public finance in emerging market economies / edited by Kálmán Mizsei.
    p. cm.
    ISBN 0-913449-36-9. — ISBN 0-8133-2198-0 (Westview) : $23.84
    1. Finance, Public—Central Europe.   2. Budget—Central
Europe.   3. Economic stabilization—Central Europe.
4. Post-communism—Central Europe.   5. Finance,
Public—Spain.   I. Mizsei, Kálmán.
HJ1000.7.D48   1993
336.47—dc20
                                                                93-23606
                                                                CIP

Contents

Foreword

In February 1993, the Institute for EastWest Studies held a conference on "Public Finance Reform in the Transitional Countries of East Central Europe" in the Czech town of Řež. The purpose of this conference was to organize a group of regional experts to discuss the formidable problems facing East Central Europe during its difficult transition period. It was intended that a cross-fertilization of ideas among the experts would provide some framework for future long-term reforms. A critical component of the transition to market economies of these countries is undoubtedly reform of the state budget. Major budget restructuring is badly needed in order to achieve fiscal balances and to promote the efficient use of financial resources while improving the government's ability to provide better-targeted social services.

An introductory chapter presents many of the themes that arose during the discussions and ties together the papers, which are updated and revised versions of those presented at the conference. The participants observed that in the course of economic transition, the fast-track reform countries in the region, with the exception of the Czech Republic, have run into growing imbalances in their national budgets. These countries are experiencing a reduction in real GDP, a decrease in tax revenues, and high unemployment. This will lead to continued transitional deficits that are unlikely to improve until a period of sustained growth can be achieved. With the expenditure side of the budget being reduced by 30%–45% in real terms, due in large part to subsidy cuts, the short-term problem would appear to come on the revenue side. However, in the long term, it was decided that deep structural reform on the expenditure side would prove to be a more challenging obstacle for these governments.

I believe that this volume should command the attention of both regional policy makers and analysts as an up-to-date assessment of the difficult but crucial goal of achieving macroeconomic stabilization during the first years of transition.

Anthony M. Solomon
Chairman, IEWS Economics Program
January 1994

Editor's Acknowledgments

I would like to thank Jacek Rostowski for his accurate advice in conceptualizing the project. From the Institute for EastWest Studies, I am particularly grateful to Jean de Fougerolles for his vital assistance in organizing the project, conference, and book, and to Rosalie Morales Kearns, former Publications Editor, Amy Lew, IEWS Word Processing Officer, and Richard Levitt, Director of Publications, for their dedicated work finishing this volume.

I also wish to thank the Pew Charitable Trusts for financing my position as Pew Economist in Residence at the Institute for EastWest Studies. I am grateful for the additional support of IEWS programs provided by the Ford Foundation, the Rockefeller Brothers Fund, the William and Flora Hewlett Foundation, the Arcana Foundation, the John D. and Catherine T. MacArthur Foundation, and the Scherman Foundation.

1

Fiscal Crises During Economic Transition in East Central Europe: An Overview

KÁLMÁN MIZSEI
JACEK ROSTOWSKI

1. INTRODUCTION

One of the most pressing problems of the transition economies, even the "first wave" ones (i.e., those that have achieved preliminary macroeconomic stabilization and an important degree of transformation into market economies), is a large and growing gap between public revenues and expenditures (see figure 1 at the end of this chapter). This problem affects Hungary and Poland in particular, but, as this introductory chapter argues, the better performance of the Czechoslovak budget was partly (although not entirely) a consequence of the postponement of hard decisions on microeconomic restructuring. This volume analyzes the reasons for growing budgetary gaps in most of the transition economies of East Central Europe; it also tries to assess the longer-term implications of large budget deficits for debt and inflation.

In the short run, the Central European fiscal crisis has been caused by a fall in revenues, while in the long run the major problem is overspending. The latter problem is exacerbated by the fact that the level of budgetary redistribution (especially in the former Czechoslovakia and Hungary) is similar to that in the Scandinavian countries, which have some of the highest levels of GDP in the world, rather than to middle-income countries of similar levels of development. Even as regards the "short-term" problem of the fall in revenue, it is unclear to what extent this is due to the depression in registered output and is therefore cyclical—so that it can be expected to disappear as output recovers—and to what extent it is mainly structural, resulting from the fundamental changes in the nature of these economies. One example of such changes, stressed by McKinnon (1991), is that the state is no longer able to interfere directly in the management of state-owned enterprises (SOEs). Another, stressed by Rostowski (1993a), is the very rapid shift in the composition of GDP from the state sector to the private sector.

2. PROBLEMS ON THE REVENUE SIDE

The short-run cyclical causes of lower revenue levels in Central Europe operate through a number of channels. Tougher monetary regimes (as in Poland) squeeze liquidity on the micro level; lower inflation disburdens the enterprises from the bulk of the previous inflation tax, but simultaneously strains them financially because of a lack of automatic liquidity financing. Moreover, the measures taken by Poland's Balcerowicz plan in 1990 (followed by a similar set of reform steps in Czechoslovakia in 1991) increased domestic *and* foreign competition on the internal markets. Finally, the well-known effects of the collapse of the CMEA (Comecon) in 1991 also contributed to the liquidity squeeze, well demonstrated by the Polish data of de Crombrugghe in this volume. Similar phenomena occurred in each of the first wave reform countries. The problem, however, is different in the rest of the region. In the Balkan countries as well as in the former Soviet Union—with the exception of Estonia and Latvia—more or less automatic liquidity financing still prevails. Yet this has not saved these "non-stabilizing" countries from budgetary problems that are of at least equal severity to those of the Central European stabilizers.

Turning to the structural or systemic causes of the fall in budget revenue, we again have a number of elements involved. The disintegration of the system of hierarchical control in the economy left few countervailing forces against SOEs' natural tendency to minimize profits. In Poland, managers of SOEs who are responsible to the workforce rather than to owners have little reason to make profits, 40% of which they would then have to pay in corporate income tax. In fact, it is surprising and encouraging that Polish workforces have sufficiently long time horizons to induce them to maintain the capital of the firm rather than consume it. This can be seen from the fact that the overall profitability of the SOE sector is positive in spite of quite high depreciation allowances, which are counted as costs (see the chapter on Poland by Alain de Crombrugghe). However, once profit attracts tax at a 40% rate, it becomes pointless for a Polish SOE.

In all three countries, the time horizon of the managers has become very short as the prospect of privatization has approached, or as future enterprise governance became increasingly unpredictable. In all three countries there were, and are, important opportunities for managers to participate as purchasers in the privatization process. Reducing the paper and real profitability of the SOE puts off outside buyers and increases managers' ability to buy a larger share of the firm. If it is believed that an outside takeover is unavoidable, asset stripping to the benefit of an outside company owned by the management may be the optimal strategy. Finally, under most circumstances, the unavoidable lack of clear rules for privatization means that the maximum return to managerial effort is likely to be through what has been called "property rights seeking behavior" (Rostowski 1993b). Managerial concentration on this must result in a reduction in the profitability of the ordinary commercial activity of the firm.

Like privatization, restructuring has also resulted in a reduction of taxable enterprise profits. Revealing which enterprises are unprofitable enables them to set operating profits against reserves, which cannot be taxed. One can see this most clearly in Hungary, where the structural reforms are the most advanced. Moreover, there is a rollover effect from the revelation of the true financial state of the real sector compared to that of the financial sector. In Hungary, the latter lost profitability one to two years after the real sector, as the previous profits of the banks were based on the lack of a realistic assessment of low-quality assets. Similarly, market-oriented tax regulations, such as more realistic reserves against losses and amortization rules, also reduced the effective corporate tax rate.

However, success in completing restructuring can be expected to play an important role in improving the tax base of the economies concerned in the medium term. Here the effectiveness of wage policies can have a crucial significance: the lower a country has been able to keep real wages, the more chance it has to maintain enterprise profits at levels that make the financing of restructuring possible (as well as generating more tax revenue in the short term). The most restraint in this respect has been shown by Czechoslovakia from 1990 to 1993 (and this has been reflected in continuing large revenues from the corporate income tax in that country), although Hungary and Poland have not lagged all that much behind. However, while Czechoslovakia seems to benefit from the highest profitability in the state-owned enterprise sector, providing the resources necessary for restructuring, it also seems to be experiencing the smallest amount of actual restructuring, as can be seen from its very low level of unemployment. This seems to be a result of the absence of financial pressure on SOEs, which is the other effect of low wage pressure in that country. An exception to this apparent lack of industrial restructuring in Czechoslovakia is the very important contribution of foreign investors in that country.

While real wages in domestic currencies have decreased, they have increased sharply internationally in these years, as currencies have appreciated in real terms. It seems that the relatively high Polish real wages are both an expression of the successes of Polish transition so far, but also of relatively weak wage restraint due to the strong position of trade unions. Still, on balance the performance of Polish governments in controlling wages in these years is something few expected, given the disadvantageous political system in that country in the early years of transformation.

The explosive growth of the private sector in these countries is a further structural cause of the fall in budget revenues: the tax administration has been faced in a matter of a few years with hundreds of thousands of new taxpaying businesses (a huge increase), all of which are highly motivated to evade taxes, in place of the several tens of thousands of state enterprises that provided the tax base in the past. The technique of tax administration has had to be completely overhauled: whereas in the past, the accounts of every taxpaying SOE were examined individually, the new circumstances require the development of Western-style random mechanisms of control. The requisite change in systems, organization, and mentality could not happen overnight. However, it does suggest that one may expect a J-curve in effective taxation rates, with a sharp fall as the private sector expands explosively in the first few years of transition, followed by a steady improvement as the tax administration slowly adjusts to the new situation. The danger is that one will in fact have an L-curve rather than a J-curve, if habits of evasion, built up in the first years of the transition, become entrenched. One can also think of implementing much more severe penalties than now exist for tax avoidance; however, one has to keep in mind that the societies of East Central Europe will accept such measures only if they are accompanied by at least some lowering of the marginal tax rates.

Thus, during the early years of transition, general government revenues have decreased sharply; the most spectacular fall has occurred in Czechoslovakia (data are still somewhat confused, but according to what are probably reliable IMF computations presented in this volume, general government revenues fell from over 70% to 52% of GDP between 1989 and 1992), while in Hungary the fall was smaller, partly because the basic elements of a market- oriented tax structure had been in place since 1988. Hungary is the only country of the region where personal income tax, profit tax, and VAT were in place before the political turmoil of 1989. Poland, with its history of near-hyperinflation and stabilization, presents a picture rather like a seesaw, with revenue falling in 1989, rising sharply in 1990 and then falling steadily in the subsequent two years (see de Crombrugghe).

The tax systems and marginal tax rates show a very strong convergence between the three countries: corporate income tax rates vary at around 40% to 50%, as do marginal personal income taxes; VAT has gradually become a more important source of government revenue, with Hungary having the highest rates, but the two other countries have similar structures, and rate differences are actually minor. The social security system is one of the most significant burdens everywhere, resulting in high linear contributions on wages (those in Czechoslovakia being somewhat lower than in Hungary and Poland). Payroll and wage taxes are everywhere a significant component of the revenue side.

3. PROBLEMS ON THE EXPENDITURE SIDE

Before 1990, the engagement of general government in redistributing the national product was very large in all three countries, though it was smallest in Poland and the highest probably in Czechoslovakia. At present, the most extensive system of expenditures of the three countries is to be found in Hungary. In that country, the last communist governments had planned, but for political reasons did not introduce, a comprehensive reform of the "state household." Its aim was to cut energetically the generous social welfare expenditures that got out of control at the end of the 1980s. However, not only did the last communist governments fail to undertake the necessary measures, but the first democratically elected government also postponed them.

Consequently, while revenues have decreased not only in absolute terms but also relative to the declining recorded GDP, the proportion of expenditure relative to GDP has not changed significantly in the last four years, implying a fall in real government expenditures of about 20% since 1989. Furthermore, only very modest structural reforms have been undertaken in order to disburden future taxpayers. Most striking is the high share (above 10%) of the pension system in GDP; reforms introduced in 1993 are too modest and will not relieve the central budgets' burden in the foreseeable future. Child allowances are also generous. Finally, large-scale unemployment has contributed to the deteriorating budgetary position.

It is instructive to compare the efforts made on the expenditure side by the various countries. As we have seen in Hungary, real expenditures have fallen by about 20% since 1989; in Poland, the fall has been about 30%; according to van der Willigen (in her chapter in this volume), it has been an astonishing 45%–50% in Czechoslovakia. The huge size of the expenditure reduction in Czechoslovakia is partly explained by the enormous share of government expenditure to GDP in 1989 (over 70%). Much of this was cross-subsidization within the state industrial sector, which has proved relatively easy to eliminate in all three countries. In 1992, general government expenditure as a share of GDP was about 55% in Czechoslovakia, significantly below the Hungarian level of about 64% (which has remained roughly constant as a share of GDP since 1989), and significantly above the Polish figure of 45%.[1] However, consolidation of financial transfers between different levels of government is unfortunately still very primitive, even in the three most advanced postcommunist economies; as Semjén shows in this volume, general government expenditure varied widely according to different estimates, with the lowest estimate being 57% of GDP. A great degree of caution in interpreting the figures is, therefore, well advised.

The relative size of general government revenues in Poland (approximately 38% of GDP) is much lower than in Czechoslovakia (52% of GDP in 1992) and Hungary (58% of GDP). Thus both Hungary, with the highest share of expenditure in GDP, and Poland, with the lowest, have excessive deficits (roughly 7% of GDP in each country), while Czechoslovakia had a relatively small one in 1992 (3% of GDP according to van der Willigen). The smallness of the Czechoslovak deficit was due on the one hand to the thoroughness with which expenditure was cut in that country, and on the other to the relative buoyancy of tax revenues (in particular corporate income tax revenues). What these figures show is that if deficits are to be reduced (as they need to be—see section 6), then this must take the form of expenditure reduction in Hungary, but in Poland it may be possible to increase revenues through better tax administration, though probably not through increased tax rates.[2]

4. THE CZECHOSLOVAK PARADOX

The markedly different performance of the Czechoslovak fiscal sphere is one of the most interesting developments in Central Europe. Czechoslovakia showed considerable restraint in its social policies between 1990 and 1992. Consequently, the share of these expenditures in GDP has only slightly increased, i.e., their real value has diminished while enterprise subsidies dried up. This is not much different from what has happened in the two other countries, but the Czechoslovaks were marginally tougher than anyone else. On top of this, wage policies were very restrictive in the same period. This has resulted in a situation in which profits have not plummeted the way they have in the other first wave reformers. This is the crucial difference between Czechoslovakia and the other two countries, and it is an extraordinary achievement given that recorded GDP has fallen in the period by 20%. The share of profit tax in GDP has remained virtually unchanged between 1989 and 1992, as the numbers of van der Willigen in this book indicate.

On the other hand, it is also true that the economic transformation in the former Czechoslovakia is in many respects behind that in Hungary and Poland. Microeconomic restructuring has only started. This has helped enterprises whose output has decreased considerably not to fire employees. In the Czech Republic, unemployment virtually does not exist, therefore it is no large burden on the budget.[3] Unemployment benefits have been constructed from the very beginning to discourage unemployment rather than encourage it. However, there have been no enterprise bankruptcies at all, i.e., the threat of business failure has not pushed firms towards economizing labor costs.

Beginning in the fall of 1993, microeconomic adjustment will finally begin to appear in the Czech Republic: the capital market will value the assets privatized with vouchers, and bankruptcy rules will slowly start working. These effects, combined with the abolition of formal wage controls and the unpleasant consequences of the breakup of the country, may increase the pressure on the budget.[4] Deficits, as shown by van der Willigen, had already started to build up in 1992—particularly in Slovakia—and may increase in 1993. Still, the low public debt inherited from the past may allow the successor states to avoid the further expenditure cuts (and possible tax increases) required of Hungary and Poland. The expectations are widespread that in this respect also the Czechs will do better than the Slovaks. However, recent events in Slovakia seem to show that expectations about extreme differences between short-term developments in the two countries are probably exaggerated.

5. THE CRISIS IN THE BANKING SECTOR

The way the countries will handle the bad debt problem in the banking sector is an issue that will have a direct impact on the size of public debt in the years to come.[5] In Czechoslovakia, the Konsolidacni banka was formed in the initial phase of transition to take over working capital financing loans from the banking sector; subsequently, some of the privatization revenues were used to recapitalize the banking sector. As of 1993, the bad debt problem has already recurred, as a suitable incentive structure in the financial sector is not yet in place.

At the end of 1992, Hungary implemented a poorly designed loan consolidation program. Bad assets were replaced, to the value of 150 billion forints (less than $2 billion) by long-term government bonds. Again, the bulk of these assets will not be recovered and the bonds are going to increase the public debt. Bank recapitalization was supposed to come in 1993, again without any mechanism or conditionality to secure improvement in bank lending. The government's inability to act on a complex subject like this on the eve of the 1994 elections has postponed the new loan consolidation; "debtor consolidation," however, is going ahead without much guarantee that this is the last bailing out of firms. The generous government guarantees to ailing firms is especially worrisome because it implicitly increases the public debt; its real extent will be faced by the new, post-election government.

The Polish "Banking Agreement" regulation, which will be in effect for three years from early 1993, tries to look at the issue in a more complex way. Its initial phase is recapitalization of the banks to the level of 12% capital adequacy ratio (according to the Cook Committee weighing). Subsequently, enterprises can apply for financial restructuring at their lead banks (since the courts are generally unable as yet to deal with insolvency procedures sufficiently rapidly or on a sufficiently large scale). The banks then organize the agreement, and consent of 51% of the creditors (and of the credits they represent) will be enough to strike the deal. The law also tries to generate a secondary market for debts and provide incentives to concentrate the ownership of bad assets outside the banking system, as debt-for-equity swaps are envisaged for claims exceeding 30% of the capital of the debtor firm.

6. IMPLICATIONS FOR INFLATION AND NATIONAL DEBT

In spite of the increasing budgetary gap in all three countries, inflation has decreased significantly over the last three years. Each of the countries has experienced a "corrective inflation," i.e., one that eliminated shortages through price liberalization. The impact of this was obviously less in Hungary (but still noticeable) and the strongest in Poland. Besides price liberalization, the introduction of new taxes, especially of VAT, has caused large price jumps. Over time, however, fewer such one- time operations were left and consequently their effect has been declining. If we take the producer price index as a good indicator of where the consumer price index is tending, then we can expect inflation to decline over the next few years in all three countries. In Hungary, for instance, PPI inflation was 12% in 1992 while CPI inflation was 22% (see figure 2). However, the level of "underlying" inflation cannot be calculated simply by cleaning headline inflation of relative price adjustments and by ending up with something quite close to the producer price index: the deficit and debt levels in the various countries will play a crucial role in its determination.

Hungarian economists believed in the 1980s that the elimination of subsidies to enterprises would close the budgetary gap. However, as we have seen, the combined effects of the shrinking tax base, as well as increasing expenditures on certain welfare items, have on the contrary resulted in growing deficits. However, the impact of the deficit on inflation has been modest so far. The primary reasons for this are that household savings have soared and, at the same time, the banking sector has reduced credit to nongovernment. The initial cause of the latter has not been crowding out by government borrowing, but was rather the weak financial situation of the enterprises. Tougher financial regulations have caused a very cautious lending policy by the banks towards enterprises. Consequently, deposit rates have been able to sharply decrease below the consumer price index. Government paper has been priced only slightly above the deposit rates and yet loan rates have remained high.

In this way, the savings of the households, and to some extent those of the business sector, have financed the budget deficit through the intermediation of the financial sector, while the credit crunch imposed by the banks has resulted in sharply falling deposit and government paper rates through 1992 and the first months of 1993, in spite of the government's growing demand on the money market. As a result, in 1992 the public debt actually might have decreased in real terms (data is quite messy in this respect as well; see Semjén in this volume) and has not increased in terms of (the falling) GDP. However, this should be regarded as an exceptional situation. Persistence of high deficits will inevitably lead to further increasing public debt (now about 80% of GDP), increasing interest rates, and growing inflationary pressure. Without serious measures here, one cannot hope that consumer price inflation will in fact fall to the level of producer price inflation. As of the writing of this introduction, one is rather witnessing the accumulation of inflationary pressures.

In this respect, the situation is similar in the three countries, although the problem is the most intense in Hungary. Trade balances have deteriorated in 1993, primarily because in 1991 and 1992 exchange rates have increasingly been used as primary tools of anti-inflationary policy. Consequently, domestic currencies got increasingly overvalued; the European recession added to the problem. As devaluations have become inevitable, their impact adds to the pressure of growing public debt.

The situation is similar in Poland to the extent that the bulk of recent government deficits has been financed by the crowding out of credit to nongovernment through the financial sector's intermediation. As in Hungary, banks have tightened their lending policies considerably, so that increased government borrowing has been accompanied by falling, rather than increasing, interest rates on government paper. However, it must be remembered that were it not for continuing government borrowing, loan rates could be even lower, improving the profitability of the corporate sector, making it possible for banks to lend more to that sector safely, and possibly even increasing government tax revenue.

Furthermore, at present about 40% of the net domestic assets (NDA) of the Polish banking system consists in credit to government. Since NDA constitutes about 22% of GDP, and has remained at this level since the end of 1990—suggesting that there is no reason to expect it to increase significantly in the medium term—the noninflationary financing of a deficit of current dimensions (approximately 7% of GDP) is clearly impossible. It would require a 50% fall in real credit to nongovernment in the first year, and the total elimination of such credit in the second year of such a deficit.

In order to avoid such a situation, the National Bank of Poland (NBP) ensures that the banking system has sufficient liquidity to finance the deficit without excessive crowding out of credit to nongovernment. The deficit is thus financed from four sources: crowding out, NBP emission for the purpose of deficit financing (which accounted for about one-third of the deficit in 1992), NBP emission so as to maintain the liquidity of the banking system (increase in rediscount credit made available to commercial banks), and increased nominal money (and therefore credit) creation through NBP acceptance of an increase in the money multiplier. Credit to non-banking in Poland is about 13% of GDP, a very low figure indeed by international standards. If we accept that further real crowding out is therefore possible only to a very limited extent, then in the medium term any large deficits in Poland will have to be financed by emission.[6]

This is how we come up against some very unpleasant monetarist arithmetic for Poland. Zloty M2/GDP is about 23%, and has remained at about this level for two and a half years.[7] With a money multiplier of about two, a deficit of 5% of GDP financed through emission implies a rate of inflation in excess of 40% per annum. Sharply growing foreign debt service obligations from mid-1994, as well as recently growing current account deficits, add to the vulnerability of the Polish situation.[8]

The above problems of financing the deficit are smaller in Hungary, where the deficit is of approximately the same size as in Poland, but where the money supply was equivalent to 53% of GDP at the end of 1992. For the moment, such problems are effectively absent in the former Czechoslovakia, where the deficit was 3% of GDP, and the money supply was the equivalent of 80% of GDP.[9]

Looking at the question of the impact of fiscal deficits on inflation in a longer-term framework, it is useful to examine the ratio of total national debt to GDP. This ratio may be—surprisingly—quite similar in all three countries. According to official figures, the ratio is about 70% in Hungary (according to our figures in this volume, at the end of 1993 this actually might be as high as 80%), 55% in Poland[10] and about 40% in the Czech Republic.[11] However, the picture may change radically once the contingent liabilities of the budget resulting from bad debts in the banking sector are taken into account. Here the fact that the ratio of credit to nongovernment to GDP is very high in the Czech Republic (roughly 80%) works against that country, whereas Poland's very low ratio of CNG/GDP (13%) works in its favor. Hungary lies in between, with a CNG/GDP ratio of about 55%. If about a quarter of CNG needs to be taken over by the budget, then this would imply a total consolidated national debt relative to GDP of about 60% in the Czech Republic and 50% in Poland.[12] In Hungary, the 1992 loan consolidation has already shifted part of the debt to government, but other large-scale operations may take the national debt as high as 90%. A lower net loss to the banking system would mean a greater differentiation between the three countries, as well as lower consolidated debt levels all round.[13] However, the obverse of high ratios of CNG/GDP is high ratios of money supply to GDP, which, as we have already noted, makes the noninflationary financing of large national debts far easier in Hungary and the Czech Republic.

We thus end with the conclusion that both Hungary and Poland have probably reached the end of their opportunities for running large budget deficits that have also seen a decline in inflation such as has been witnessed since 1989. As we have already noted, clear signs of the reversal are already there. Since accelerating inflation would probably have very severe consequences for medium-term economic growth (particularly through its effect on foreign direct investment), both countries are faced with an absolute need to cut budget deficits sharply. In Poland, this may occur partly as a result of increased revenues due to the ongoing economic recovery and an improved tax structure and administration (1993 has seen the introduction of both a unified personal income tax and of the VAT). However, expenditure cuts are also likely to be necessary, particularly as the deficit will be increased by an annual 4% of GDP from mid-1994 because of the need to service foreign debt.[14] In Hungary, almost all of the burden will have to be taken by expenditure cuts. However, a heavily unpopular government is waiting for the elections, expected in the spring of 1994, and thus there is no way to expect the necessary tough decisions with a long-term structural impact to be launched before early 1995.

The Czech Republic is clearly best placed, with both low deficits and probably the lowest national debt, as well as a very high demand for real money balances. However, even here it requires only a somewhat pessimistic estimate of bad debts in the banking system to suggest that the country is almost at the limit of what can be considered a safe ratio of national debt to GDP.

The country study on Spain (as well as the comment on it) in this volume shows that East Central Europe faces disproportionately more difficult tasks than countries that have had the fortune of not experiencing several decades of communist economy. Spain started out after Franco with low taxes, very low public debt, and a fairly capitalist economy—characteristics that not even the fast track reformers (with the partial exception of Czechoslovakia) of East Central Europe share. Spain could expand its state welfare services and accumulate a manageable level of public debt while increasing the tax-raising capacity of the state. The Hungarian and Czech governments, taxing away around 60% of GDP certainly do not have this option; they, as well as the Polish government, have to let the capitalist structures develop, and, at the same time, must make very hard decisions in cutting budgetary expenditures—a task certainly unprecedented in modern economic history.

Figure 1
Government Budget Balance

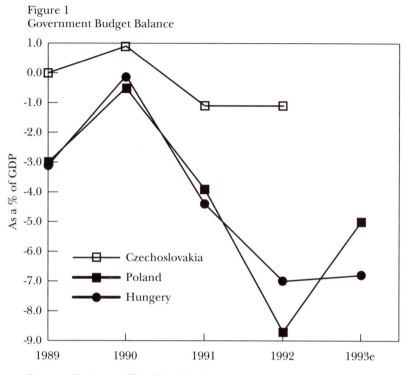

Source: Institute of EastWest Studies.

Figure 2
CPI, PPI, and Exchange Rates

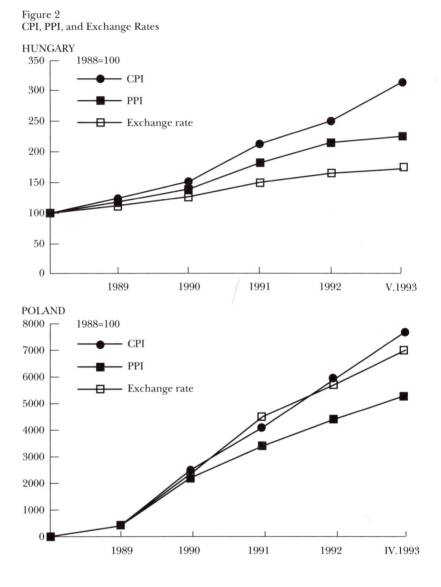

Figure 2 (cont.)

CZECHOSLOVAKIA

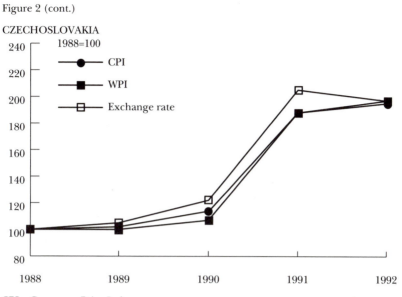

CPI: Consumer Price Index
PPI: Producer Price Index
Source: Institute for EastWest Studies.

NOTES

1. Down from about 55% in 1988.
2. The larger size of the Polish agricultural sector, usually difficult to tax, is another problem. However, this should not be overstressed, as agriculture contributes less than 10% of Poland's GDP.
3. Although underemployment is, of course, a burden on the enterprises.
4. Before what appears to have been a politically motivated revision, the Statistical Office of the Czech Republic registered a 10% fall in industrial output in the first quarter of 1993. This has now been revised to -2%.
5. The authors do not share the opinion formulated by many Western analysts that the old debt of public enterprises should simply be taken over by the state; their recovery after such a transaction would become more doubtful than ever (see Begg and Portes 1992; Mizsei 1993).
6. Increases in the money supply due to increases in the money multiplier have the same effect as emission. Imagine a 50% increase in the nominal money supply as a result of an increase in the money multiplier, of which half goes to finance the deficit: inflation will be 50%. Exactly the same effect would obtain if the money multiplier remained constant at a value of two, and base money were increased by 50%, with all of the additional central bank liabilities constituting additional credit to government. It goes without saying that emission has the same effect whether it results from direct lending by the central bank to government or whether it is due to the central bank maintaining the liquidity of the banking system in the face of government borrowing from the commercial banks.
7. Net foreign liabilities of the banking system (i.e., foreign currency deposits) are roughly equivalent to net foreign assets (i.e., net international reserves), leaving NDA roughly equal to zloty M2.
8. The Polish budget benefited greatly from effectively not servicing its international debt in the critical period of 1990 to 1993.
9. The money/GDP ratio is about the same in the two successor states.
10. On the assumption of a $45 billion foreign debt, a $90 billion GDP and an internal debt equivalent to 10% of GDP.
11. The latter figure is based on an estimate of Czech GDP of $30 billion, and a foreign debt for the Czech Republic of $7 billion, as well as an internal debt of 17% of GDP (see van der Willigen).
12. This would be the equivalent of a loss of 50% on 50% of the loans made to nongovernment by the banking system, which may be somewhat overpessimistic.
13. If the loss is 15% of CNG, then the Hungarian debt becomes 78% of GDP, the Polish 57%, and the Czech 52%.
14. In the absence of any other changes the deficit would then reach 10% of GDP.

REFERENCES

Beggs, D., and R. Portes. 1992. *Enterprise Debt and Economic Transformation: Restructuring of the State Sector in Central and Eastern Europe*. Discussion Paper Series, no. 695. London: Center for Economic Policy.
McKinnon, R. 1991. *The Order of Economic Liberalization*. London and Baltimore: Johns Hopkins University Press.

Mizsei, K. 1993. *Bankruptcy and the Post-Communist Economies of East Central Europe*. New York: Institute for EastWest Studies.

Rostowski, J. 1993a. The Implications of Rapid Private Sector Growth in Poland. Discussion paper. Center for Economic Performance, London School of Economics.

————. 1993b. Comment on "Privatization in Russia, the First Steps" by Shleiffer and Vishny. Proceedings of National Bureau of Economic Research conference on Russia and Eastern Europe. Chicago University Press: forthcoming.

2

Some Fiscal Problems During Economic Transition in Hungary

ANDRÁS SEMJÉN

1. METHODOLOGICAL CAVEATS CONCERNING FISCAL ANALYSIS FOR HUNGARY

It is not an easy task to analyze the state of Hungarian fiscal affairs. The first difficulty to overcome is the lack of reliable and internationally comparable fiscal data. The Hungarian budgetary and statistical system has never been good at providing such figures, but the difficulties also result from the effect of economic transition on data collection. Part of the problem is due to the marked general deterioration in the coverage (and in some cases the quality) of the Hungarian statistical system. The performance of the monitoring and short-term forecasting unit providing the government with preliminary data and estimations for budgetary planning is also rather weak and perhaps even open to political pressures (or just bound by wishful thinking?). Preliminary and expected data used for budgetary planning often differ from facts very significantly. The Central Statistical Office (CSO) is also not at its best when publishing preliminary estimates, and revisions of preliminary data take sometimes more than a year.

However, part of the problem might be due to the complexity of the Hungarian budget structure. The *general government* encompasses the *central government* containing the *state budget*, the activity of *budgetary chapters* (mainly *ministries* and the *central budgetary institutions* they administer), the activities of numerous *local governments* (sometimes too small to operate efficiently) responsible for their own *local budgetary institutions* (like schools, nurseries, local theaters and museums, etc.), a variety of extra-budgetary funds, and the Social Insurance Fund (SIF). The financial flows between the different entities are almost innumerable; there are extensive transfers among and within the different subsectors of general government, i.e., transfers from extra-budgetary funds to central budgetary institutions, to the state budget and local governments or to other extra-budgetary funds to complicate the picture. According to Hungarian accounting standards, fiscal accounts (presented to the Parliament each year) are not consolidated. Let's suppose that the state budget allocates some money to a budgetary chapter (e.g., a ministry), which then transfers it to a local government as a grant, part of which will be used to pay social security contributions to the SIF, which will use it to finance its expenditures on pensions. The first sum clearly contains "pure" public expenditure, however, as we move downwards along this tree, we will count some part of the original expenditure again and again at each level. László (1993) wittily pointed out that according to this methodology the share of general government redistribution to GDP in principle might easily reach more than 100%. However, as the World Bank observes, "data limitations preclude a proper consolidation of Hungarian fiscal accounts, and the authorities, while recognizing the problem, are unable to make an informed guess about the amount of double-counting of revenues and expenditures" (World Bank 1992).

Another problem is caused by the economically not always very meaningful concepts (categories) used in Hungarian fiscal accounts, which significantly differ from the structure (the rows) of General Financial Statistics (GFS) (World Bank 1992, 14–15).[1] It is evident, however, that both presentations contain serious double-counting, and overstate the size of the public sector or government.

International organizations like the IMF, the World Bank, and the OECD have been instrumental in bridging the gap between Hungarian and international accounting standards, forcing and helping Hungarian authorities to compile internationally comparable data. However, not only do the GFS and the Hungarian presentation of the consolidated general government budget for 1991 give very different results due to differences in accounting methodology[2] and consolidation,[3] but there are also some differences between OECD (1993) and World Bank data (even the GDP figures for 1988 or 1989 are slightly different). This means that one should be very cautious when using data from different sources. However, despite the numerous differences among data sources, the main conclusions are likely to be the same, whatever source is used.

2. THE SIZE OF GOVERNMENT

It is a commonplace that the government is oversized in Hungary. While this is certainly true, because of some features of the Hungarian budgetary system described earlier, it is not easy to tell how large the government actually is.[4] In 1991, the difference between the Hungarian presentation and the GFS presentation of general government revenue and expenditures ratios to GDP amounted to 8.5%–9% of GDP (World Bank 1992).[5] As table 1 (at the end of the chapter) shows clearly, this difference is significant in international comparison as well. While the Hungarian presentation would place Hungary beyond the top of the range of developed countries, using comparable GFS data would "only" place Hungary in the middle of the group of welfare states, amidst the Netherlands, Denmark and Sweden.[6]

Nevertheless, one thing is certainly clear whichever presentation of data is used: Hungary has a big government, too large proportionate to its economic performance. Though there were serious efforts taken to reduce government spending during recent years, some newly emerging needs calling for an enlargement of the safety net during the transition, together with the long-lasting economic depression deeply rooted in the accumulated "adjustment debt" of the economy, falling output figures, and the contraction of the economy led paradoxically to a relative growth in the size of government spending (illustrated in table 2), despite a considerable fall in expenditures in real terms.[7] (Total general government expenditure in real terms is estimated to decline to 79.8% from its 1989 level by 1993, or to 77.7% excluding interest payments for public debt.)[8]

3. THE REVENUE SIDE

The structure of the revenue side of the Hungarian budget is comparable to that of Western market economies. This relatively favorable situation is due to widespread tax reforms introduced well before the transition process started. Hungary was the first country in Eastern Europe to introduce a market-oriented tax system. The value-added tax and the personal income tax were introduced in 1988, while a corporate income tax, the enterprise profit tax (EPT), was introduced in 1989. In the socialist years, the bulk of government revenues was raised by the taxation of enterprises (as in all socialist countries) and by a complex system of numerous turnover taxes, while direct taxation of individuals raised only very little revenue.[9] The "old taxes" were phased out with the introduction of the new system.

Due to the legacy of the socialist system, the share of enterprise profit tax revenues was too large when it was introduced to replace differentiated profit taxes and some other production- related taxes in 1989.[10] This preponderance was especially obvious when EPT was compared with personal income tax (PIT) revenues. Since then, both the statutory tax rate for the enterprise profit tax and EPT's share of GDP have decreased, the latter partly due to numerous tax reliefs granted to offset the effects of the extremely conservative depreciation rates.[11] Generous tax relief was provided from the very start of the system (e.g., to attract foreign investors), available mostly in the form of reduced tax rates, though accelerated depreciation rules, tax deductions, and investment tax credits have also been used.[12] The relief made budgetary planning quite unreliable; as early as 1989, right at the start, EPT receipts totaled 40% less than anticipated, due to tax exemptions, refunds, and arrears. No wonder that the reduction of tax relief and the broadening of the tax base started early, in 1990. The year 1991 saw the tightening of EPT relief for joint ventures, food processing, and retail business, together with the introduction of some new relief (e.g., for capital used in environmental protection, restoration of historic relics, etc.). The overall scale of relief was, however, supposed to diminish. In 1992, shorter asset lives were introduced for new assets to make depreciation more realistic (in accordance with the new Act on Accounting), a necessary fiscal innovation, though reducing the revenue-making capacity of the tax.[13] EPT is now levied on a relatively large base, and can make the cost of capital high in international comparison.[14] However, remaining tax relief (as it was not granted on a uniform basis but reflects sector, location, type of ownership) can still distort investment decisions quite seriously. The revenue-making capacity of EPT has been further eroded by making provisions for bad debt possible (otherwise a most welcome measure) and extending the length of loss carry-forward. There are some other reasons contributing to lower revenues: Kornai (1992a) gives thorough attention to the growing difficulties of tax collection during the transformation process. While in the old system it was relatively simple to collect revenues due to state ownership, the monobank system, and the low number of economic units (the business accounts of a state-owned firm could be easily checked and the monobank could simply deduct the tax due to the budget from the firm's account), with the rapid growth of economic units the administrative complexity of taxation increased dramatically. "These days . . . it is not easy to collect money even from state-owned firms," according to Kornai. Privatization and the rapid growth of new enterprises make things even more complicated, especially as a great part of the new private activities belong to the twilight world of the underground economy.[15] However, if access to legal credit and the capital market is positively tied to tax compliance, there is a chance to improve the situation. The government also contemplates the introduction of some minimum lump-sum taxes; this should also be paid by loss-making enterprises or by those that were granted tax relief.

Graduated personal income taxes were introduced in 1988, with 10 brackets ranging from 20% to 60%. Earnings in the state sector were grossed up to leave net income unaltered; due to widespread overtime work and second jobs, however, after-tax incomes did change. The progressivity of the tax schedule was rather steep, and the same (highest) marginal rate applied to a very wide range; from modest to extremely high incomes. Taxes on some forms of capital income (dividends, interests) were levied using a flat rate (20%) and withheld at the source.[16] Small-scale payments could also be taxed at the source with a flat rate, further reducing the base of the progressive tax. The relatively high basic allowance, the widespread exemptions for different types of incomes (social incomes, etc.), the deductions, the very generous treatment for "small-scale" agriculture and "intellectual activities," and the tax-exempt status of fringe benefits meant that PIT was levied on only about 40% of total household incomes.[17] While the average rate of taxation was rather low (14.5%), the actual rate of taxation on taxable income was much higher. The PIT rules left considerable room for tax avoidance, while at the same time the relative importance of the "hidden economy" made tax evasion quite widespread.

Despite these shortcomings, the introduction of the PIT was a major step toward increasing public awareness of the costs of the public sector. Nevertheless, the Hungarian PIT schedule was not very up-to-date; it was conceived in the spirit of the traditional Swedish-type tax system (a well-known failure by that time), with strong disincentive effects and a clear motivation to tax evasion. Though the steep progressivity of the system might have been considered instrumental in gaining public support, it clearly undermined tax compliance at the very beginning and did not serve the interests of the emerging market economy. The tax base was far from comprehensive; it can be considered surprisingly narrow in the light of the tax reforms of the 1980s.[18]

In 1989, the number of PIT brackets was at first reduced to eight, while the top and bottom rates slightly decreased (the new range was from 17% to 56%). Increased personal, child, and retiree allowances also contributed to a slight reduction of average tax rates. A year later, the PIT schedule was modified again; the number of brackets was reduced to five, and the top marginal rate was lowered to 50%. The first democratic Parliament voted for the increase of the number of tax brackets to seven (a step backwards), and diminished the bottom rate to 12%. However, as the rates were not adjusted fully for inflation, bracket creep could ironically lead to an increase in effective tax rates in 1991. For 1992, the number of brackets was drastically decreased, and the highest marginal tax rate was also reduced to 40%. The same tax rates (0%, 25%, 35%, 40%) are still in effect in 1993 (despite some half- hearted efforts by the Ministry of Finance to raise them again).

Self-employment and small businesses gained importance in the pattern of employment with the expansion of the private sector, making the collection of the PIT more difficult; tax evasion now constitutes a major obstacle to the full utilization of the revenue-raising capacity of the PIT. This is just another example of Kornai's famous fiscal trap: "The larger the private sector's share of production, the harder it becomes to collect taxes" (Kornai 1992a). Though gross household incomes have reached 65%–70% of GDP, households' taxable cash income totaled only 37%–40% of GDP. The narrowness of the tax base required relatively high statutory tax rates that gave strong incentives to tax evasion and avoidance. The combined marginal taxation of wage costs (including employers' payroll taxes and contributions to the Solidarity Fund) through PIT, employers' and employees' social security contributions, and unemployment insurance premiums is very high; this, together with the increasing cost-consciousness of the business sector, resulted in serious changes in the structure of remuneration packages. A rapid growth of tax-exempt fringe benefits took place (mostly in the private sector), reducing tax revenues and raising important questions concerning horizontal equity.

Equity concerns can also be raised in connection with tax relief (deductions up to 30% of taxable income) given to promote investment and raise the domestic demand for privatization.[19] These problems can be used to justify the importance of the broadening of the tax base. The Budget Law for 1993 was brave enough to tackle some of the problems; one-third of the estimated fringe benefits (totaling 65 billion forints) became fully taxable, and the tax treatment of "intellectual" work and small agricultural producers became less permissive, which is expected to broaden the tax base by some 7.5 billion forints. Another way to increase PIT revenues can be to bring social income (especially cash benefits) under the umbrella of taxation. Taxing family allowances has been recommended by many, including the IMF (Kopits et al. 1990); it is also on the agenda of the new fiscal consolidation program of the government (Pénzügyminisztérium 1993a).[20] However useful this could be for the revenue side, there are serious doubts whether this is the right way to achieve better targeting.[21] A controversial issue of reforming the PIT is the taxation of interest and dividend income. There are demands from political parties to reduce these taxes in accordance with the preferential treatment of savings and investments. Dividends paid by companies liable to 40% EPT can become tax-exempt in line with the new consolidation program (if companies enjoying a preferential EPT status pay the tax difference), and tax rates on interest can be reduced while levying the tax on deposits in foreign currency as well.[22]

Nevertheless, despite the serious efforts put towards tightening the tax system, there has been very little success so far in translating the legal broadening of the tax base into revenue. The government was not determined enough in the relatively new corporatist system of negotiations between the "social partners," and always agreed to give some new relief in place of the old ones being phased out, thus sacrificing the very sense of the whole process.

Value-added tax was introduced with three rates, 0%, 15%, and 25%, and there were also some commodities exempt from VAT. The standard 25% rate (generating nearly 95% of VAT revenues) applied only to some 40% of consumer expenditures; the 15% rate applied to most services, while the zero rate was "levied" on most food products, fuels, pharmaceuticals, household heating services, some cultural goods and services, etc. An additional excise tax was levied on items like tobacco and beverages. The VAT applied to imported items as well, while exports were entitled to a rebate.[23] There was also an investment VAT-rebate; in 1988 it was only 20% due to revenue considerations, next year it was raised to 40%, and in 1990 to 60%, with a full rebate made available for investments in disadvantaged regions. In 1991 the investment rebate was increased to 80%. The government contemplated a modest VAT reform for 1993; the main elements of this were the complete abolition of the zero rate, while introducing a two-rate (10% and 20%) schedule; and the elimination of some VAT refunds, especially for self-constructed housing. It was estimated that 35% of all purchases would have been in the 10% bracket. However, this proposal was found too radical and faced strong opposition from the public, the trade unions, and the political parties (even within the coalition). The government retreated and submitted a less radical proposal to the Parliament, where a compromise was reached; the zero rate was maintained for household energy and pharmaceuticals only, while the preferential rate was lowered to 6% (instead of the 8% proposed by the government), while the normal rate remained 25%. The government first seemed to be happy with this "two and a half rate" VAT, although the difference between the two positive rates seemed to be too big, and certainly contributed to evasion.[24] The mid-year increase of the lower (preferential) VAT rate to 10% in 1993 (in connection with the supplementary austerity budget made to meet IMF requirements) and the narrowing range of goods with a zero rate (to pharmaceuticals) made the Hungarian VAT rates very high in international comparison. Though the uniformity of the system may attract some purist tax theoreticians, it would be found rather unusual in most developed European market economies and may further increase the temptation for tax evasion. The new regulation forcing every shopkeeper to give receipts to customers for all purchases seems to be unlikely to achieve perfect compliance (see note 24).

Customs and tariffs also contribute to government revenues; nevertheless, as Hungary has to open its markets gradually to Western competition according to the EC Association Agreement, the share of these revenues cannot be expected to rise parallel with the growth of imports. This is reflected in the fact that the share of customs duties to imports, reaching 15.2% in 1989, was down to 8.9% in 1992.

The Act on Local Government was a milestone in local government finance. It conferred upon local governments the right to impose certain local taxes; however, the different taxes (the "local tax menu") were clearly defined by the law, and the tax base was more or less also regulated centrally. Local governments could only decide whether they wanted to impose a certain kind of tax from the "menu" or not, and could also determine the rates to be used. The 1991 budget projected revenues of 26 billion forints from local taxes; however, the actual revenues collected turned out to be more modest, about 18 billion forints, due mainly to the reluctance of local governments to exercise their taxing power and risking their re-election probabilities. The law also declared that some of the PIT revenues should go to local governments, although it left determination of the exact share to the annual budgets.[25] This share was set at 50% at first, but in the 1993 budget it was reduced to 30%. Not even these reductions proved to be effective in enforcing the widespread use of local taxes.

If we deal with the general budget, we should not forget about contributions to the Social Insurance Fund, a major extra-budgetary fund financing social security and public health. The contribution rate is distortionally high, and international comparisons show that the share of GDP spent on social security is very high, too.[26] (We shall return to this question later.) Other wage-related contributions (e.g., employers' and employees' contributions to the Solidarity Fund paying unemployment compensation) make the wage bill even higher. Though the above-mentioned contribution rates are already too high and should be reduced to avoid over-taxing and a loss of international competitiveness due to high labor costs, they raise too little to cover the expenditures of the funds, so some central government transfers are also needed to keep the SIF afloat. Another problem is the high and ever-growing level of arrears in contributions from enterprises. As some of these enterprises are practically bankrupt, there is little chance that the SIF can ever get hold of this money. Certain large public sector enterprises (e.g., the national rail, MAV) are also among the largest debtors at the SIF.

Though even those budgetary institutions that were formed

originally to administer traditional public sector responsibilities (e.g., schooling, etc.) engaged more and more in activities of a commercial nature during the 1980s, the revenues of budgetary chárges and user fees still constitute only a minor revenue item; it can gain more importance in the future for local government budgets, however, especially if measures are taken to improve the cost recovery of local public services.[27]

Though the above sources and the structure of government revenues are more or less in line with the requirements of market economies, there are certain "built-in" destabilizers, some problems that can make such a system very vulnerable in the course of transition.[28] Some econometric results indicate that during the transition the share of the black or underground economy will be even higher than before. This makes collecting the revenues rather difficult and tax evasion a major problem.[29]

Another problem arises from the fact that most revenue sources are connected to economic performance; whenever a recession or a crisis occurs, revenues are bound to fall, threatening the economy with the danger of deficit.[30] During the last three years, the budget had to face several shocks (one-time and reform-induced events) endemic to the transition process, as the formulation of a new regulatory and legal framework gradually took place, privatization and a proliferation of economic units changed the ownership structure and the size pattern of the economy radically, and continuous economic inefficiency led to many bankruptcies, etc. These processes, though clearly showing some promising signs of a basically healthier way of development for the economy on the one hand, will cause a catastrophe for the budget on the other, since in the short run they lead to shrinkage of the tax base, growing tax and social security contribution arrears, and all in all the melting of budget revenues. The most important such developments and their impact on the budget are summarized in table 3.

4. THE EXPENDITURE SIDE

It is the expenditure side, where the dispersion of data amongst different sources is great, that makes the analysis most difficult. However, despite limited possibilities for comparing data referring to different years, or data "borrowed" from different authors, there seems to be some consensus concerning the main line of reasoning.

Administrative expenditures (reflected in the "General government services" and "Public order & safety" rows of table 4) were touched upon by Kornai (1992a), based on calculations using IMF data. Kornai's figures are somewhat lower than the ones we have in table 4, but even so, he found the Hungarian figures inadmissibly high, especially in comparison with countries like Germany, Chile, or Denmark. He also demonstrated the simultaneous effect of two opposing trends during the transition: one allowing for a reduction of administrative expenditures,[31] and one calling for higher expenditures in many fields.[32] Though Kornai is not very optimistic concerning the prospects of serious cuts in administrative expenditures, the figures envisaged by the Ministry of Finance show great progress in this field. However, this favorable trend is not completely in line with some recent experiences. The government tends to use the creation of new administrative bodies and offices to demonstrate its devotion to facing challenges and solving new problems. Deteriorating standards of living and widening income differences may lead to an increase in the crime rate, calling for a stronger police. There are also vested interests preventing radical cuts in administrative expenditures.

In 1988, fiscal policy proved to be effective in reducing both consumer and production subsidies. The subsidy reduction program brought subsidies down from over 13% of GDP to 7% in 1991 (World Bank 1992; housing subsidies included). This program was necessitated not only by fiscal considerations. Assistance to loss-making firms had to be discontinued anyway to promote market selection, or, in other words, to "harden" the previously soft budget constraint (see Kornai 1992a and his earlier writings on soft budget constraint) and increase the motivation of producers to be economically efficient. Subsidies to consumer prices also had to be eliminated to reduce distortive effects on consumption and on the allocation of resources. However, as subsidy reduction started long before the political change, there was much less to be done in this respect in Hungary than in other post-socialist countries, which meant there was less scope for possible gains for the budget. Nevertheless, the steps already taken had a significant effect on the structure of general government expenditures. Table 5 (borrowed from Muraközi 1992) clearly demonstrates that the turning point was around 1988, when a considerable restructuring of budget expenditures had started. While the share of business subsidies and transfers (capital expenditures or investments, financial assistance to firms, price subsidies to consumers) diminished considerably from 26% of GDP to less than 10% during the 1987–1991 period, social spending and subsidies to the traditional domain of public activities made up for the difference (they rose from 39% to 57% of GDP), not allowing public spending to diminish (see Muraközi 1992). The main tendency is clear; expenditures towards the business sector decreased while transfers to the population started to rise.

Subsidies to enterprises are expected to be reduced further, to

4.5% of total expenditures in 1993 from 10.2% in 1989, while consumer subsidies will mount only to 1.1% instead of 3.9% in 1989. The World Bank suggested that "continued progress in reducing subsidies should permit the elimination of all except urban public transport subsidies, lump-sum housing purchase grants, and, possibly, agricultural export subsidies" (World Bank 1992, 29). Though subsidy reductions are certainly the most important steps taken on the expenditure side in the right direction so far, their net effect on the budget might not be as positive as it seems at first glance. Subsidy cuts might increase the number of bankruptcies, thus leading to loss of tax revenue and an increase in unemployment, requiring more public expenditure on labor market policies; the elimination of price subsidies may increase the poverty line and contribute to increased needs for social assistance. However, their beneficial effects on economic behavior and efficiency certainly far outweigh these side-effects in the longer run.

Another relatively successful chapter of the story was the cutting of housing subsidies. The provision of low fixed-interest housing purchase loans imposed a significant burden on the budget even under low inflation, and might have some perverse redistributive effects. High inflation then converted this subsidy into a bomb threatening to explode in due time. Measures introduced in 1991 reduced the burden on the budget significantly: nevertheless, there are some reasons to worry.[33] Proposals for an indexed mortgage system were not accepted, the repayment subsidies for post-1989 loans already started to have a significant effect on the budget, partly due to the high inflation experienced. Despite all efforts taken, the share of housing subsidies is still high enough (see table 4) and, what is worse, these costly subsidies were ineffective in providing means for maintaining a modest level of new investment in housing. Public housing investment disappeared, and private investment in housing is also at an unprecedented low level, obviously contributing to the recession.[34] In the longer run the unresolved problems of the housing sector might also have significant impact on the budget. Though low rents in the council housing sector are not financed by visible public transfers, but rather by neglecting maintenance work and renewal, the resulting deterioration of physical capital will lead to higher expenses in the long run, or will result in a loss of assets. Although privatization of public services and responsibilities can be a good way of reducing public spending, in the housing sector it might prove to be a failure. The selling off (or sometimes practically giving away) of the housing stock far below the market price will not only leave some of the localities without the most valuable part of their assets, but also will deprive them of the means for an adequate housing policy. If the supply of rented accommodation falls sharply, this might create a need for new types of housing subsidies or might lead to a severe shortage of "social housing," requiring costly investment programs in the future.

The level of social spending has risen dramatically during the last decade. Its share of GDP grew by more then 10% from 1985 to 1991, when it exceeded 37.1%, including consumer price subsidies. The share of total benefits to gross household money income has risen from 33.3% in 1988 to 35% in 1992, while the share of benefits less taxes to gross household money income reached its peak at 20.6% in 1991 (OECD 1993). The same tendency is reflected by a continuous increase in central government transfers as well.

International comparisons in Andorka, Kondratas, and Tóth (1993) indicate that until the mid-1980s, the share of social expenditures to GDP was below the level of OECD social welfare states (Belgium, Denmark, Finland, France, Netherlands, Norway, Sweden), though already at that time exceeding that in lower-income OECD countries (Greece, Ireland, Portugal, Spain, Turkey). However, around the turn of the decade, Hungary caught up with the welfare states in this respect, though ironically on the basis of a decreasing economy. Though to some extent this rise is justified by the increasing need for social assistance due to the transition (unemployment benefits, means-tested local social assistance, etc.), it is certain that such a high share of social expenditures to GDP is unsustainable at the present level of economic development of the country; moreover, the experience of the welfare state may also lead one to question the desirability of this development path and might provide a good case for reducing this very high share anyway.

One of the main problems behind this development is the steadily increasing share of pension payments. This is partly due to unfavorable demographic characteristics and trends and partly to the inclination of the new democratic Parliament to correct some of the "unfair" developments of the system with little or no regard for the present economic conditions.[35] However, the core of the problem is the very low average age of retirement (around 54 years), reflecting relatively low legal retirement ages (55 years for women and 60 for men) and a continual misuse of disability pensions. The widespread use of disability pensions was necessitated by the temporary lack of a proper unemployment insurance scheme in the period when unemployment started to climb; however, after the introduction of such benefits and some elements of an unemployment-related early retirement scheme, the problems embedded in the misuse of disability pensions have remained. Though these problems of the pension system were already well known at the beginning of the transition period, very little progress was achieved in this respect (a parliamentary resolution to raise the retirement age gradually starting after the end of the first democratic government's term, and some legal progress to make a two- or three-tier pension system possible). The great fuss created about the formation (election) of self-governing bodies to manage a separate Health Insurance Fund and a Pension Fund can hardly hide the fact that these bodies are highly unlikely to solve the fiscal problems inherent in the present situation.

Another fiscal sustainability problem is caused by the fact that the Hungarian welfare system has been characterized by universal benefits that benefited not only the poor but the middle classes as well. Though this can be considered bad targeting, this feature was instrumental in creating social support for a system that at least provided some benefits and protection to marginal groups (like the Roma) within the society. Better targeting is urgently needed to focus the resources on the needy, although this cannot be achieved without jeopardizing social consensus concerning the benefits. The restructuring of the system seems to be inevitable in the longer run, and it is a pity that the first democratic government was not determined to do something while its "grace period" (honeymoon with the electorate) still lasted. However, it should be kept in mind that better targeting is not necessarily identical with means-testing, and some benefits administered according to objective demographic characteristics may be quite well targeted. In spite of all this, the present system of family and maternity benefits is unlikely to last long; there must be a trade-off between political and fiscal considerations. Equity considerations in many cases would point in the same direction as fiscal ones; however, their impact on the public or on politicians is not strong enough to enforce the change needed.

5. THE PUBLIC SECTOR DEFICIT

Hungary has a long tradition of accumulating public debts. Kornai (1992a) and Muraközi (1992) give a detailed picture for the 1980s and show that during the decade there were only three years (1984, 1988, and 1990) in which the budget was near equilibrium or had a small surplus, while in the rest of the decade the deficit usually exceeded 1% of GDP and sometimes even reached 4%. (Nevertheless, having an 8% deficit is something new to Hungary.)[36] Muraközi even shows (though with some reservations about the reliability of earlier statistical data) that while during the years of the traditional command economy the normal budget outcome was a surplus, the market-oriented reform of economic management in 1968 marked the beginning of a new tendency: general government budget has been normally running deficits during the last 25 years. There is nothing unusual in running deficits; many governments do the same even in the long run. However, there are serious reasons why this should be avoided in a weak economy. The burden of financing the deficit may become a major obstacle to economic recovery.

Figure 1 uncovers an embarrassing tendency: the government is losing control of the deficit, due to the fact that budgetary planning has a tendency (or perhaps motivation) to overestimate the size of legal and taxable economic activity and so the revenues, while it is far more accurate in estimating the size of the expenditure side. This is not surprising, as a decline of budget revenues is a typical symptom of economies in transition experiencing a severe recession (cf. McKinnon 1991 and 1992). Nevertheless, the scope of the continuously growing deficit is almost unequivocally considered threatening, and it is a political commonplace (echoed by the bulk of the actual Hungarian literature on economic policy) that the deficit, or at least its ratio to GDP, should be reduced considerably to make economic growth possible.[37]

As it is widely recognized that Hungarian marginal tax rates are already too high and raising them any further would threaten strong disincentive effects, cutting expenditures and maintaining a restrictive fiscal policy seems to be the only viable solution for many. Erdős (1992) is nearly the only one in recent economic literature to challenge this view, arguing that a budget deficit in itself does not necessarily mean that the economic policy is expansive. He suggests that the full employment deficit (surplus) should be analyzed instead. He also questions on Keynesian grounds whether cutting expenditures would be a good idea in a recession, saying that "the budget can hardly diminish its deficit by reducing its own expenditures or increasing tax rates, as the consequence of these measures would be a drop in GDP and in tax revenues. It is only the private household that can easily sustain financial equilibrium by cutting expenditures or increasing revenues."[38]

Another unorthodox but very reasonable view is to say that the deficit in itself would not be a major problem if it had been used to finance the necessary investments (e.g., in infrastructure) to enhance economic growth. However, the low level of investments clearly demonstrates that this was not the case in Hungary.

It is interesting to see what reasons are usually held responsible for the large and ever-growing public sector deficit. A recent analysis prepared by the Ministry of Finance (Pénzügyminisztérium 1993b) investigates the reasons behind unexpectedly high deficits and argues that external factors are to blame. The significant and lasting drop in output is considered the main reason for the deficit. This drop is said to be mainly due to:

- the collapse of traditional economic relations with East European countries;
- shocks endemic to the transition to market economy;[39]
- overall recession of the world economy.

The recent experience of some Nordic countries (Sweden and Finland) is used by the authors to demonstrate that the increase in the Hungarian budget deficit was rather moderate if we consider the scope of the drop in GDP.[40] Nevertheless, there is nothing to be proud of. The budget obviously was unable to meet some reasonable adjustment targets,[41] and though the structure of its expenditures now differs significantly from what we had six years ago, the most important changes had started well before the transition "officially" started.[42] This led Muraközi (1992) to say that there was "no systemic change" in fiscal policy at all. It is also startling (though rather typical) that the Ministry refers only to unfavorable external factors as possible reasons for the deficit, while it is clear that the government and the fiscal policy pursued can also be blamed to a certain extent. The government seemed to lack the dedication or courage to implement fundamental and politically risky changes (pension reform, family allowance, health reform, higher education finance reform) on the expenditure side of the budget, and this was a major factor behind the huge deficit, together with the revenue shortfalls due to poor economic performance.

6. THE FINANCEABILITY OF THE DEFICIT

The fiscal deficit can be financed in three major ways: by foreign borrowing, domestic borrowing, and monetary expansion (seigniorage).[43] Throughout the 1970s and the 1980s foreign borrowing had a crucial role; the National Bank of Hungary borrowed from abroad and provided loans to finance general government budget deficits. The real debtor of this credits is the Hungarian state, though technically the burden of servicing foreign debt lies with the NBH. This process led to the accumulation of the $21 billion external debt that is now a major source of the increase in domestic public debt through a devaluation item (as changes in the exchange rate of the forint change the size of the public debt measured in forints).[44]

As is well known, the accumulation of one of the highest per capita external debts in the world took place in two waves (see Oblath 1992a); the first wave started in 1974 and lasted into the beginning of the 1980s. This was mainly due to the lack of structural adjustment after the oil shock and to the political will to conceal the price (the economic failure) of slowing down the reform of economic management started in 1968. Foreign borrowing helped to maintain economic growth and a relatively high level of personal consumption in an unhealthy economy, and was used to conserve the system. However, the mistake of stopping reform in 1973 became obvious very soon, and the only viable political alternative remaining was the resumption of economic reform in the 1980s.[45] From 1981 to 1984, the level of external debt seemed to stabilize (or even diminish, due to the strengthening of the dollar). In 1985 a new wave of debt accumulation started that lasted till 1991. In this period external debt nearly doubled. The major factor behind the increase of net external debt was the deficit of current account in both periods; however, while during the first wave of debt accumulation current account deficit was mainly due to the deficit of the non-interest current account (NICA), during the second wave NICA had a significant surplus and interest payments were responsible for the rapid growth of gross external debt.[46] The present level of external debt seems to be so high that any possible intention to increase it further (e.g., to finance an economic upswing) would not only threaten the availability of the already endangered export surplus through increased domestic demand but would certainly run into supply constraints on foreign capital markets as well.[47] However, as domestic borrowing may also run into supply constraints, there is a chance that external debt will be marginally increased in 1993.

Hungary has consistently pursued a policy that assigned high priority to servicing the debt in order to remain solvent and keep its access to external capital markets at any price. However, as some of the developing and some ex-socialist countries were successful in getting temporary debt relief, there appeared some voices advocating a turn in the official strategy of debt management (see Oblath 1992a for a survey of recent critical political and professional approaches to this strategy).[48] As the share of sovereign debts has been relatively insignificant in Hungary (see table 8), achieving debt relief would be even technically more difficult than in countries with a higher share of intergovernmental loans.

Nevertheless, the macroeconomic consequences of servicing the debt are rather serious, especially so if one excludes a possible influx of foreign capital.[49] Without capital inflow, servicing foreign debts would sooner or later push the economy into a vicious circle of spiraling recession that would undermine in the long run the very ability of the economy to achieve a trade balance surplus crucial for debt service.[50] However, actual developments have presented the country with a unique opportunity. As Oblath (1992b) shows, the inflow of foreign capital (a relative success story of the Hungarian transition process) and unilateral transfers provide an excellent opportunity for servicing the external debt without necessarily running into a recession trap. The debt management strategy chosen by the present government also relies heavily on the influx of foreign working capital; however, until now it was not able to avoid recession, anyway[51] (though the recession certainly would have been deeper without the foreign capital received).

Domestic borrowing started to play a significant role in the 1990s: the stock of state bonds and treasury bills has been rapidly growing recently, as is demonstrated by table 9. With increased savings of the population and the likewise increasing entrepreneurial money demand, the public sector deficit can be financed from domestic sources without major difficulties for the time being.

While the growth rate of government securities is impressive, this does not necessarily mean a similar growth in "real" domestic (private) borrowing, as a considerable part of these securities is held by the NBH, and so belongs to the realm of monetary expansion (see note 44). Despite the impressive pace of change in deficit finance, securities markets are still relatively underdeveloped in Hungary (see Király 1992). Király considers the Hungarian treasury bill market typically vertical, and shows that the lack of a centralized secondary market for treasury bills restricts the central bank's ability to signal and perform open market operations and so to fine tune the monetary base.[52]

As mentioned above, rising domestic savings (see table 10) contributed to the serviceability of external debts and the financeability of budget deficits. Hungary's performance is relatively good in this respect; with the widening of wage differences and a greater level of employment risks and income fluctuations, household savings show a remarkable increase.

Várhegyi (1993) reports a significant increase in enterprise savings as well (22% within the 1989–1992 period), and remarks that the increase in propensity to save contributed to an increase in the level of monetization of the economy. The share of currency holdings within the monetary base has been decreasing, while the monetary base as a percentage of GDP increased by 7% in 1991 and by 3% in 1992. The increase in the propensity to save is a welcome phenomenon and makes it easier to finance the budget deficit, but it is somewhat misleading to refer to high household savings as the major basis of financing the deficit, as private investors were allowed to play only a minor and indirect role in the market of government securities still dominated by publicly owned big commercial banks. It is also worth mentioning that even the NBH had to play a crucial role in buying government securities.[53]

Monetary expansion also played a significant role in financing the growing deficit.[54] The monetary base doubled between 1989 and 1992 (especially due to a sharp increase in reserve requirements) and broad money (M2) also grew from 707.2 billion forints in 1989 to 1487 billion forints in 1992 (NBH 1993b). According to recent calculations by Oblath and Valentinyi (1993), seigniorage (the sum of inflation, tax, and changes in real base money) received by the government rose from 3.6% of GDP in 1989 to 5.8% in 1992. The World Bank (1992) uses cross-country statistical evidence to show that the amount of seigniorage positively correlates with the rate of inflation in the relevant range.[55] This means that if Hungary really wants to bring inflation down, a fiscal adjustment amounting to 2% of GDP could be required to offset the loss of seigniorage revenue.[56]

7. MACROECONOMIC IMPACTS OF THE DEFICIT

A long-term tendency to run a budget deficit inevitably leads to the accumulation of a sizeable public debt, which should be serviced and so can also contribute to preserving huge budget deficits. Public debt is a hot issue in Hungary. It might be argued that the enormous numbers often referred to by the press and in political debates are somewhat exaggerating the real scope of the problem, as the public sector deficit is defined in Hungary from the point of view of the NBH. If one calculated domestic public debt in a narrow sense, subtracting all the debated items (including devaluation items, which do not cause real problems provided the amount of external debt is held constant, and direct NBH credits to government, including credits to the State Development Institute and state bonds held by the NBH, as suggested by Oblath), the remaining domestic public debt would not look very serious (table 11). Nevertheless, it does not seem to be technically possible to simply write off NBH credits to government. The different character of the various items of domestic public debt is, however, reflected by the differentiation of interest rates to be paid. The debt due to accumulated devaluation items does not bear any interest, while the government pays a below market rate interest after the stock of its direct NBH debt accumulated prior to 1991. Even so, interest payments entail a significant burden for the budget.[57]

One tendency is clear enough: domestic public debt is rising at a rapid pace, but this certainly has nothing to do with the much criticized inclusion of NBH direct lending to central government, as the share of the latter to GDP remained roughly constant. Even if one considers devaluation items an inheritance from previous governments (though they certainly incorporate some effect of the actual fiscal and monetary policy as devaluation has something to do with the rate of inflation), there is an increase in deficit of the magnitude of 8% of GDP in 1991 and of a 4% magnitude in 1992 that cannot be so easily explained by the faults of the previous governments.

The role of servicing the enormous public debt or financing the public sector deficit in the lasting recession is a rather controversial issue. There is a line of reasoning implying that there is a considerable crowding out taking place: the treasury, pushing interest rates up to the sky in order to finance the public sector borrowing requirement, crowds out private investors from the money market. Although interest rates are really high enough in Hungary to discourage private investors from borrowing, the reasons behind this seem to be more complex. This might be perhaps illustrated by the fact that commercial banks did not use up their refinance credit lines (provided for foreign exchange deposits) because they might have found it too risky to lend. It was certainly not the lack of liquidity in the banking sector that prevented private sector credits from an expansion. However, it is certainly not easy to determine the exact effects of the public sector's money demand on interest margins and private sector lending interest rates. Interest rates might have been lower, had the banks not been offered gilt-edged securities to buy from the treasury.

Even if crowding out may not be a real problem in the short run, it can become a more serious issue in the longer run unless the deficit is diminished. Valentinyi (1992) constructs a simple theoretical macroeconomic model to demonstrate the macroeconomic impacts of the public sector deficit. Assuming that interest payments after the public debt amount to an average 5% of GDP while the difference of real interest and real growth rates is around 7% on the average within a period of five or ten years (reasonable assumptions if we compare them to the actual figures), he concludes that interest payments may amount to 7% of GDP in five and to 10% of GDP in ten years. If there is a primary debt as well, there is an even larger gap to fill in. Crowding out may certainly occur to a serious extent and contribute to a deepening recession, and/or the government will have to more and more rely on monetary expansion, as in the longer run the public will likely become reluctant to buy government securities. This line of reasoning illustrates that maintaining a sizeable budget deficit in an economy in recession would certainly lead to a dramatic increase in inflation. International experience can also show that a large deficit can only be sustained without inflation provided there is a relatively high rate of economic growth in the country.

All in all, a deficit of this magnitude is obviously an obstacle to the growth of the private sector (especially so as it is not so much used to financing policies aimed at the creation of better conditions for the private sector, but to conserving an old and anachronistic expenditure structure) and implies a high risk of accelerating inflation. This means that in spite of certain achievements the main step is still ahead in the process of fiscal reform. Despite the technical financeability of the deficit, all possible efforts should be taken to reduce its share of GDP.

Table 1
Summary of General Government Operations: International Comparison

Country	Year	Revenue	Expenditure
Austria	1989	46.9	49.7
Canada	1989	40.3	43.9
Denmark	1989	59.6	59.4
France	1989	46.2	47.8
Greece	1988	32.7	46.3
Netherlands	1989	51.1	56.6
Portugal	1988	40.7	45.0
Spain	1987	35.0	38.6
Sweden	1988	59.1	56.9
United States	1988	34.3	36.5
Germany (West)	1989	45.7	45.9
Hungary[a]	1989	61.3	63.7
Hungary (GFS)	1991[b]	53.4	56.9

[a]These data correspond to the Hungarian presentation, while all other data refer to GFS.

[b]Preliminary data.

Source: Kornai 1992a, based on IMF data; GFS data for Hungary are from World Bank 1992.

Table 2
Summary of Fiscal Measures: Central and Consolidated Government
(Billion forints; percentage of GDP in parentheses)

	1988	1989	1990	1991	1992	1993 Budget
Central government[a]						
Revenue	789.9	926.6	1,105.9	1,120.8	1,364.3	1,694.6
	(54.8)	(53.8)	(52.9)	(48.6)	(51.5)	(54.1)
Expenditure	793.1	939.3	1,089.2	1,294.9	1,586.8	1,882.4
	(55.1)	(54.5)	(52.1)	(56.1)	(59.9)	(60.1)
Subsidies	186.5	207.0	184.7	151.0	138.4	143.7
	(12.9)	(12.0)	(8.8)	(6.5)	(5.2)	(4.6)
Transfers	261.6	321.4	387.4	488.5	587.2	695.7
	(18.2)	(18.7)	(18.5)	(21.2)	(22.2)	(22.2)
Balance	−3.2	−12.7	16.7	−74.1	−222.5	−187.8
	(−0.2)	(−0.7)	(0.8)	(−3.2)	(−8.4)	(−6.0)
Consolidated government[b]						
Revenue	892.9	1,046.3	1,204.2	1,292.1	1,458.6	1,793.3
	(62.0)	(60.7)	(57.6)	(56.0)	(55.0)	(57.3)
Expenditure	892.3	1,087.4	1,194.5	1,354.1	1,682.2	1,972.4
	(61.9)	(63.1)	(57.2)	(58.7)	(63.5)	(63.0)
Balance	0.6	−41.1	9.7	−62.0	−223.6	−179.1
	(0.0)	(−2.4)	(0.5)	(−2.7)	(−8.4)	(−5.7)
GDP	1,440.4	1,722.8	2,089.3	2,308.4	2,650.0	3,130.0

[a]"Central government" refers to the state budget, budgetary chapters, central budgetary institutions, extra-budgetary funds, and the SIF.

[b]"Consolidated government" refers to the central government and local governments.

Source: OECD 1993, p. 34.

Table 3
The Impact of Shocks Endemic to the Transition
(billion forints)

	1991	1992	1993
Revenue loss			
Act on Accounting			
provisioning for losses		3.0–4.0	
change in depreciation		4.0–6.0	
Banking Act[a]			48.0[b]
Temporary agreement with EC	1.0		2.0
Visegrád agreement			1.0
EFTA			0.5
Collapse of ex-CMEA markets	82.8		
Increase in expenditures			
Solidarity Fund	18.5	35.5	52.0

[a]Including the effects of bankruptcies and liquidations.
[b]Cumulated for 1991–1993.

Source: Pénzügyminisztérium 1993b.

András Semjén

Table 4
General Government Expenditures by Functional Category
(in percent of GDP)

	1989	1990[a]	1993 (exp.)
Total Expenditure	63.1	57.4	58.1
I. Traditional Domain: Public Goods	10.6	11.7	7.2
General government services	8.6[c]	8.1	5.6[c]
Public order & safety		1.8	
Defense	2.0	1.9	1.6
II. Social Welfare	32.0	34.8	37.5
Merit goods	11.0	13.6	10.4
Education	5.6	6.9	5.4
Health	3.7	4.9	4.0
Recreation and culture	1.7	1.7	1.0
Income maintenance programs	21.0	21.2	27.1
Pensions		9.7	
Maternity and child care	11.8[d]	0.9	14.5[d]
Sickness benefits		1.2	
Housing & community amenities	5.9	4.8	3.5
Family allowances	3.0[c]	3.1	3.5[c]
Other			
Social assistance	0.3	1.6[c]	5.6
III. The Mixed Economy[b]	20.5	10.9	13.5
Fuel & energy**	2.9[c]	1.4	0.8[c]
Mining, manufacturing & construction**		1.2	
Agriculture, forestry & fishing**	2.3	2.5	1.0
Transport & communication**	2.8	3.1	4.4
Other economic affairs & services*	7.9	5.7	2.0
Other expenditures*	4.6	−3.0	5.3

[a]As 1990 data are not from the same source as the others, there might be differences in the definition of categories for the different years, distorting the comparison of data. (This is most likely to apply to categories marked with "*.")
[b]Consumer price subsidies to sectors marked with "**" might also be considered part of social expenditures.
[c]Figures represent the sum of 2 categories.
[d]Figures represent the sum of 3 categories.

Source: World Bank 1992 for 1990; Pénzügyminisztérium 1993b for the other two years.

Table 5
Change in General Government Expenditures 1989–1992
(1984 = 100)

	1984	1985	1986	1987	1988	1989	1990	1991*	1992**
Capital expenditures	100	95	96	101	94	86	72	54	51
Subsidies & transfers to firms	100	105	118	116	95	66	43	22	18
Consumer price subsidies	100	88	99	102	59	50	32	27	9
Business subsidies (subtotal)	100	98	107	108	87	69	51	34	27
Health care & social assistance	100	104	108	110	124	143	148	147	135
Education	100	106	106	106	120	142	147	172	160
Research	100	103	99	112	93	103	88	78	48
Defense	100	101	104	106	119	107	97	47	43
Safety & public order	100	97	88	123	101	145	155	198	177
Public administration	100	110	111	116	152	187	219	268	233
Economic & communal services	100	112	115	109	111	105	92	106	115
Budgetary institutions (subtotal)	100	104	106	108	117	127	125	140	133
Social security	100	103	105	106	127	135	134	128	120
Out of which: pensions	100	103	106	108	110	113	113	108	105
International & other expenditures	100	82	102	98	96	163	129	90	79
Total	100	99	106	106	105	110	98	92	87

*Preliminary data.
**Budget estimates.

Source: Muraközi 1992, based on CSO and national budget data.

Table 6
Public Expenditures for Social Programs in Hungary, 1991

	Social public expenditures (billion forints)	as % of general government	as % of GDP
Pensions	262.8	19.1	11.4
Education	148.2	10.8	6.4
Health	117.1	8.5	5.1
Family benefits	105.3	7.6	4.6
Housing subsidies	72.8	5.3	3.2
Social services	43.1	3.1	1.9
Consumer subsidies	40.4	2.9	1.8
Pharmaceuticals	39.4	2.9	1.7
Sick pay	29.0	2.1	1.3
Employment policies	30.3	2.2	1.3
Total	888.8	64.5	38.5
General govt. expenditures	1,378.2		
GDP	2,308.4		

Source: Andorka, Kondratas, and Tóth 1993, p. 5.

Table 7
Central Government Transfers
(billion forints; and as % of GDP [in parentheses])

	1988	1989	1990	1991	1992 (prelim.)	1993 (budget)
Central govt. transfers[a]	261.6 (18.2)	321.4 (18.7)	387.4 (18.5)	488.5 (21.2)	587.2 (22.2)	695.7 (22.2)
Social security pensions	130.0 (9.0)	156.5 (9.1)	202.1 (9.7)	260.8 (11.3)	307.8 (11.6)	355.1 (11.3)
Other social security benefits	85.7 (5.9)	113.0 (6.6)	158.6 (7.6)	184.7 (8.0)	211.5 (8.0)	239.6 (7.7)
Extra-budgetary funds	35.8 (2.5)	29.4 (1.7)	22.7 (1.1)	37.3 (1.6)	56.1 (2.1)	77.9 (2.5)
Other current transfers[b]	10.1 (0.7)	22.5 (1.3)	4.0 (0.2)	5.7 (0.2)	11.8 (0.4)	23.1 (0.7)
Transfers/ central govt. expenditures	32.1	33.6	33.0	33.7	36.6	37.7

[a]Net of transfers within the general government.
[b]Includes transfers abroad and transfers to nonprofit institutions.

Source: OECD 1993, p. 44.

Table 8
Hungary's Gross External Debt
(end of each year, million US $)

	1988	1989	1990	1991	1992
Convertible currency debts					
Total	19,602	20,390	21,270	22,658	21,438
Maturity structure:					
Short-term	3,363	3,306	2,941	2,177	2,286
Medium- and					
long-term	16,239	17,084	18,329	20,481	19,152
Type of loans:					
Financial	17,469	18,060	17,587	18,135	16,211
Commercial					
(trade-related)	1,626	1,763	1,980	1,777	2,011
Intergovernmental	0	0	472	1,512	1,446
Other	507	567	1,231	1,234	1,770
Inconvertible currency debts					
Total	583	361	235	154	217
Maturity structure:					
Short-term	120	87	80	38	16
Medium- and					
long-term	463	274	155	116	201
Type of loans:					
Financial	136	88	71	35	13
Commercial					
(trade-related)	0	0	0	0	0
Intergovernmental	439	260	140	104	190
Other	8	13	24	15	14

Source: NBH 1993a.

Table 9
Stock of Government Securities
(billion forints)

	1988	1989	1990	1991	1992
Govt. bonds outside					
the NBH (1)	17.5	22.7	36.6	49.2	187.8
Govt. bonds held					
by the NBH (2)	0.5	4.5	4.5	7.1	121.5
Govt. bonds total					
(1) + (2)	18.0	27.2	41.1	56.3	309.3
Deficit finance	9.0	13.0	13.0	26.3	149.5
Nondeficit finance	9.0	14.2	28.1	30.0	159.8
Treasury bills (3)	9.7	8.6	10.2	60.0	157.2
Govt. securities					
outside the NBH					
(1) + (3)	27.2	31.3	46.8	109.2	345.0
Govt. securities total					
(1) + (2) + (3)	27.7	35.8	51.3	116.3	466.5

Source: Oblath and Valentinyi 1993, based on NBH and Ministry of Finance data.

Table 10
Household Disposable Income, Consumption, and Savings, 1988–1992

	1988	1989[a]	1990	1991	1992
Billion forints, at current prices					
Disposable income[b]	932.0	1123.0	1424.9	1858.9	2179.0
Consumption[c]	876.9	1064.8	1288.2	1565.2	1891.1
Savings	55.1	58.2	136.7	293.7	287.9
Household	47.0	57.1	56.2	−25.0[e]	37.9
Financial[d]	8.1	1.1	80.5	318.7[e]	250.0
Percentage of disposable income, at current prices					
Savings	5.9	5.2	9.6	15.8	13.2
Household	5.0	5.1	3.9	−1.3	1.7
Financial[d]	0.9	0.1	5.6	17.1	11.5

[a]Estimates.
[b]Including the value of health care, education, and social welfare provided free to households.
[c]Private national consumption.
[d]Net savings of households not used or designated for house purchase.
[e]Including loans forgiven by the government.
Note: Várhegyi (1993) has also published household savings data covering a slightly longer period. However, as her figures differ somewhat from the above, we confine ourselves to the above period.

Source: OECD 1993, p. 15.

Table 11
Domestic Public Debt, End of Year
(billion forints)

	1990	1991	1992 (prelim.)	1993 (budget)
Direct NBH credit to central govt. (net of SDI credit)	498.7	583.6	568.6	560.1
NBH credits to SDI	259.5	253.5	247.0	241.9
State bonds held by NBH	4.5	7.1	121.5	
NBH direct lending to central govt.	762.7	844.2	937.1	
Percent of GDP	36.7	36.0	35.4	
State bonds in the hands of banks, insurance companies, & financial institutions[a]	17.5	30.1	28.0	385.8[c]
Treasury bills	10.2	59.9	157.2	124.5
Other[b]	47.6	124.0	183.7	365.6
Total public domestic debt (net of devaluation item)	838.0	1058.0	1306.0	1677.9
Percent of GDP	40.3	45.1	49.3	53.6
Fiscal liability from forint devaluation	519.2	777.9	862.5	862.5
Percent of GDP	25.0	33.2	32.5	27.6
Total public domestic debt	1357.2	1835.9	2168.5	2540.4
Percent of GDP	65.3	78.3	81.8	81.2
GDP	2079.5	2346.0	2650.0	3130.0

[a]Due to differences among data sources, data referring to government bonds are slightly different from the ones in table 9.

[b]Credit to budgetary institutions, extra-budgetary funds, and local governments; housing loans forgiven (1991); capitalizations for: treasury bonds to replace housing loans, Housing Fund finance, bonds for NBH ruble claims, other items (1992), plus Bank Credit Consolidation (1993); Social Security deficit bonds.

[c]Including state bonds held by the NBH.

Totals may slightly differ from the sum of the items due to rounding errors.

Source: OECD 1993; NBH 1992; Oblath and Valentinyi 1993.

Figure 1
Hungarian State (Central Government) and Consolidated
General Government Budget Deficit (or Surplus), 1989–1993
(percent of GDP)

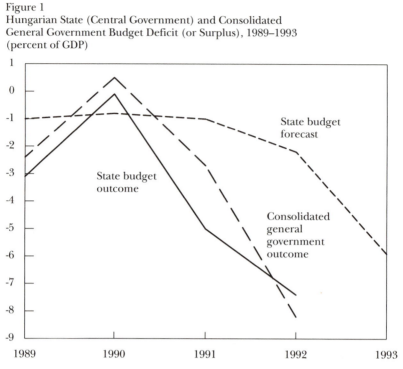

Source: OECD 1993, p.35, based on Ministry of Finance data.

NOTES

The author is very much indebted to László Antal and Werner Riecke, whose conference paper ("Reforming Public Finances in Hungary") served as a starting point of the present study. However, all responsibility for the views expressed in the present paper lies with the author, who is also grateful to István György Tóth and Ákos Valentinyi for their valuable comments on an earlier version of the paper.

1. The Ministry of Finance is surprisingly reluctant to adopt international accounting standards. One cannot help having the strange impression that this might have something to do with political considerations. The government might perhaps face less opposition if the accounting concepts in the budget prevent the public (including the MPs) from getting a clear-cut picture of the structure of public spending according to different uses. Nevertheless, there might be a breakthrough approaching, as in a recently prepared document intended for the members of the Committee for the Rationalization of General Government Budget (Pénzügyminisztérium 1993b) the Ministry published expenditure data in functional breakdown.

2. The Hungarian presentation includes amortization payments as expenditures, and changes in credits and cash balances as revenues (for all but the state budget).

3. There is less consolidation among the components of general government in the Hungarian presentation; e.g., social security contributions paid by budgetary chapters, central budgetary institutions, and local governments to the Social Insurance Fund are not consolidated.

4. László (1993) surveys recent *Közgazdasági Szemle* articles on the subject, and confronts their (and other experts') opinions concerning the redistribution rate with calculations using his own consolidated budget data. The range is considerably wide, with estimations varying between 52.6% and 70%.

5. This is to emphasize that standard (unconsolidated) Hungarian data should be viewed with great caution, remembering that revenue and expenditure levels and ratios may be significantly overstated.

6. We also should mention that using 1989 GFS data (if there were any) would give even more favorable, i.e., significantly lower, results for Hungary, which can be demonstrated by comparing the Hungarian presentation data for 1991 (61.9% and 66%, respectively) with the GFS data for Hungary presented in table 1.

7. Structural adjustments called for but not accomplished due to the rigidities of the socialist system have accumulated, and now constitute a "negative dowry" to make the transition to a market economy even more complicated.

8. Most expenditure items (according to the functional breakdown) declined in real terms; social insurance and family benefits increased slightly, while subsidies to transport and communication and interest payments for public debt increased more (20%–30%). There was, however, one item that skyrocketed: social assistance (comprising previously nonexistent items like means-tested benefits administered by municipalities and unemployment benefit payments) increased dramatically in real terms (Pénzügyminisztérium 1993b).

9. This was implemented through three main channels: a property tax on net assets, a municipal profit tax, and a wage bill tax. In this old system the factors of production were taxed at different rates. The share of enterprise

direct taxes to operating surpluses was 28.2% in 1988 (31.8% in 1989; 26.0% in 1990; 30.8% in 1991). However, this figure went down to 14.2% in 1992, partly due to a dramatic decrease in the profitability of financial institutions in connection with increased bank provisioning for bad and doubtful loans (a consequence of the banking law).

10. Differentiation was made by sector and type of enterprise (public vs. private, cooperatives vs. enterprises).

11. 1989: 50% plus a 4% temporary surcharge; 1990: 40% (a preferential rate of 35% to be applied for the first 3 million forints of taxable income).

12. These made the effective tax rates much lower than the statutory ones. Though this was partly foreseen, owing to the reliefs the actual drop in the tax rate was significantly bigger than planned, and this led to unanticipated refunds due to the overpayment of tax obligations endemic to the system of tax installments. The tendency of budgetary planning to underestimate the effects of tax relief on the tax rate is evident from the comparison of data based on budget estimates to statistical data referring to the gradually growing rate of tax relief to taxes + relief. The ratio of relief to taxes + relief was 22.6% in 1989 (though estimated at 14.8%), and 23.1% in 1990 (compared to the estimate of 15.9%) (Source: World Bank 1992).

13. The new depreciation rates were not extended to existing assets; these were categorized in six categories due to revenue considerations. Even this change resulted in a slight reduction of effective asset lives.

14. The relative cost of capital is also influenced by the rates of inflation, the method of financing (debt vs. equity), the tight rules for loss carry-forward, etc.

15. Kornai (1992a) is instructive about a possible way to ensure adherence to the law. He suggests that adherence should be made advantageous to the "gray" private sector by a "deal"; if the entrepreneurs receive the rule of law as a service, they will be willing to pay taxes as the price for this service. "Private entrepreneurs will be attracted toward legality if that is the only way they can gain legal protection for their property." Nevertheless, we must emphasize that this deal would not be costless for the budget. Due to the lack of finance and serious bottlenecks, the speed of justice is very slow nowadays; actually it is so slow that the value of the legal protection offered tends to zero. Kornai's line of reasoning may suggest, however, that it would be a good public investment to "speed up" the working of justice.

16. This later was reduced to 10% for dividends provided that the company already paid its EPT liability.

17. According to some CSO estimates, there was some 30 billion forints income realized in small-scale agriculture in 1992, out of which only less than 1 billion forints figured in the personal income tax base.

18. See Jenkins 1991 and Khalilzadeh-Shirazi and Shah 1991.

19. This allowance is especially criticized in World Bank (1992), where other allowances are said not to "pose significant administrative or allocational burdens." This latter view might, however, contradict Jarvis and Micklewright (1992), who dislike the child allowance on equity grounds, and consider its extension a "most regrettable" step. As this allowance (a monthly 1,300 forints per child eligible for family benefit in 1992) is worth nothing to those not liable to personal income tax (i.e., the most needy) and worth the most for those who face the highest marginal tax rate, its effect on income distribution can indeed be called regressive. This child allowance has been recently converted (for the

1993 tax year) into a (non-refundable) tax credit (monthly 300 forints per child eligible for family benefit; for families with three or more eligible children, the value of the tax credit is 400 forints per child), which raises far less serious equity problems. The consolidation program elaborated in the Ministry of Finance for 1994–1996 contemplates an increase in the amount of this allowance (tax credit) to offset the effects of bringing the family allowance under the personal income tax.

20. Most proposals suggest grossing up the benefits (using some lower tax rate for this). It would lead to an absolute increase in benefits for those without a tax liability, while those facing a higher marginal rate would receive less than at present.

21. See Jarvis and Micklewright 1992. We will come back to the issue of targeting later. It has to be mentioned that the reduction in the progressivity of the PIT rates (especially the lowering of the top rate) also reduced the possible revenue gain that could be obtained from taxing family allowances; this will be further aggravated by any kind of grossing up. If we consider the administrative costs and difficulties (slightly exaggerated in Jarvis and Micklewright) of this measure, we have to realize that there is not too much to gain from all this. Taxing the allowance without grossing it up would be a different story, however.

22. Taxing interests on foreign currency accounts has already been raised several times; it is rather ironic that this idea has been supported by the National Bank of Hungary, which should have felt worried about the possible drop in currency deposits, while the Ministry of Finance evidently disliked the proposal despite its concern for revenue gains.

23. As the VAT was not originally levied on individual imports (including cars), there was a financial incentive to import individually, which resulted in the dramatic slippage of the convertible currency travel balance in 1989. Later this failure was corrected, and official and individual imports are now treated equally.

24. The problem of VAT evasion can be quite substantial in the case of certain products or sectors, e.g., clothes, vegetables, etc. The problem is covered by Kornai (1992a). He says: "The more active the legal protection of buyers becomes in the future, the more common it will become for buyers to demand a receipt, even if that means paying a higher price, covering the value-added tax." Nevertheless, the present stage of development in some fast- changing markets, with new enterprises emerging and disappearing each moment, lacks the stability needed to make buyers interested in paying a higher price, as the chances of enforcing a legal claim seem to be weak in these markets.

25. The PIT was originally intended to be the main source of local government finance. However, its role has gone through a series of changes since 1988. Originally, it was redistributed among localities on an equal per capita basis (a small amount over a guaranteed maximum was, however, retained by the central budget); then in 1989 tax revenues on interest income were earmarked to the Housing Fund. Since 1990, transfers to local governments have been based upon the average PIT payment within *each* locality. The average per capita PIT paid in a reference year (two years earlier; in 1990 this meant 1988) serves as the basis of the transfer. Settlements with a per capita PIT under a certain minimum limit (4,000 forints) were to receive supplementary transfers to make up for the difference. It was a drastic change

when the 1991 budget declared that only 50% of the PIT revenues collected two years prior would be transferred directly to localities. (Supplementary transfer for the poorest localities remained in effect.)

26. It is a commonplace that the contribution rate is "53% of enterprise wage bills, the highest in the world" (World Bank 1992). However, this statement is partly due to misinterpretation of the data. If a worker is paid 100 forints, his contribution will be 10 forints, while the employer is due to pay 43 forints. The ratio of total contribution to pre-tax (but net of social security contribution) wage is 53 to 90; this is nearly a 60% burden. Nevertheless, if we take the total wage bill, i.e., 143 forints as 100%, the share of total contribution will be only 37%, which is still high enough, but not that high in international comparison. At present the employers' contribution is already 44%, the employees' 10%. Contributions to the Solidarity Fund were raised to 7% and 2%, respectively.

27. The World Bank cited the opinion of a Hungarian official on the "freedom" of risking public funds: "Rather than funds, the government transferred freedom."

28. Kornai (1992a) also warns that the hardening of the budget constraint during the transition may lead to a sharp contraction of economic activity, reducing the tax base and budgetary revenue.

29. Lackó (1992) constructed and fitted a monetary model (based on the demand for money) for the 1970–1989 period to estimate the share of the underground economy. According to her results, this share increased from 13% to 18% between 1973 and 1987, and then came a dramatic increase: it rose to 26% in 1988, 31% in 1989, and 34% in 1990. She considers these results lower approximations of the real size of the underground economy, and concludes that the period of transition will be characterized by an underground economy significantly bigger then during the socialist era. This conclusion is in line with the reasoning of Gábor R. (1992), who warns that the rapidly shrinking employment in the previously state-owned corporate sector and the occurrence of mass unemployment pushes labor into the small enterprise sector, making underground economic activity and tax avoidance all too easy for small entrepreneurs during the transition.

30. Hungary (as is usual for economies in transition) is experiencing a severe and lasting recession; the decline of GDP (in real terms) was 3.7% in 1990, 10.2% in 1991, and 4.5% in 1992; industrial output in 1992 was about 65% of that in 1985.

31. The elimination of double bureaucracies (party and government), some reduction in the responsibilities of central government (central planning, price control), etc.

32. The democratic political system also needs a professional political apparatus; the new system of local governments and the decentralization of the public sector also can justify some increase in administration. The courts will have to play a greater role in settling disputes, and the proliferation of independent economic and legal entities will also increase the number of legal procedures. There are new governmental responsibilities as well, part of them endemic to any transition to a market economy (like privatization, counseling for the unemployed, etc.), and part of them undertaken "voluntarily" by the government to fulfill its political promises (e.g., restitution, mass privatization, etc.).

33. Holders of pre-1989 housing loans were asked to choose between

paying back the loan in higher installments, i.e., paying higher but still subsidized fixed interest (15%), or having half of their outstanding principal forgiven but paying market interest rates on the remainder. A surprising majority of loan-holders chose the second option and paid the remaining outstanding debt back at once.

34. However, the facts also leave some room for another opinion, according to which the low level of housing investment is good as it is, because the housing stock in Hungary is relatively oversized due to previous constraints restricting productive private investments, and so the government should avoid creating incentives for new housing construction in order to encourage a higher level of productive investment. However, there is little evidence that the drop in housing investment had anything to do with higher productive investment.

35. In spite of relatively high activity rates of the population, the ratio of labor force to pensions is very low in Hungary (about 1.9:1 in 1990, while, for example, in the US it is about 3.2:1).

36. Their data differ, as usual, because Kornai uses mainly IMF data while Muraközi sticks to CSO statistics.

37. However, it is rather difficult to evaluate government views concerning the undesirability or desirability and the impacts of the deficit. Medium-term fiscal policy programs prepared by finance ministers (Iván Szabó is the third one during this term) usually aim at substantial reforms both on the expenditure and the revenue side so as to reduce the deficit (or at least to curb its rapid growth). It is indeed amazing how similar are the views held by members of financial government, the big opposition parties, and IMF sources in this respect. However, despite this general consensus, there is considerable disagreement when we come to the deeds, or when medium-term programs are translated into budget proposals. Then the government argues that the proposed size of the deficit (usually found by the opposition to be extremely high and still underestimated) is needed to sustain a certain level of domestic demand and to lessen the recession.

38. Though Erdős's paper can be considered a most welcome attempt to show the relevance of Keynesian macroeconomics in the present situation, there are serious doubts whether the old and somewhat unfashionable Keynesian recipes that were meant to treat recessions within a normal business cycle can be used in a totally different context, for economies in a deep structural crisis aiming at transition to a market economy.

39. These have been listed in table 3.

40. In Sweden a 1.4% drop in GDP turned a 4.7% surplus into a 1.4% deficit in 1991. In Finland an 8.1% decrease in GDP due to external shocks in the 1990–1992 period led to a deterioration in budget outcome amounting to 9.2% of GDP. If we contrast the Hungarian performance (deficit grew from 4.9% to 7.1% of GDP, a 2.2% deterioration reflecting a 16% drop in GDP in 1991–1992) to this background, it can be considered quite favorable. However, here again we have an example of inadequate comparison: more or less healthy and rich market economies responding to an external shock can afford running budget deficits that would kill a weak economy in transition.

41. The World Bank (1992) sets some of these rather ambitiously, not allowing for domestic borrowing or the use of privatization proceeds. The Parliament set less severe constraints for the budget; nevertheless, the government was not able to fulfill those either.

42. Important expenditure trends (besides the already mentioned reduction in business subsidies) during the term of the present government include a sharp reduction in military spending and an expansion of spending on education and on public order and safety. However, the most marked is the skyrocketing of administrative expenditures (table 5), which may partly be due to decentralization and an increase in the importance of local governments. Nevertheless, this is certainly not an achievement to be proud of.

43. Two potential sources of financing are neglected here. Public deficit can theoretically also be financed to some extent by "eating up" foreign exchange reserves or selling public property. As foreign exchange reserves have been growing, the first opportunity is not the case in Hungary; and although some part of the privatization proceeds are now used to finance the current expenditures of the budget (i.e., the real size of the deficit would be even bigger without this), the scope of this is not too significant. However, it is generally agreed that privatization proceeds should be used to repay (external) public debt.

44. Domestic public debt in Hungary (unlike in most countries) is usually defined from the point of view of the NBH. Outstanding loans provided to the government by the NBH are counted as part of domestic public debt. However, there is a characteristic view that questions this practice (Oblath 1992b), reasoning that as the NBH itself is part of the public sector, this calculation involves double-counting to a serious extent.

45. As Kornai (1992b) points out, this (although increasing the role of private sector, and through this the level of well-being) was no real solution either; as economic reform involved a certain level of political liberalization, it only accelerated the disintegration of the old political system. According to Kornai's fresh and provocative analysis, market socialism has never been a robust concept, and it could not even prove its superiority to a "classical" socialist command economy. He implies that at the beginning of the transition the macroeconomic situation was more favorable in those countries that never tried market socialism, as those countries which tried to implement market-oriented reforms tend to have higher inflation, higher budget deficits and bigger external debts. Nevertheless, it seems to me that keeping away from economic reform was in no sense any better for conserving political stability.

46. Interest payments during the 1980s amounted to $10.9 billion, roughly the same amount as the country's accumulated gross external debt in 1981 (see Oblath 1992a).

47. There was no foreign trade surplus in Hungary in the last two years, according to customs statistics; however, subtracting items not affecting the balance of payment, the trade balance already showed a small ($91 million) trade (export) surplus in 1992 after a $369 million deficit in 1991. This small surplus was the combined outcome of a month-by-month diminishing export surplus experienced in the first half of the year and a growing foreign trade deficit in the second half. This year the trade balance shows an annoying deteriorating trend (NBH 1993b).

48. He lists four differing lines of reasoning; two are political- ethical, one is a so-called global political economics approach, and the fourth one contains economic approaches aiming at finding a "third way" between servicing and rescheduling the debt, mixing the elements of debt relief with remaining solvent.

49. Oblath (1992b) analyzes the different ways of servicing the external

debt in the absence of foreign capital inflow. Net resource transfer to the lending countries can be achieved without inflation by restricting enterprise credits, or producing a budget surplus or a steady and significant growth in private savings. However, it seems to be very difficult to avoid the inflationary pressures of the resource transfer. Economic policy has several options, however; some of these are inflationary, some lead to a recession, while the combination of these is likely to bring about stagflation.

50. There are serious signs indicating that despite considerable capital inflow this might happen in 1993, as the export performance of the country deteriorated seriously, while imports grew.

51. The influx of foreign working capital (in million US$) at the end of each year showed a rapid increase in Hungary: 1988: 23; 1989: 215; 1990: 569; 1991: 2,107; 1992: 3,424.

52. She classifies the different segments of the money market as horizontal or vertical, according to the character of the typical transactions in each segment. A transaction is said to be vertical if it changes the amount of high-powered money in circulation.

53. The other side of the same coin is a decrease in short-term commercial bank lending to the business sector. This trend is mainly due to the high business risks involved, the lack of proper credit evaluation and appropriate collateral, and high interest margins resulting in considerably high real interest rates—far too high to be paid from normal enterprise profits. The low level of competition in the banking sector is also to be blamed.

54. Additional demand of the budget financed by money creation raises both the real value or the volume (through an increase in demand) and the nominal value (through higher prices) of transactions. Both factors will contribute to an increase in the demand for money and thereby is a revenue (amounting to the increase in money held by economic actors) for the government, which receives additional goods and services "free."

55. This relationship might change if the inflation rate exceeds a certain limit; in hyperinflationary periods economic actors are becoming less willing to hold currency.

56. CPIs for Hungary during the recent years are as follows: 1987: 108.6%; 1988: 115.5%; 1989: 117.0%; 1990: 128.9%; 1991: 135.0%; 1992: 123.0%.

57. Interest expense of the central government budget is rapidly increasing. The interest paid in 1989 were around 62 billion forints, while in 1991 they amounted to 93 billion forints (OECD 1993); preliminary 1992 data show a considerable increase to 170 billion forints (NBH 1993a).

REFERENCES

Andorka, Rudolf, Anna Kondratas, and István Gy. Tóth. 1993. Overview: The Hungarian Welfare State in Transition: Structure, Development and Options for Reform. Reforming Social Policy in Hungary. Policy Study #3 commissioned by the Joint Hungarian-International Blue Ribbon Commission, Budapest.

Erdős, Tibor. 1992. A gazdaság stabilizálásáról (On the stabilization of the Hungarian economy). *Közgazdasági Szemle* 39, no. 11, pp. 985–1000.

Gábor R., István. 1992. A második gazdaság átalakulásának kérdőjelei (The second economy today—Question marks of the transformation). *Közgazdasági Szemle* 39, no. 10, pp. 946–53.

Jarvis, Sarah J., and John Micklewright. 1992. The Targeting of Family Allowance in Hungary. Welfare State Program Discussion Paper. London: STICERD, London School of Economics.

Jenkins, Glenn P. 1991. Tax Reform: Lessons Learned. In *Reforming Economic Systems in Developing Countries*, ed. Dwight Perkins and Michael Roemer, pp. 293–311. Cambridge, MA: Harvard Institute for International Development.

Khalilzadeh-Shirazi, Javad, and Anwar Shah. 1991. Introduction: Tax Policy Issues for the 1990s. *World Bank Economic Review* 5, no. 3, pp. 459–71.

Király, Júlia. 1992. Pénzpiaci szegmensek—szegmentált irányítás (Segments of money market—segmented monetary control). *Közgazdasági Szemle* 39, no. 7–8, pp. 642–53.

Kopits, G., R. Holzmann, G. Schieber, and E. Sidgwick. 1990. Social Security Reform in Hungary. Washington, DC: Fiscal Affairs Department, IMF.

Kornai, János. 1992a. The Postsocialist Transition and the State: Reflections in the Light of Hungarian Fiscal Problems. *American Economic Review* 82, no. 2.

———. 1992b. Még egyszer a piaci szocializmusról (Market socialism revisited). *Közgazdasági Szemle* 39, no. 9, pp. 773–96.

Lackó, Mária. 1992. Az illegális gazdaság aránya 1970 és 1989 között (The weight of illegal economy in Hungary between 1970 and 1989). *Közgazdasági Szemle* 39, no. 9, pp. 861–82.

László, Csaba. 1993. Mekkora valójában az államháztartás szerepe az újraelosztásban (The real extent of the role of general government budget in redistribution). *Közgazdasági Szemle* 40, no. 1, pp. 63–79.

McKinnon, R.I. 1991. *The Order of Economic Liberalization: Financial Control in the Transition to Market Economy*. Baltimore: Johns Hopkins University Press.

———. 1992. Taxation, Money and Credit in a Liberalizing Socialist Economy. *Economics of Planning* 25, pp. 97–112.

Muraközi, László. 1992. Az államháztartás a kilencvenes évek Magyarországán (Public finances in Hungary in the nineties). *Közgazdasági Szemle* 39, no. 11, pp. 1050–66.

NBH (National Bank of Hungary). 1992. *Annual Report 1991*.

———. 1993a. *Monthly Report, 1993/1*.

———. 1993b. *Annual Report 1992*.

Oblath, Gábor. 1992a. Külső adósságfelhalmozás és adósságkezelés makroökonómiai problémái Magyarországon I (Foreign debt accumulation and macroeconomic problems of debt management in Hungary I). *Közgazdasági Szemle* 39, no. 7–8, pp. 605–23.

———. 1992b. Külső adósságfelhalmozás és adósságkezelés makroökonómiai problémái Magyarországon II (Foreign debt accumulation and macroeconomic problems of debt management in Hungary II). *Közgazdasági Szemle* 39, no. 9, pp. 797–814.

Oblath, Gábor, and Ákos Valentinyi. 1993. Seigniorage and Inflation Tax in Hungary. KOPINT-DATORG Discussion Paper. Budapest: forthcoming.

OECD. 1993. *Economic Review of Hungary*. Paris: Center for Co-operation with European Economies in Transition, Economics Department.

Pénzügyminisztérium. 1993a. *Az államháztartás konszolidációja 1994–1996*. Munkaanyag (Consolidating public finances in Hungary in the 1994–1996 period. Interim report).

————. 1993b. *Tájékoztató az államháztartásról.* Az államháztartási racionalizálási bizottság számára (Public finance bulletin. For the members of the Public Finance Reform Committee).

Valentinyi, Ákos. 1992. Stabilizáció és növekedés Magyarországon—néhány elméleti megfontolás (Stabilization and growth in Hungary—Some theoretical considerations). *Közgazdasági Szemle* 39, no. 10, pp. 908–23.

Várhegyi, Éva. 1993. A monetáris politika a gazdasági folyamatok tükrében (Monetary policy as reflected by the economic processes). *Közgazdasági Szemle* 40, no. 5, pp. 396–414.

World Bank. 1992. *Hungary: Reform and Decentralization of the Public Sector, I–II.* Country Operations, Central Europe Department, Europe and Central Asia Region.

3

Comments on Semjén

FABRIZIO CORICELLI

András Semjén gives an extremely insightful account of the main fiscal pressures affecting the Hungarian economy, where the budget deficit is proving one of the major obstacles to successful transformation. The author rightly stresses that these fiscal pressures are by and large an inevitable outcome of economic transition. Following Kornai (1992), he emphasizes the main channels through which economic transformation adversely affects the budget.

On the revenue side, the fall in revenues is determined not only by the overall economic recession but also by the very nature of the transition.[1] First, the redistribution of economic activity from state to private sectors produces a fall in the tax base, as the tax burden on private activities is much smaller than that on state enterprises. This is due both to the presence of tax incentives for private activities and to difficulties in tax collection. Second, the attempt to impose hard budget constraints is likely to affect output of state enterprises negatively and thus reduces tax revenues. An example of this is given by the new bankruptcy law, which has triggered a large number of bankruptcy procedures, exempting firms involved from any tax obligations.

Both channels highlight the trade-off between structural change and budgetary pressure (see also Tanzi 1993 for an excellent discussion). It is worth noting that Hungary is subject to fiscal pressures similar to, if not larger than, those affecting other economies in transition despite the fact that Hungary had a tax system comparable to Western economies *before* beginning its radical market reforms in 1990. This seems to contradict McKinnon's view, which ascribes the decline in tax revenues in economies in transition to the tax system, in particular to the absence of a VAT tax (McKinnon 1991). The Hungarian experience suggests that the transition itself implies adverse effects on tax revenues.

On the expenditure side, the main pressures seem to come from social expenditures. While pensions represent the main source of expenditure, unemployment benefits are becoming a significant burden for the budget (more than 2% of GDP). It should be added to the discussion by the author that the unemployment benefit scheme in Hungary is by far the most generous in the whole of Central and Eastern Europe (see Burda 1992). As unemployment is still increasing, the burden on the budget is going to increase in the near future. If one considers unemployment as a necessary by-product of the process of reallocation of resources across sectors—mainly from state to private activities—the budgetary pressures arising from unemployment can also be considered a manifestation of the restructuring process.

In sum, the budgetary problems of Hungary are largely a symptom of the transition process, not of macroeconomic disequilibrium and loose fiscal policy. In principle, a country should be able to borrow to smooth the initial costs of transition and defer the fiscal adjustment to a future of more favorable aggregate conditions. In turn, this implies that the public debt of the country is bound to increase unless there is a counterbalancing increase in private savings. The recent increase in domestic debt financing of the deficit—in the form of government bonds—has been viewed as a welcome development. However, the burden of the service of the total debt, domestic and foreign, may represent a strong deterrent for investment and thus growth. The shift towards domestic debt may have given a greater degree of freedom to domestic economic policy, as domestic debt can be curtailed, for instance by devaluing the exchange rate, while the same policy would increase the domestic currency value of the external debt.[2] However, as domestic debt increases, people would begin to realize that the government has an incentive to pursue a price level jump via a devaluation of the exchange rate. Anticipation of such a policy would trigger a move away from the forint, with extremely negative effects for the economy. Thus, debt management is an important area for Hungary, and perhaps the increase in domestic debt should be viewed more cautiously.

The heart of the fiscal problem in Hungary is that it inherited from the past an external debt that in per capita terms is among the largest in the world. Therefore, increasing the debt may have adverse long-term macroeconomic effects.

As noted above, whatever its composition, the burden of total debt may force the Hungarian economy into a persistent state of low growth. As shown recently by Calvo (1993), the presence of a large government debt is likely to generate a situation in which two distinct outcomes, one "bad" and one "good," can arise. Indeed, if the economy grows fast, the burden of the debt in terms of domestic output (GDP) is low. Thus, investment is not discouraged by the expectation of high taxes levied to raise revenues to service the debt. By contrast, if growth is slow, the burden of the debt discourages investment, thus pushing the economy into a persistent low growth equilibrium.

The challenge for the Hungarian government is to find policies that increase the likelihood of a good equilibrium. In this respect, international organizations like the IMF, the World Bank, and the EBRD could help in devising schemes that link debt service to the performance of the economy, thus ensuring that the burden— taxation—of the debt service is distributed on a wide base during periods of relatively favorable macroeconomic situation. This should help remove disincentives for private investments. Moreover, debt-for-equity swaps, which can be linked to foreign direct investment that raises total factor productivity in the economy, should also be pursued on a significantly large scale.

In sum, while the choice of the Hungarian government to avoid a unilateral default on external debt is likely the correct one, effort should be directed at ensuring that the heavy burden of the debt does not jeopardize the success of the extremely costly economic transformation that the Hungarian economy is currently undergoing.

NOTES

1. Other factors that account for the decline in corporate tax revenues are the rationalization of depreciation rules and the provisions for bad debts. While welcome from an efficiency point of view, these measures have significant adverse effects on budget revenues in the short run.

2. Deflating the external debt through revaluation of the exchange rate does not seem a feasible option, as the negative impact on exports would lead to a sharp contraction in domestic output.

REFERENCES

Burda, M. 1992. Unemployment, Labor Market Institutions and Structural Change in Eastern Europe. INSEAD Working Paper, 92/68/EP.

Calvo, G. 1993. Growth, Debt and Economic Transformation: The Capital Flight Problem. International Monetary Fund, mimeo.

Kornai, J. 1992. The Postsocialist Transition and the State: Reflections in the Light of the Hungarian Fiscal Problems. *American Economic Review* 82, no. 2.

McKinnon, R. 1991. *The Order of Economic Liberalization*. Baltimore: Johns Hopkins University Press.

Tanzi, V. 1993. Fiscal Policy and Economic Restructuring of Economics in Transition. International Monetary Fund, Working Paper Series, WP 93/22, March.

4

The Polish Government
Budget Stabilization and Sustainability

ALAIN DE CROMBRUGGHE

1. INTRODUCTION

The government budget is at the center of Poland's economic transformation. First, the structure of the budget is bound to reflect the desired move from a centrally planned economy to a market-oriented one. Second, the budget is a key element in the necessary macroeconomic stability. Third, the timing of the budgetary reforms and deficits is determined by the policy makers' objectives and the constraints of the economic transformation.

This study tries to put the budgetary experience of Poland into a more general perspective on the transition to a noninflationary market economy. It starts from the implications for the budgetary policy of the objective of creating a full-fledged market economy. It tries to identify general patterns and constraints. A first set of constraints and opportunities is given by the inheritance from the past: financing constraints, limited resources, incomplete information. A second set of constraints is of a more political nature and includes credibility and strategic considerations. A third set of constraints is related to the transformation itself, including price liberalization and the reallocation of goods and factors, even of property rights. Moreover, external shocks and accidental events can never be excluded; they require some margin of maneuver in policy and in economic responsiveness.

This chapter starts with an overview of the 1989–1993 budgetary developments. Section 3 looks at the creation of a budget suited to a market economy. Section 4 looks at the constraints, which are divided into three groups: financing, politics, and structural (including exogenous shocks). Throughout the text, an attempt is made at quantifying the impact of the variables on the stabilization and fluctuations of the budget. Section 5, the conclusion, stresses the importance and the fragility of the recent achievements and the need for further caution and efforts to really create a "free economy" (Kornai 1990).

2. OVERVIEW OF BUDGETARY DEVELOPMENTS 1989–1993

During the last four years of transition, most macroeconomic and budgetary variables went through dramatic fluctuations. The process could be characterized as a sequence starting from bankruptcy, followed by a strong stabilization, and then a slow economic recovery and institutional reconstruction. This "statistical" description should not hide, however, the dramatic economic transformation that was irreversibly allowed to take place in January 1990: the liberalization of price signals and of the supply of goods and factors to create a full-fledged market economy.

Figure 1 presents the main components of the budget (i.e., excluding extra-budgetary funds) while table 1 gives the main general government aggregates as well as GDP and inflation figures (see also tables 2–4). All these yearly figures inevitably hide even wider variations of some indicators within a year, as for instance the outburst of near-hyperinflation at the end of 1989. Real GDP must have started declining in 1989 (after a relatively good year in 1988). The poor export performance, the extreme price pressures in what was already an overheated shortage economy, and the high share of inventories (see, e.g., Berg and Sachs 1992) all indicate that the official 0.2% real growth in 1989 is an overestimate.[1] In 1990, a 6%–12% fall in GDP was recorded, driven by adjustments in domestic demand, despite buoyant exports to the West. Another 4%–6% fall came in 1991, despite high domestic demand, under the pressure of costs and the especially dramatic trading difficulties with the former CMEA partners, mostly the Soviet Union. GDP stopped falling in 1992, and 1% or 2% real growth could have been recorded if a severe drought had not hit agricultural output. Prospects for 1993 are a cautious 1%–2% real growth and a consumer price inflation slowly stabilizing around 32% over the year.

The consolidated public sector deficit averaged 7% of GDP in 1989, while 1990 recorded a 2.7% consolidated surplus (against a planned 0%–1%). 1991 had a 4.4% GDP consolidated deficit (see figure 1), and 1992 ended up close to 7%, above the planned 5% and below the revised 7.5%. The 1993 budget foresees again a 5% GDP deficit.

The budgetary situation in 1989 largely deteriorated under pressure of wage increases and partial price liberalizations as well as turnover and profit tax revisions or exemptions under the last communist government.[2] The plan was losing control of the economy and a complicated system of taxes and subsidies could not help it allocate goods and factors efficiently. The budget deficit was fought by a reduction in public investment and in some subsidies and aided by only a limited fall in profit tax revenue. The year started without systemic reform projects but with a "Round Table" with the Solidarity union, which led to wage and political concessions and eventually to a Solidarity government at the very end of August.[3]

A budget surplus emerged in 1990, peaking in the summer. Profit taxes were buoyant as global price liberalization in January offered enterprises initially higher sale prices, while costs at first remained low. Budget expenses were kept low: consumption subsidies were cut, a first step toward a market economy. Real wages increased only at the end of the year, and social expenditure did not yet face unemployment and increased benefits. Taxes aimed at containing wages became a key element of the income policy.[4]

The budgetary situation then reversed itself. Costs increased, wages rose. Social expenditure (pensions and unemployment) rose in real terms. No new taxes were introduced.[5] Old profit and turnover taxes fell, as control over state firms weakened and new market conditions started to bite. The breakdown of trade with the Soviet Union (and the ensuing higher cost of energy) hit the production potential of the economy and demand in some sectors. Distortions in the labor market, growing impatience among the workers, and normal reallocation problems put pressure on wages, despite rising unemployment. Real wages remained too high, given the size of the shock. The monthly revisions of wages and the indexation of pensions made wage-price pressures very strong.

Deficit-cutting efforts in 1992 and 1993 involved tax reforms and expenditure fixes. On the tax side, a broadening of the turnover tax gained up to 2% of GDP compared to 1991. The personal income tax, introduced in January 1992, has produced the expected withholding and pre-payment revenue, but final settlements will not be known until April 1993. VAT is planned for June 1993, and in the meantime new excises and a temporary import surcharge will boost revenue from indirect taxes. Social security contributions were raised in March 1992 and are now quite high. On the expenditure side, no further real reforms were made. The most important measure was a temporary de-indexation of wages in the budgetary sphere and a lengthening of the intervals of pension indexation. Other savings came in the investment budget and in forcing purchases of goods and services to not exceed disposable tax revenue, which wisely helped prevent their share of GDP from rising. Nevertheless, general government expenditure in 1992 and 1993 is expected to reach up to 47% of GDP, only two percentage points less than in 1988.[6] This hides of course a much bigger real fall, since real GDP fell 15%–20% over the period, but this also puts Poland in the West European average, although its GDP per capita is much lower.

In expenditure, the highest single item used to be subsidies, which thus exhibit the most dramatic fall. Since 1991, transfers to social funds rank first, followed by health (partly because some medical subsidies changed classification). All expenditures that included a large wage component started rising in 1989, stabilized in 1990, and then continued their climb, reclaiming by 1992 almost all the savings in subsidies (in GDP terms). Long-postponed financial obligations are expected to burden the budget again by 1994.[7]

The disequilibria of 1989 and 1991 combined revenue losses and changes in expenditure. Both found their origin partly in wage pressure. Expenditure cuts could not compensate for the fall in revenue. The budget may run out of expenditure to cut, although there is still room for reform in social, health, and housing spending. Later (i.e., after completion of the base broadening of the VAT, excise, and income taxes), the budget may also run out of new taxes, especially if it wants to stimulate the supply side without distortional exemptions and subsidies. Wage and cost discipline will have to be enforced by fair taxation and by controls on owners and creditors.

3. CREATING THE BUDGET FOR A MARKET ECONOMY

3.1 FROM ACCUMULATED DISTORTIONS TO MARKET RULES

In socialist economies, production and redistribution objectives were initially pursued through the central allocation of a number of goods and services. Later, the loss of control on state enterprises was compensated by a number of "fixes": corrective incentives and direct or indirect regulation. Taxes (especially turnover taxes) and subsidies were used intensively and modified repeatedly to indirectly achieve objectives that the plan could no longer achieve directly.[8] The resulting system was both costly and not transparent. Privileges were granted, sometimes deliberately (e.g., the promotion of large industrial plants), sometimes inadvertently. Rent-seeking behavior was indeed encouraged by the interventionism of the government and the absence of bankruptcies.[9] Inflation (or shortages where prices were fixed) was inherent to such a system: it kept it alive by hiding its failures under distorted relative prices and an impression of excess demand.

The operation of a socialist budget is complicated by its interventionism. Its tendency to tax profitable activities to support less profitable ones tends to kill its sources of revenue and multiply its expenditures. The arbitrary nature of its intervention, however, offers the budget some room for maneuver. Nevertheless, by 1989, the available fixes and the acceptable inflationary fuel seemed to have been exhausted.

The budget in a market economy is quite different. As a rule, it does not try to achieve a specific allocation of resources and goods, which is left to market signals (through prices and profits). Its provision is of public goods and services, which the market cannot provide efficiently, and it makes this provision subject to severe tests of social return to consumers. Tax rates tend to be kept to levels that do not discourage effort and creativity.[10] Social assistance and income redistribution take the form of insurance or of income support for well-identified groups: children, elderly, the sick, or unemployed people. This requires resources from the taxation of consumption and of income. Finally, inflation is kept low in order to maintain clear market signals and reduce the power of price-setters. Some role by the budget and monetary policy to stabilize economic activity is recognized.[11]

Various elements of the transition to a market economy bring the budget first some relief, then new pressures. Most of the room for budgetary stabilization is offered by a cut in subsidies, justified by the desire to simplify and better target the provision of public goods and social assistance. More revenue can be provided by the elimination of numerous tax exemptions. In addition, temporary adjustment effects, such as capital gains, may boost taxable profits. Pressures come from social allowances, especially in the transition phase, when resource reallocation increases the number of retirees and unemployed. The survival of old rights at the same time as new and hopefully simpler and more efficient systems of social support are introduced may be costly. Further, due to the transformation of economic activity, the old tax base may practically vanish even before a new one is identified, let alone captured.

The subsequent paragraphs look at some key elements of the revenue and expenditure policy. They identify and try to quantify the main effects of the transformation in this area. Recommendations, when made, are guided by the traditional principles of public finance, like the minimization of economic distortions, but also by two more practical principles: the reversion of the old preference for care over opportunities and a reduction of the structural disequilibrium between revenue and expenditure.

3.2 TAX POLICY

3.2.1 Structure of Revenue and Expenditure

Figure 1 reveals a structural disequilibrium in the central budget. The government's payroll and transfers to social funds amounted to 11% of

GDP in 1991, and it has been very difficult to de-index these items from other wages in the economy. Among the taxes that could go up with this kind of expenditure, the payroll tax and the excess wage tax together raised 5% of GDP, covering less than half of the wage-sensitive expenditure. Among the taxes that do not necessarily fall with this kind of expenditure, turnover taxes and customs duties raised another 8.5%. Profit taxes tend to fall when wages rise. Historically, profit taxes accounted for more than one-third of central budget revenue.

Some efforts were made in 1992 to reduce the structural disequilibrium between revenue and expenditure. The personal income tax now applies to pensions and civil servants. It increases the cost of these people, but on the margin, it will, fortunately, recover some of the expenditure increases. In 1992, the new personal income tax raised the expected 5.5% of GDP, but the excess wage tax was lowered in the second half of 1992.

An increase in social security contributions reduced the structural disequilibrium of the social funds.[12] In March 1992, the contribution rate rose from 43% to 45%, and the base became gross instead of net wages. There was also by 1993 a 3% contribution to the unemployment fund. At this rate, the social security contributions are actually very high. The small size of the contributing labor force is a problem: meaningful contributions are collected from about 10 million registered employees; the contributions of about 6 million farmers and other self-employed people, 2.5 million unemployed, and more than 8 million pensioners are not significant.[13]

3.2.2 Direct Taxes

The profit tax rate was reduced from 65% to 40% in 1989. In 1990 and 1991, old exemptions were reduced. In 1991, depreciation allowances were increased and a three-year carry-over of losses was introduced. These moves are in line with the intended stimulation of aggregate supply.

A 20% payroll tax remained in force until the end of 1991. The personal income tax was introduced in January 1992, with the highest marginal rate set at 40%. The new tax is pretty standard in its effort to aggregate personal income (except for interest income, which is exempt) and in its deductions. The main non-income related deduction is for housing mortgages. Collection is facilitated by withholdings from wage-earners and advance payments by self-employed people.

Taxable profits have vanished and were more or less allowed to do so (through temporary exemptions for the private sector and for joint ventures, wage increases above the norm, and delays in the collection of the tax on wage increases).[14] The possible uses of profits also affect the firm's attitude towards them. Choosing between wages and profits from shares depends upon taxes. In 1991, the profit tax was 40% of gross profits; the statutory burden on "grossed up" wages can be estimated to be around 39%.[15] Actually, workers did not hold shares, and bonuses from profits were subject to some additional taxes in 1991. Anyway, the incentives for profits are not as strong under a bonus as under a dividend system, and profits are never as certain as wages.

The recent experience calls for a harder stick and a tastier carrot. The stick is a real threat of bankruptcy or of owner and creditor control. The carrot is a faster and larger distribution of free or fixed-price shares to the workers (OECD 1992) and built-in incentives for profits in the transitory compulsory dividends and excess wage taxes (e.g., credits in the profit tax; see the discussion of wage policy, below). A faster "commercialization" of enterprises would facilitate control, acquisitions, and restructurings. All this matters even more for economic efficiency than for profit tax revenue. Even after a short-run fall while production and demand are restructured, the profit tax is bound to be a lower source of revenue in a market economy than under central planning.[16]

Personal income taxes and social security contributions appear, then, as a necessary substitute for profit taxes in addition to being justified in their own right, by many of their uses, by the need to spread the sources of revenue, and by their better correlation with social expenditure than many other taxes. Excessive income taxes and social security contributions nevertheless risk raising the cost of employment, which both reduces international competitiveness and encourages the informal economy.

3.2.3 Indirect Taxes

In 1988, the Polish turnover tax was a narrow-based but well-enforced production tax. Its performance had been extremely disappointing from 1989 until 1992, despite numerous rate increases.[17] In addition to tax cheating, a fall in industrial sales and inappropriate exemptions (e.g., for private businesses), the fall in the real value of the tax can be explained by its inability to reach the rapidly expanding value added in services, distribution, and retail.[18]

The case for a value-added tax (VAT) is well known (see, e.g., Gordon 1992). This is one of the most stable sources of government revenue, and one of the least distortional ones. If anything, it favors much-needed savings against consumption and does not hurt exports. Moreover, this tax can reach the most rapidly expanding sectors of the economy, like distribution, retail, services, and imports. Tax compliance is made easier by its collection at each stage of the production and distribution process. Another major advantage of an early introduction of a broad-based VAT is the collection of a wealth of data on economic activity. Finally, the number of people to educate is limited to the number of businesses, and once they use a reliable accounting system for the neutral VAT, they can also be subject to other taxes.

The introduction of the value-added tax should have the highest priority in Eastern Europe. A transitional low rate broadening of the turnover tax (as on retail sales and services, and of course on most previously exempt items) is a necessary alternative in case of political or technical difficulties with the VAT.[19] Customs duties are also needed, but their rate should not invite evasion, hurt industrial exporters, or deprive these usually monopolistic economies from healing competition. Poland introduced comprehensive tariffs in August 1991, a relatively well-timed move.[20] It started broadening the turnover tax base in May 1992, too late, even given its desire to boost the private sector by an almost untaxed status. Rates were increased again in October 1992. Poland hopes to introduce the VAT after the September 1993 general election; it should raise at least 10% of GDP or 30% of government revenue.[21]

Precious time has been lost with indirect taxes. The performance of the broadened turnover tax in 1992 shows that at least 2% of GDP was lost in 1990 and 1991.[22] In 1993, at least one more percent of GDP will be gained by the VAT that could have been gained in 1992. The benefit of earlier action would not have been limited to revenue collection. A much lower inflation rate, and maybe also fewer popular protests, could have been obtained if the turnover tax broadening had been part of the January 1990 "big bang." In hindsight, it appears that the devaluation has exceeded the needed correction, and that prices have jumped above predictions to reach world levels. There was thus room for a broadening of the turnover tax without inflationary or competition consequences, while all small subsequent corrections generated political difficulties, inflation, and preemptive imports.[23]

3.3. SOCIAL POLICY

The social policy of a market economy differs from that of a centrally planned economy in offering people the means to fulfill (some of) their needs rather than offering them the goods directly. The dramatic fall in subsidies and the still-increasing distribution of pensions and other replacement income reflect this change in Poland. Consumption and production subsidies were indeed reduced from 16% to 3.4% of GDP between 1988 and 1992 (see table 5 for subsidies). But in the provision of health, education, infrastructure, and social safety, Poland seems to have inherited a communist preference for care above opportunities.[24]

The system of unemployment benefits introduced in 1989 offered allowances without time limits or entry tests, while retraining plans were never implemented. Time limits (one year or two job offers) were introduced in December 1991. Training programs and hiring subsidies are now being considered again. Reductions in unemployment benefits can cause a rise in social assistance expenditure, but usually not at a 1:1 ratio.[25]

Health expenditure has risen without significant improvement in health care. Import and (less importantly) production subsidies for medicines are now in the health budget.[26] There is talk of a new compulsory health insurance and of a major overhaul of the system. A clearer distinction could be made between three aspects: public health, necessary insurance, and private care. The OECD has devoted much attention recently to health provision systems (e.g., surveys of the United States and Italy) along these lines, with a special focus on compulsory insurance systems. It also showed that the share of health expenditure in GDP tends to rise linearly with per capita GDP. Spending more than 5% of GDP, Poland already exceeds the level of a few members of the EC. It should not let this percentage rise in the near future.

Housing subsidies still absorbed, in two very inefficient ways, more than 2% of GDP in the 1992 budget (see table 5). First, consumption of heating and hot water is usually not measured and supply cannot be cut: people have no incentive to save and often do not even pay the amounts they are charged. Installing meters appealed to the World Bank as a transitional investment well worth its cost. Second, interest subsidies go to cooperatives that take years to complete cheap non-mortgageable apartments, discouraging private construction. As the OECD survey of Poland shows, even the reformed construction subsidies are a potentially explosive expenditure; focused on construction, they are needlessly distortional and may fail to reduce the cost of construction.

Retirement, disability benefits, and family allowances all need reform to be better targeted and cost less.[27] A few points specific to Poland can be mentioned. Disability benefits and early retirement may have served to disguise unemployment. The old and still-surviving pension law gave very high pensions to some groups of workers. The new pension law (November 1991) provides for a quite generous treatment of the years where no contribution was paid. Pensioners' real income has fared better than that of workers, and by 1991 the real per capita expenditure in a pensioner's household was higher than in a worker's household (table 6). Such consumption data raise doubts about the necessity of the present level of pension expenditure, and may act as a disincentive to work.

A major transitional problem in reforming social insurance and services is the absence of funds to supplement current contributions. The extensive state ownership of assets (from apartments to factories) will have to be partly allocated to social insurance funds.[28]

Poland cannot sustain its present social benefits, and its present withdrawals from the labor force (disability, retirement, unemployment; see table 6).[29] Its still-growing labor force should start saving for its retirement years. Contributions are relatively easy to collect and badly needed to support the present system, although they risk overly burdening the labor market (Bruno and Sachs 1985). In addition, the cost of the present system endangers the provision of the necessary infrastructure for the future development of the economy.

For the budget, the replacement of arbitrary subsidies by indexed income support has provided only short-term relief. In fact, guaranteed indexed income support tends to put even more pressure on the budget than arbitrary subsidies. Given the slowness of tax reform, the financial position of the government has been weakened. Higher wages in the economy not only reduce profit taxes but increase wage-indexed and wage-related expenditure. The appearance of an unsustainable position in the second year of the reforms calls for fast disinflation and de-indexation, and for the early introduction of consumption and personal income taxes.[30]

3.4. ADMINISTRATION

The choice for quantity rather than quality in administration is another structural deficiency, typical of economies controlled by political parties (communist or others). The central government pays close to 3 million people, or about 17% of the labor force. Of these, 1.1 million work in education and 800,000 million in hospitals, while the army accounts for 230,000 people. At the same time, the central administration employs 270,000 people and is hiring, but its salaries are still too low to retain the best individuals. Communal and housing services, science, culture, and sports take care of the rest of the 3 million (source: GUS bulletin and 1992 budget). The civil service system must be revamped to make it suit democracy and the market economy.

One of the growth areas of the central administration is tax inspectors. Another area where increased expertise and staffing will be needed is commercial courts, where bankruptcy and competition proceedings should soon increase.

The impact on the budget is hard to judge. The central administration wage cost (wage times people) will most probably increase. In all other areas of public employment, there seems to be room for decrease, if not in wages then in people.

3.5 INVESTMENT POLICY

Public investment has fallen from 5% to 3% of GDP. This comes immediately after subsidies in its relative contribution to budgetary savings. A disproportionate burden may have fallen on the local authorities, their investment falling from 2.5% to 1.1% of GDP. Moreover, in the recent deficit years (1989, 1991, 1992, and—projected—1993), total investment expenditure has been lower than the budget deficit, while just the opposite would be required by a long-term reform perspective.[31]

Investment and borrowing policies are deeply linked. The government must expect that future tax revenue will be large enough to service the debt accumulated by the present deficits. To ensure such tax revenue from the economy, government actions should be seen as increasing its future productivity, or as investments (material or otherwise) bearing appropriate rates of return. The anticipation of future tax revenue from the economy may be over-optimistic if the preference for care over opportunities continues. Moreover, it is not even certain that the future liabilities of the government implied by new laws on pensions and social benefits are fully recognized in the present accounting system. Such liabilities should start being backed by assets or savings.

The present policy partly reflects lower subsidies to sometimes misguided industrial investments, but it also reflects a slowing down of infrastructure works and even a depreciation of existing assets.[32]

Various suggestions have been made to help maintain infrastructure provision at a sufficient level. Tied grants and loans from international institutions and foreign countries help maintain investments in infrastructure and create opportunities for environmental cleanups, but such activities have to be budgeted nevertheless. Balance sheet accounting or introduction of investment as a "financing" ("below the line") item instead of an "expenditure" item are suggestions to facilitate the budgeting of investment (Bruno 1992).

The main difficulty with an investment policy at this stage is the evaluation of the social and financial returns of the projects. The only information that the reformers could find on existing investment projects seems to have been their past and remaining costs.[33] There is thus little tradition and expertise, but a greater difficulty may be the determination of appropriate reference prices, let alone "shadow prices," in the fast changing environment of an economy in transition.

There is a case to be made for small public work programs at the local level. In addition to providing useful and desired local infrastructure, they may become an element in the control and training of some of the unemployed.

Infrastructure investment can play a crucial role in boosting the supply side of the economy and in fighting unemployment. Despite the need to carefully evaluate returns on investment, it is too easy in the short run and too costly in the long run to shift a large part of the budgetary savings on investment while still borrowing!

The investment reduction in 1989–1992 thus represents a cash saving of 2%–3% of GDP per year, but also a net depreciation of public assets by the same amount. This undue reduction explains—without justifying—a two to three percentage point reduction of the budget's share of GDP.

3.6 EXPENDITURE AND REVENUE POLICY

Past characteristics of government revenue and expenditure policies have just been described, as well as the main changes required by the transition to a market economy.

Table 7 tries to imagine what a budget could be in the medium term. Two main considerations have guided this exercise: a reversal of the preference for care over opportunities and an attempt at a better "coverage" of expenditure changes by automatic revenue changes in the same direction. The role of the budget as a counter-cyclical automatic stabilizer is not rejected by this, but simply held within more reasonable bounds. The total size of general government expenditure relative to GDP (46%) is allowed to reach the West European average, and this may be too optimistic before a major increase in GDP and administrative efficiency is attained, or this may also entail undesirably high costs of redistribution, but it is guided by what the majority of the Polish voters seems to demand.

The role of local governments is boosted slightly, to give the population a better opportunity to take responsibilities for public goods and services. A transfer from the central budget is maintained as this is an essential form of solidarity within the country and a way to pay for the use of some local services and infrastructure by external users.

Health care is moved to the social funds, leaving only public health issues (prevention, information, etc.) to the central budget. Poland still has to decide what kind of health system it wants, but a system of compulsory insurance (covering every individual directly or indirectly and allowing for some risk-pooling and solidarity) and a relatively free choice of providers (with competition between individual or group providers and complementary national guidelines for cost and quality control) may offer enough flexibility to respond to the needs and preferences of the population.

Investment expenditure is allowed to return to at least 4% of GDP. Only part of it is deficit financed. There seems to be no room for additional real debt accumulation. The allowed government deficit of 1% of GDP is lower than the expected GDP growth rate, giving room for a net amortization of part of the debt. Since social funds could wisely accumulate some assets, the suggested general government deficit is very small.

Finally, a major change in budgetary procedures is needed on the expenditure side. The first step of the budgetary process should remain the estimate of possible revenues under various economic and tax policy assumptions determined by the minister of finance in consultation with the Council of Ministers. At present the second step is the analysis of each ministry's requests (in real terms) by specialists of the Ministry of Finance. This procedure invites overstatements, and requires a lot of work from the Ministry of Finance while producing some frustrations in other ministries. The second step should, instead, be the determination by the Council of Ministers of priorities and financial "envelopes" for a number of activities and for the various ministries and agencies.[34] Then would come the verification procedure, and it would be much easier.

4. CONSTRAINTS

4.1 FINANCING CONSTRAINTS

4.1.1 Context

Note that the financing issues often appear first in the discussion of the budget. This is quite natural when the main problem is to make a budget survive until the following year.[35] In a longer-term perspective, however, an acceptable deficit is part of the general fiscal policy. Planned in this way, deficits never reach unfinanceable heights and annual deficits never amount to unsustainable debts. Governments should not live with the idea that they should always go for the maximum deficit; there may be years where the government should actually save. In the case of Poland, the inherited debt acts as a constraint on the possible sources of finance for the reforms. Nevertheless, it is also possible to see large debt in a strategic perspective: it can somehow "tie the hands" of future governments and put a limit on their profligacy (see section 4.2).

4.1.2 Indebtedness

By 1989, the previous governments had accrued a foreign debt of about $40 billion, or about 50% of GDP or 8 years of then current exports. Annual debt service obligations exceeded total annual export receipts. Nevertheless, it took quite a while for creditors and debtors alike to recognize the actual bankruptcy of the Polish government.

The first turning point in foreign finance had already taken place, in 1981–1982. Official debt was first rescheduled and then, as martial law was imposed in Poland, Western governments stopped all official lending but let interest arrears accumulate. Commercial credits virtually stopped as well. The evaporation of foreign finance not only meant the end of the government's ability to spend more than it earned, but also indirectly reduced its earnings as well. Enterprises previously supported by subsidies were bound to remit lower profit and wage taxes. During the first half of the 1980s, Poland experienced on average negative GDP growth rates.

In the second half of the decade, however, Poland's exports improved, and a foreign debt fund (FOZZ) was set up with contributions of state enterprises. Precise data on foreign debt operations are hard to obtain, as some of the fund's activities included unofficial repurchases of commercial debt on the secondary market. Nevertheless, the almost total suspension of debt service at the end of 1989 and the liquidation of the FOZZ in 1991 may represent a net but temporary freeing of resources of about 3% of GDP, after deduction of the indirect negative effects on GDP and on tax revenue.

Much more important for the long-run health of the budget was the April 1991 Paris Club reduction of 50% of the official debt. This lowered both the short-term disbursement pressure and the long-term "debt overhang" effects. Bilateral agreements were signed with all official creditors by mid-1992. The simultaneous need for an IMF agreement has delayed negotiations about similar terms with the London Club. The importance of this conditionality should not be underestimated. The past left both a burden and obligation of reform.

An often neglected part of the debts from the past is obligations-in-kind taken by previous governments. The advance sales of cars and apartments are examples. There was also a small debt in dollars in domestic banks, which could not be wiped out by inflation; worse, they tended to increase with the price liberalization. The budget surplus of 1990 gave the government an opportunity to repay some of its domestic financial debt, and bonds were issued in 1991 to take care of the rest. Obligations-in-kind are now small.[36] Table 8 summarizes the present debt outstanding.

Inherited debts were thus a large burden. Relief was needed on the foreign debt and some domestic obligations had to be modified. Progress is still needed with the Western commercial banks, whose slowness at least matches the delays they see in Polish economic reforms. Debt service will have to resume by 1994 and be foreseen in budget and balance-of-payments projections. Foreign debt service may still require at least 2% of GDP for interest and another 2% for amortization.

The main impact of the inherited debt is in allowing almost no room for further debt accumulation and thus for deficits in the transition to a market economy. Lenders are scarce, and future debt service will eventually absorb 5% of GDP, i.e., more than 10% of general government revenue.[37] The conditionality of the debt reduction put Poland under IMF supervision.

4.1.3 Deficit Financing

Monetary finance has been the main source of government finance, and almost the only one in 1989 (see table 2). The ratio of current inflation to current deficit (and even to current borrowing in the banking system) has been very unfavorable compared to other countries, but it did improve slightly in 1992 (table 9).

4.1.3.1 Seigniorage. Seigniorage, the revenue from money creation, played a variable role over the period. In principle, this revenue accrues to the National Bank of Poland, which remits part of it to the budget. Table 10 gives some measures of seigniorage and of money creation. The most common (demand-based) measure of seigniorage is the annual increase in the monetary base (the sum of the cash issued by the central bank and the compulsory reserves of the banks at the central bank). A second measure, which better reflects the budgetary value of seigniorage, is central bank profits transferred to the budget. This measure can be extended to include profit taxes on the banks and other profit transfers from the banks to the budget.[38]

In 1989, due to the partial price liberalization, the monetary overhang and the monetary finance, prices rose faster than money creation. As a consequence, real cash fell by one-third and real M2 by almost two-thirds. According to NBP estimates, the GDP velocity of M2 rose from 3.5 to 7. Nevertheless, up to 10% of GDP was collected in seigniorage. The 1990 stabilization brought a recovery of real money, mainly backed by the acquisition of foreign reserves through a trade surplus of almost 3% of GDP. From December 1989 to December 1990, M2 rose by a factor of 4.9, prices 3.5. High reserve requirements helped the collection of seigniorage despite the low increase in the real demand for cash. In 1991, prices and money rose by about 60% but real cash declined somewhat. Velocity stabilized around 5, and M2 never recovered its real 1988 level. Figure 2 shows these developments for M2.

In 1992, seigniorage seems close to steady-state values (i.e., the inflation rate times the monetary base).[39] Profits transferred to the budget are far below the first measure of seigniorage. It is possible that the budget, as well as other borrowers (e.g., some state enterprises), benefited indirectly from the seigniorage in the form of low interest rates.

The pattern of monetary stabilization in figure 2 is not uncommon. The return of flight capital, a trade surplus, and the reconstruction of real money balances have been observed in many economies where stabilization occurred together with a large devaluation and efforts to restore credibility with budgetary discipline and positive real interest rates. The budgetary discipline paradoxically is needed to encourage the reconstruction of the monetary base, but prevents the government from directly benefiting from it in the form of increased borrowing from the central bank. Only the extra profits of the banks benefit the budget (totally or via tax revenues, depending on institutional arrangements).

A further increase in real money demand will be hard to achieve without a renewed effort to reduce at least the primary budget deficit. This time, the induced reserve increase may become useful to service and amortize the remaining foreign debt (see section 4.1.2). In 1992, real money demand and foreign reserves increased slightly, but a trade deficit appeared in the last two months of 1992 and deepened in the first quarter of 1993.

4.1.3.2 Banks. There are differences between central bank and commercial bank finance. First is the demand for cash (central bank) and deposits (banks). The move toward deposits (credit multiplier: December 1989 = 1.9, December 1990 = 2, December 1991 = 2.4) forced the government to borrow relatively more from the commercial banks than from the central bank, despite high compulsory reserve ratios. Second is the bargaining position. Commercial banks tend to extract more surplus from the government (higher cost) than the central bank but, by so doing, enforce more discipline.[40] Third, the banks are more likely to refinance themselves in the public with (less money-like) long-term certificates of deposit. In mid-1990, however, the central bank itself began to sterilize part of its (foreign) assets by selling 4- to 26-week bills, before it started dealing actively in treasury bills and treasury bonds in mid-1991.

4.1.3.3 Bonds. Bonds were first issued in 1989 and 1990. They offered options to buy shares in the privatization program, and to pay taxes. Issues ended when the budget went into surplus. Since mid-1991, there has been an active market for short-term discount treasury bills, ranging from 4- to 26- and now even 52-week maturities, auctioned weekly and tradeable among the banks. Treasury bills and bonds now account for a bit more than two-thirds of the outstanding government debt in the banking system, but half of them are held by the central bank.

Long-term domestic bonds were launched in mid-1992.[41] They could affect financial discipline. Public secondary trading can provide a good indicator of confidence. Non-negative real interest rates will be needed, or at least rates competitive with foreign currency and durable goods investments. Instruments whose value is hard to affect without outright default may signal discipline. If the government bets on success (i.e., real sustainable appreciation), foreign currency indexed three- or five-year bonds (payable in domestic currency only) may be a good form of finance as long as inflation uncertainty remains, despite the appearance of maintaining a two-currency economy. As for the internal convertibility of the zloty, access to guarantees in foreign currency may increase the credibility and use of the domestic currency.

A critical mass in the bond market and a large constituency of holders may come sooner than the government originally thought. Bonds will be a necessary element of any recapitalization and privatization of financial institutions. There are indications that civil servants would also accept bonds as partial payment. The political weight of bond holders may add to the credibility of the government's macroeconomic policies.

4.1.3.4 Foreign finance. Presently, foreign finance is negative on net, despite continuing loans from the World Bank. Existing sources of foreign finance have not been used very actively. For the $4 billion of pledged multilateral assistance, the government has been slow in setting investment and restructuring priorities, although it has also rightly complained about procedural complications. Indirect (i.e., balance-of-payment) support could come from IMF borrowing (a tranche was drawn in May 1991), and from export credit guarantees. In November 1992, a new letter of intent was agreed on with the IMF, which should open the way to a standby $700 million credit the IMF board approved after the 1993 budget was passed in the Sejm. More importantly, the restoration of good standing with the IMF opens the way to the implementation of debt reduction agreements.

An active use of bond and foreign finance is possible and needed to move away from monetary financing. But government borrowing still has costs, whether it takes money, credit, or foreign currencies away from the rest of the economy.

4.1.3.5 Interest rates. The lower limit for deposit interest rates is the alternative in foreign currency, determined by the announced annual depreciation of about 24% plus a normal nominal interest of about 10%. The refinancing rate of 38% and the auction-determined rates of 37%–43% (depending on maturities) for treasury bills thus incorporate a small additional devaluation risk premium. The difference between the growth of producer and consumer prices still distorts the credit market: in 1992, the first grew by 27%, the second by 45%. This leaves negative real interest rates on treasury bills and on zloty deposits for private savers, but at the same time quite high real borrowing interest rates for a number of production sectors[42] (nominal credit rates varied, in 1992, between 44% and 57% per annum).

This is where two main pieces of the stabilization puzzle meet. Except for a drought-induced jump in food prices in the third quarter of 1992, the continuing consumer price rises are largely due to price rises in the service sector, taxes, and administered prices (thus in fact to delayed steps to stabilize the budget deficit). The need to maintain the international competitiveness of enterprises in the face of persistent wage pressures, which also hurt the budget, makes it impossible to slow the crawling peg for the exchange rate. Wage restraint and a one-time adjustment in government services, housing, and energy prices, together with a stabilization of indirect taxation on a broad base, would permit a slowing of the crawling peg and a fall in nominal interest rates and in real interest rates to industrial borrowers. One sees here one of the advantages of a successful "shock therapy": a shorter period of price distortions and of high real interest rates.

Progress is needed in finance. After being cut from foreign finance in the 1980s and relying excessively on monetary finance, the government has to focus its efforts on finding domestic non-monetary sources of finance for the deficit, but only those it can justify on long-term investment grounds. The next section turns to strategic and timing considerations about the deficit.

4.2 POLITICAL, STRATEGIC, AND TIMING CONSTRAINTS

4.2.1 Credibility and Timing Theories

The theory of credibility was recalled in De Broeck, de Crombrugghe, and Kudlinski (1992). In the simplest theoretical approach, the government is assumed to target low inflation and lower unemployment than the wage setters are willing to deliver. The wage setters' assumed objective is to maintain high real wages, but they can only set nominal wages periodically. Both face the constraint that high real wages reduce employment and that inflation can be used to (temporarily) reduce real wages (there is thus an assumed inflation-unemployment trade-off or Phillips Curve). A lack of credibility of the government's low inflation target produces higher inflation and the same level of unemployment than if the government did not try to stimulate employment by using inflation to reduce real wages. To establish its anti-inflation credibility after the many Polish experiences of corrective and even hyperinflationary price increases, the government may be forced to accept high costs in terms of high unemployment and reduced expenditure.

Then comes the issue of timing. In a multiperiod version of the game just outlined, the government can choose to reduce inflation either gradually or very fast. The employment (or output) loss will be spread over a long or short period. In various simulations of such a multiperiod game, Oudiz and Sachs (1985) have shown that a fast disinflation leads to lower accumulated inflation and unemployment costs than a slow one. Additional political considerations may, however, enter into the game and modify this result. Alesina and Drazen (1991) have built a model in which two constituencies delay the stabilization of the economy and incur a high cost, which serves to reveal each constituency's strength and tolerance level, until one eventually wins. Nevertheless, when very high inflation has to be stabilized, it usually has to be done in one shot in order to minimize distortions, i.e., to restore meaningful relative prices (including intertemporal ones).[43]

As for the strategy of indebtedness, Persson and Svensson (1989) have suggested that a conservative (anti-inflation) policy maker may decide to leave a high budget deficit to a spending-prone successor in order to force him to spend less.[44]

4.2.2 Anchors and Implementation

In practice, the inflation-unemployment trade-off appears somewhat simplistic, but the insight it offers into the credibility issue is still relevant. As Balcerowicz (1992) notes, a stabilization program based only on the threat of bankruptcy and unemployment is unrealistic, and even more so in an economy where bankruptcy institutions and asset markets are lacking and where the labor market does not operate in a competitive way. On the other hand, numerous Latin American experiences show that wage, exchange rate, and (worst of all except in a few monopolies) price freezes provide only short-lived stabilizations and false hopes: hidden problems just become worse until the program collapses. Price liberalization was a necessity in Poland, to heal the markets, credibly show the change of system, and open the way to competition in the goods market. The art of the matter was then to give an indication of where prices and wages would stand and to complement the unemployment and bankruptcy threats with other safeguards.[45]

To offer an indication of where prices should stand, the program offered a convertible currency at—for at least three months—a fixed exchange rate. Foreign competition through imports, as well as on the export markets, should keep an upper limit on prices, which it indeed did, although perhaps at too high a level, but this is less hard to reach for enterprises than the opposite. To offer an indication of where' wages should stand, and to automatically penalize deviations, the tax on excessive wage increases was devised. Balcerowicz (1992) defends it strongly, and it was adopted under some form in most subsequent Central and East European stabilization programs. This tax is discussed below with the income policy. In addition, to protect state and enterprise assets from excessive costs and wages claims, a compulsory dividend was levied on the state assets of the enterprises and amortization was increased. Nevertheless, real wages had recovered their average 1989 level by the end of 1990 and continued to rise in 1991, then finally stabilized in 1992.

Three major policy concessions or dents in credibility can be identified. First, in the second half of 1990, the indexation coefficient of wages exempted from the tax on excessive wage increases was raised, and the interest rates at the NBP were lowered (Winiecki 1992, Balcerowicz 1992). Second, in 1991, talks of policy changes and of "industrial policy," together with more emphasis on sectoral privatization studies, gave conflicting signals to the state firms. Simultaneously, tax collection, even in state firms, proved somewhat problematic, especially in 1991. Arrears accumulated then to more than 2% of GDP, especially in the tax on excessive wage increases and in the compulsory dividend on state assets. This may indeed have hurt the budget twice (direct loss plus cost-raising behavior of firms) and the credibility of the program. Figures 3 and 4 suggest indeed that some big loss-making firms did not hesitate to incur *popiwek* (tax on excessive wage increases) obligations.[46] Third, in 1992, these two taxes were reduced, one argument being that they should be "payable" to make sense. Nevertheless, given the firms' ability to effectively determine their costs, it can be asked what impact this had on the behavior of firms. Turnover tax arrears took, in 1992, some of the room left by the reduced *popiwek* and *dywidenda* (compulsory dividends on promoter's funds) obligations.[47]

Another problem with firms in arrears is the bankruptcy or restructuring procedures, and the manpower to implement them. "Too big to fail" was not the only obstacle; "too many to fail" may have played a role, too. Action has been taken by the government in some of the worst loss makers, like the Ursus tractor factory and the national railways (PKP).[48]

As for the strategy of indebtedness, it remains an open question whether a stronger adjustment in 1990 could have got rid of more debt and more inflationary pressure. Despite the extraordinary boldness of the program and the fact that it was the first of its kind, some possibilities have been identified (albeit after the fact) for avoiding the mid-1990 policy relaxation and improving the turnover tax earlier. The question that can then be asked is what would have been done with the accumulated cushion. Unfortunate industrial policy experiments could also have undermined the credibility of further reforms. Of course, some debt repayments (but only after the completion of renegotiations) or further improvements in the tax administration (but only after tax reforms) or faster privatizations could have been useful expenditures to prepare even larger margins of maneuver for the long run.

Credibility and clear indications of where economic policy is going for some time are the elements with which any stabilization program stands or fall. The Polish governments did relatively well on this, especially given that the upturn of measured economic production in 1992 occurred without a new burst of inflation or major concession to enterprises or workers.[49] Unfortunately, serious progress on inflation was not recorded recently, either. Wage pressures remain strong, while bankruptcy and privatization procedures remain slow. Tax

arrears slowed in 1992, but will still accumulate to 3% of GDP by the
end of the third year of stabilization.

4.2.3 Political Pressures

The move to a democracy at the same time as the move to the market
may not be easy, but each one tends to support the other. Nevertheless, in times of elections, the political logic of attracting votes may run
against the economic logic of rigor. Poland faced these difficulties from
the second half of 1990 until the end of 1991. It was only in mid-1992
that it got a stable government. The success of the Polish democracy is
that whoever got a say in economic management eventually came back
to the fundamental principles of market mechanisms and macroeconomic stability. Strikes were often successful but they have not
managed, so far, to throw the economy off course. Even if elections
corresponded with some releases of macroeconomic fuel, the slowing
of macroeconomic progress had to be weighed against the risk of a
total rejection of the reforms by the voters.

Many stabilization programs have foundered because politicians
claimed victory too early and wasted their gains before completing the
reforms, or because politicians or voters lacked the courage to carry
on. Poland, so far, has managed to stay on course, even if the course
may still seem too slow or on a knife-edge. Single-digit annual inflation
rates and well-functioning labor and capital markets are still not in
sight. Better functioning goods markets and slowly increasing production are already unquestionable achievements. The last part of this
chapter is devoted to these structural transformations. They may affect
the budget only indirectly, but it turns out that their impact is actually
very strong.

4.3 Economic Transformation and External Shocks

4.3.1 The Costs of Making the Transition

The transition from central planning to market signals requires a
number of transformations. These transformations may be more or
less controlled by wise policies, but they have to take place anyway and
bring with them a number of shocks that also affect the budget.

4.3.2 Inflationary Habits

After long experience with inflation, people learn how to live with it.
Most contracts are indexed on past price changes, others anticipate an
ever-rising rate of inflation. In this case, a reduction of inflation can

prove extremely costly for all those who are bound to payments contracted in the past, because their revenues suddenly drop compared to their obligations. Debtors are hit, moreover, by the high real interest rates needed to convince savers to lend again when a stabilization is attempted. Finally, inflation hurts some businesses more than others, skewing progressively the economic structure of a country, and a fall of inflation only slowly supports the reconstruction of a diversified economy.

In Eastern Europe, inflation-proofing of the economy had been pushed less far than in countries where state control was even weaker and the private sector larger. Nevertheless, Poland faced wage indexation, an organized labor force, and a large dollarization, and had understood the profitability of trading activities under inflationary conditions.

The cost of inflationary habits in Poland is mostly reflected in the downward rigidity of nominal wages and prices, which force almost every single relative price adjustment to produce an average price increase. This also slows the perception of relative price changes and the response of production factors to areas of higher demand. Moreover, a weaker responsiveness of government revenue than government expenditure to inflation is a danger for the budget. Budget finance became more and more dependent on central bank borrowing and so did enterprise finance as well.

4.3.3 Price Adjustments

It needs to be recalled that, before the 1989–1990 price liberalization, Poland faced shortages of many final and intermediate goods. Queues were a common sight. Leisure and working time wasted in shopping or in trying to reach autarky have never been fully measured. In addition to maintaining artificially low prices, the system also decided quite arbitrarily on relative prices.

A major reason that price liberalization and open trade have to happen early is that they are a determinant of the reallocation of factors. The difficulties linked with the reallocation of labor and capital are described in the subsequent subsections. Factors being less mobile than goods, their adjustment to demand and supply conditions is slower. Moreover, factors should be seen as scarce, and used thriftily; their allocation should be strictly determined by demand for their products, i.e., the satisfaction of people's needs, not by any desire (communist or other) to create structures (centralized, competitive, technological, or other). Even what will be said below about capital and labor mobility (wage and profit dispersion indicators) is subordinated to the usefulness of this mobility for the satisfaction of final demands.

In Poland, price liberalization could occur early and quite successfully. The risk of abuse of monopoly power, while still existing, was reduced by the creation of an anti-monopoly agency, the lifting of most trade restrictions, and the adoption of a low and uniform tariff. Moreover, the country had a diversified and partly decentralized economic structure, numerous urban centers, and easy access to Western markets. Arguments heard in China or Russia about monopoly power and distribution problems do not apply to Poland.

The price liberalization represented a one-time gain for the budget in 1990 and at the end of 1989, as most capital gains (e.g., on inventories) of enterprises were considered taxable profits. Almost all the extra income from profit taxes in 1989 (1%–2% of GDP) may be traced to capital gains, while only part of the extra income from profit taxes in 1990 is from this source, a good additional chunk coming from the positive effect of the devaluation on exports and on foreign currency balances. The rest of the extra profit tax revenue in 1990 came from real wage restraint, lower employment, and the banking sector. These profit tax gains compensated the impact of the 1989 Tanzi effect of hyperinflation on real tax revenue: even under a monthly collection of taxes, a 50% inflation rate can erode half of the real value of taxes between their computation and their collection. This effect seems to have hit the turnover and excise taxes more than any other one.

4.3.4 Wage Adjustments

In the personal income area, at least three adjustments have to take place. One is the stabilization of average wages (and allowances) to a realistic level. A second is the adjustment of relative wages in the vertical dimension (skill and responsibility compensation) and a third is their adjustment in the horizontal dimension (industry-specific differences for similar work).

4.3.4.1 Wage level. An initial adjustment of the average wage level is relatively easy to obtain through devaluation, market price liberalization, and administrative price rises. It is much harder to maintain, depending on the wage-setting institutions. Figures 5 and 6 compare the evolution of real gross wages in three reforming countries. At the aggregate level, factors like indexation, inflationary expectations, lack of government or central bank credibility, weakness of the owners or creditors, and strength of the unions can easily destroy the initial adjustment. The role played in Poland by these well-known macroeconomic factors has been reviewed in paragraphs devoted to them. An additional difficulty in maintaining the average wage level in formerly centrally planned economies is due to the huge needs for relative wage adjustments.[50]

Wage pressures have pervasive effects on budgetary performance. Increases in real wages reduce profits and profit tax revenue, and Czechoslovakia is the only country in the region that shows both stable real wages and stable real profit tax revenue (see the relevant chapters in this volume). The payroll of the government rises as wages rise, and so does indexed replacement income as pensions and unemployment benefits. Real wage pressures also reduce employment, entitling more people to pensions or unemployment benefits (see table 6). Wage taxes rise with wages but fall with employment.

4.3.4.2 Skill rewarding. Central European economies were relatively egalitarian. The rates of secondary and vocational education were pretty high, but higher and university education were less widespread. Both in the administration and in state enterprises, wages poorly reflected the level of education and of responsibility. In a market economy, by contrast, wage differentials are supposed to induce people to acquire the skills and positions that are most in demand and pay best. If too many people invest in the same skills, their relative reward falls. The exact operation of this reallocation mechanism, the possible role of factors other than wage differentials, and the social implications are the object of numerous studies, but at any rate the existing wage differentials in Poland were too low to stimulate investments in skills and responsibilities. As with relative prices, the adjustment tends to happen only in an upward direction. A great deal of nominal and real wage inflation can come from this source, despite the existence of mass unemployment.

Relative wage adjustments can be expected to occur gradually, mainly after the prices are left to the market. Indeed, demand for skills will largely be derived from the demand for goods and services. The scarcity of skills will be observed only after firms start to reorganize and once foreign firms enter the labor market. In Poland, Boeri and Keese (1992) report some indications of widening wage differentials by function within sectors; another indication is increasing parity of wages in the "material services" (more clerical positions) with those in industry (see table 11).[51] The budgetary impact of relative wage adjustments is hard to measure, except insofar as they disproportionately raise the average real wage. A negative budgetary impact is felt on profit taxes while a positive one is felt on wage taxes. Nevertheless, a rise in marginal wage or personal income tax is not necessarily an appropriate policy here: gross salaries for scarce skills will have to rise even further to find their equilibrium, and tax evasion or avoidance (fringe benefits) will be more attractive, reducing profits and profit taxes even more. A tax on increases in the total wage bill of the firm or on average wage increases (like the *popiwek*) allows an adjustment of relative wages within firms using a wide enough spectrum of skills (with the first formula inducing somewhat more labor shedding than the second one). Hard budget constraints and credible macroeconomic policies are the best guarantees against the inflationary impact of relative wage adjustments, but important nominal downward rigidities of wages and widespread indexation mechanisms may still explain a second round of price increases (after the first round due to price liberalization).

4.3.4.3 Inter-industry differences. Another characteristic of employment and wages in Central European economies is the communist preference for large industrial enterprises. Coal miners enjoyed the highest wages in Poland in 1989, earning twice the average of clothing industry workers; they were followed by the non-ferrous sector, the fuels industry, and iron and steel. The coal sector was also the largest industrial employer. Some of the lowest wages were found in the service sector. Now, some non-trade or oligopolistic services, such as banking and the former foreign trade monopolies, top the wage list.

Inter-industry wage differentials are also justified in a market economy on the basis of various characteristics (skills, risks, efficiency wages) that were not necessarily taken into account by the central plan. The reallocation of labor may even temporarily justify different wages for the same work in different sectors. Here is thus an additional reason for upward nominal average wage pressures. Nevertheless, there is also a risk for a very unpleasant combination of high unemployment with high inflation.

A costly combination of high unemployment and high inflation can find its origins in unwarranted sectoral wage evolution. The most profitable sectors, the sectors with the strongest labor force, and those with the highest capital intensity are able to raise wages. Other sectors, including state pensions and civil servants, follow by some form of indexation to average wages and this makes the inflation dynamic.

The unemployment dynamics of this sectoral pressure on wages is based on an "insider-outsider" operation of the labor market. Wages are raised by insiders, and even in profitable firms this discourages additional hiring. The insiders are able to ignore the large numbers of unemployed outsiders when they bargain, even with a real profit-conscious owner. A capitalist can indeed care more about the dedication of its workforce than about its price.[52] A perfectly rational decision at the firm level may thus fail to take into account the economy-wide externalities of such a decision. Even the increased purchasing power of the wage-raising group will fail to fully benefit the economy: access to the most demanded and profitable sectors will be barred by the "insiders" to the "outsiders." This problem, however, will develop only in the presence of monopoly power, either of the firm in its goods market or of the workers in their segment of the labor market.

The wage-price spiral here is based on a very simple circle of copied or indexed wage increases, breeding a larger deficit, leading to money printing and rising prices. Each round may cost a few more unemployed people and widen the gap between the pay in the strongest and the weakest sectors.

A test of the hypothesis of insiders' market power would start from the observation of high unemployment and high inflation, low labor mobility, and high differences in wages across sectors. It would then check if there is a systematic relation between wages on the one hand and profits, concentration of sales, and concentration of labor on the other. The results for Poland are presented in table 11. The regressions and the wage dispersion indicator (coefficient of variation) support the hypothesis of strong pressures from powerful groups, especially in 1991. For the other years, the effect of the inherited communist wage dispersion (based indeed on big unionized factories) dominates new tendencies to appropriate profits.[53] Figures 3 and 4 show a U-shaped relation between profitability and excess wage taxes due. The left side of the U may be explained by credibility issues (see above) and the right side by profit appropriation, but the top of both sides is made of sectors with a high number of (unionized) employees per firm. Table 12 shows that one-third of the unemployed are younger than 24 and almost two-thirds are younger than 35 years. This paints a very worrying picture of the access of outsiders to employment (even if the share of unemployed school-leavers seems to be falling).

There is also some anecdotal evidence of insider behavior and of demands for indexation. Strikes in the summer of 1992 took place in concentrated and profitable sectors: the copper combine in Lublin and the most modern FIAT car factory in Tichy. The FIAT workers eventually lost the sympathy of the population when it appeared that their requests would put them far ahead of any other worker in Poland. In December 1992, the coal miners, who saw an erosion of their relative wage position (but who still top the list in industrial wages and represent the most concentrated sector), went on strike. In the same month, the Parliament refused to permanently de-link public servants' wages from industrial wages (but accepted later a temporary break in indexation for the 1993 budget).

International evidence also points to the damaging effect of monopolistic insiders' behavior in economies in transition.[54] Employment and wage inflation problems appear indeed in unified Germany, where a sectoral wage bargaining system led by the metal workers (insiders) raised the cost of unification dramatically. The poor inflation and employment performance of monopolistic wage bargaining systems by comparison to fully centralized and fully competitive systems has been shown for the OECD area (Bruno and Sachs 1985; Calmfors and Driffill 1988; OECD 1988). The difficulty in evaluating the Polish system, as with any system, is its hybrid nature: wage determination is in principle left to the firm under a tax-enforced (*popiwek*) national guideline for wage growth (not level), but the market power of some firms and the indexation mechanisms are reminiscent of the sectoral wage determination systems.

The negative budgetary impact of insider monopoly power can be large. Strikes in big factories are an old Polish characteristic, but after the price liberalization, new incentives appear to capture profits. Given a high level of uncertainty, profit appropriation tends to occur only after profits are observed and thus may start around the end of the first year of the reforms. The budget then gains increased revenue from wage-based taxes (in Poland, at most 2.5% of GDP from the *popiwek*, and even a slight loss from the flat wage and social security taxes, the lower number of taxpayers overcompensating for their higher pay). The budgetary costs are found both on the revenue side (loss of profit taxes, up to 4% of GDP) and on the expenditure side, with an increase in the number and allowances of pensioners (at most 2.5% of GDP) and unemployed (up to 1.5% of GDP) and in the wages of civil servants (up to 2.5% of GDP). The maximum budgetary cost in 1991 thus reaches 8% of GDP, of which at least half can be traced to excessive wage increases.

4.3.4.3 Wage determination mechanisms. Whatever the present situation, Poland still has to find labor market institutions that can deliver low inflation and low unemployment, easy access for the young, retraining rather than retirement or subsidization for the old, economic growth, and sufficient tax revenue. This is hard to find. A breakup of labor and goods market power is difficult to obtain even in Germany (and, in the labor market, it may have undesirable social consequences). More centralization of wage bargaining may be unpopular at this stage. Nevertheless, efforts will have to continue to increase competition on the goods market and to improve the attitude of firms and unions toward competitiveness, while centralized wage bargaining institutions may have to give broad guidelines and discipline to the labor market (given the still small size of Poland, its relatively large openness, and its history of strong unions, domestic competition may not suffice).

Credible instruments of income policy are not easy to find and to use. The recent attempt by the government to negotiate "state enterprise pacts" will certainly improve the relations within state enterprises. The obligation for enterprises to agree on a business plan including an ownership structure will remove a lot of uncertainty in enterprise management and encourage long-range decisions. The exchange of the power of the workers council in the enterprises for a minority representation on the board (the German model) will clarify and strengthen the position of management while granting the workers access to information and influence on the decisions not available in many countries. In retrospect, the involvement of workers in the privatization process may have been too low (Balcerowicz 1992).

The tax on excessive wage increases was devised first to support the real wage adjustment part of the stabilization program, and it succeeded in this at least until mid-1990. It also served a second objective: protecting the enterprise from a complete appropriation of its cash flow by the workers in the absence of an active owner. The success here was limited, but at least some of the lost cash flow went to the budget instead of to the workers. A tax on excessive wage increases is difficult to administer, although it is much more efficient and resistant than a simple wage freeze. The main difficulties are with the definition of the wage norms: firm-specific (under its 1990 wage bill or 1991 average wage form), or sector- or skill-specific (under other possible forms), annually adjustable or not.[55] Another problem with the tax is the indexation of the underlying wages: activities (sectors or skills) able to pay the tax drive up average wages (and prices) and so exempt less profitable activities from the tax: as any indexation mechanism under high inflation, this works as a brake on the reallocation of resources and an accelerator on inflation.[56]

A few adaptations in Polish tax-based wage policies may be considered. One policy, started in August 1992 to stimulate workers' interest in profits, is the exemption from *popiwek* of bonuses paid to employees from taxable profits (up to 8.5% of an employee's wage to avoid cheating). A second policy, to limit the costs of wage indexation, is to switch the reference wage for indexation from wages including bonuses from profits to wage costs. These two first changes could have been done earlier. A third policy is a greater attention to inter-industry wage differentials in the determination of the norm of an industry or firm (attempting to reduce unjustified differentials). A fourth policy may be suggested, once employment promotion in profitable firms becomes an objective: a reduction of *popiwek* charges for firms increasing their workforce permanently (but not by mergers), prefer-ably even offering training to their additional workforce, provided these firms also maintain their profits.[57] Some of this idea is captured by the 1991 switch from wage bill to average wage as the basis for the computation of the *popiwek*, but now more can be done despite the general impression that Polish firms are still overstaffed. Ideally, the incentive should be part of a larger system of retraining of the unemployed, but by using the *popiwek* it would reduce the latter's unpopularity by explaining one of the reasons it is there: to fight increased inequalities obtained by insiders.

As for the compulsory dividend, it could have all the qualities of a lump-sum tax on cost or of a lump-sum crisis levy, provided its base can be calculated correctly to ascertain its nature. It can still play a useful role of revenue raiser, reminder of ownership rights of the state, and instrument of control on profitability.[58]

The indexation of wages and pensions paid directly by the government has been extremely hard to reduce. Substantial savings have nevertheless been achieved by lengthening the intervals between indexations. For pensions in 1992, the gain may have been close to 1% of GDP.[59]

There is still a serious risk of rising wages, prices, budget deficits, and unemployment. If indexation is to remain for the long run, it should at least be suspended for the time still needed for the adjustment of relative wages, prices, and taxes to the new market conditions. At the same time, the adjustment of relative wages should not be allowed to occur at the expense of the "outsiders" in wage negotiations. The tax on excessive wage increases seems to still have a role to play for some time, even in profitable enterprises, but part of the bonuses from profits can be exempted from it.

4.3.5 CMEA Trade

The breakup of the CMEA and the shift to the dollar for trade with the Soviet Union should first be seen as a supply shock (January 1991). The Soviet Union was the provider of gas and oil. The substitution of domestic coal seems to have been very limited for technological reasons and because of the problems of the domestic coal sector itself. The share of energy and material cost in total revenue increased for all industrial sectors between 1989 and 1991, except in the liberalized food and power sectors and the labor-intensive clothing sector.

How much of the growth of exports to the OECD area is a successful reorientation of CMEA trade and how much is the independent product of a new openness to the West is still debated. In a smoothly functioning economy, it matters little to know that pieces of cotton formerly sold to Russia are now sold to Germany or that original sales of furniture to Germany have doubled. In practice, the reallocation of factors is not so smooth (as some specialized segments of labor and capital cannot easily be reallocated) and it has even been slowed by some of the wage issue problems in the labor market.

The effect of the trade shock on the budget need not be much larger than on GDP, except insofar as budget revenue tends to be procyclical and budget expenditure countercyclical. Due to the heavy reliance of the budget on profit taxes and its large role in replacement income, the budget is indeed strongly affected.

The timing of the trade shock in 1991, in a year of rising real wages, was especially unfortunate (the second year of an adjustment program is often a year of wage catch-up, and the risk of an exogenous and unforeseen shock is never absent; in the case of the CMEA it was even partly foreseen, though). The burden of the adjustment was thus shifted to the firms and the budget. Nevertheless, in 1991, the share of materials and energy costs in total income rose less than in 1990 and less than wage costs in 1991. The budgetary difficulties of 1991 can thus hardly be traced to the trade shock alone (even taking into account the rise in wages coming from indexation to the price increases generated by the trade shock).

The main impact on the budget is through the profit tax (at most, 4% of GDP lost) and the social benefits (at most, 2.5% of GDP in pensions and 1.5% in unemployment). It is fair to assume that not more than half of these costs can be traced to the trade shock in 1991. The trade shock could thus have a budgetary impact of up to 4% of GDP and probably less.

4.3.6 Capital and Labor Reallocation and Economic Restructuring

Just as with investment in skills, investment in fixed capital and creativity has to respond to market signals. Data on profit dispersion in the last three years are not encouraging: the dispersion is narrowing. Fortunately, part of the narrowing is due to loss-making firms that lost less money on their total sales in 1992 (three-quarters) than in 1991, although sectoral profits seem to converge to a very low average (3.3% of sales by mid-1992).

Apart from the reallocation of capital and labor, the transformation of the economy represents a net loss of part of the existing physical capital and acquired labor skills, thus an impoverishment of the economy and a one-time reduction of its potential income level. Insofar as this correction took place in 1990, it was largely borne by a fall in real wages. But in fact, as the reallocation progresses and old production is eliminated, part of the labor force never returns to work and its retirement has to be financed. This is where the process of reorientation of the economy hurts the budget most, even if it takes place without the profit appropriation described in the paragraph on intersectoral wage differentials.

Given the accelerated economic depreciation of the firms' capital under the reforms, allowed amortizations were increased; they went up from less than 2% of sales in 1989 to 3% in 1990, and close to 6% in 1991 and 1992. This element of the reforms, helping firms to restructure, has not been celebrated enough, maybe because too many firms decided to use the extra cash to make up losses or pay the tax on excess wage increases.

It is striking that all economies of Eastern and Central Europe have gone through a 20%–30% fall of their industrial production over the first two years of reforms. Such a similar pattern in sign and magnitude cannot be observed for the other variables like inflation, budget deficits, unemployment, and trade balances, although the signs of most variables are also similar. There seems to be thus room for local conditions and policies to affect these other variables, while one can expect that the opening of the economy to the forces of domestic and foreign competition, and to prices reflecting real demand and cost conditions has hit similar production patterns in a similar way (e.g., all economies suffered from excessive factor and input consumption, excessive inventories, excessive vertical integration, insufficient services and consumer goods).

It is thus hard to assess conclusively the impact of economic restructuring on the budget. Certainly part of the unemployment and early retirement costs should be counted here. The lower wage tax revenue due to lower real wages (only in 1990) is compensated by lower wage and pension expenditures. Part of the fall in profit tax should be counted too, as some of it was deliberately produced by increased amortizations, but part of it should be borne by the wages.[60] Part of the accelerated economic depreciation of capital and labor was due to the collapse of CMEA trade. The restructuring of the economy alone may then explain up to one-third of the 8% of GDP shock to the budget due to factors like wage pressures, the trade shock, and economic restructuring.

4.3.7 World Recession

Developments in the world economy cannot be ignored. Trade liberalization and economic reform took place in Poland at the end of an economic cycle in the West. Given the starting point of the Polish economy, however, their downturn had a very limited effect. Polish exports to the West doubled in two years and show no sign of falling. In fact, Poland exploited the opportunities coming from its new openness, and a boom in the West would have only marginally accelerated the process. For the continuation of the export growth, however, more favorable conditions in the West may have a positive impact, both on demand and on access.

As for foreign direct investment, the uncertainties in the West do not help, but are probably negligible compared to the uncertainties in the East.

4.3.8 Privatization

Privatization has managed to remain the most urgent and the most delayed element of the transformation of the Polish economy, just as with almost any other former socialist economy. And as with other of the aspects of privatization, its impact on the budget is the object of much debate.

A first form of privatization of the economy is the development of free enterprise. The number of individual businesses rose from 800,000 at the end of 1989 to 1.5 million by mid-1992, while the number of private corporations grew from 11,000 to 50,000. The broadly defined private sector (including former cooperatives and private agriculture) was said to employ more than 50% of the labor force and to produce around 45% of GDP by the end of 1992. Due to its infancy and investment burdens, unequal presence across sectors, and numerous tax exemptions, the private sector contribution to budget revenues is especially low, but comprehensive data are not published. Table 13 gives some indication of the private sector contribution to tax revenue. This low taxation is partly deliberate. The private sector contribution to the re-development of the economy and the difficulty of tracing it during the transformation period were sufficient reasons not to curb it with inapplicable regulations. It is nevertheless unhealthy to let the private sector grow for too long on the margin of the economy. The control of the 1992 personal income tax returns in early 1993 and the introduction of the VAT in the second half of the year will be major steps in the integration of the private sector in the tax base of the economy.

A second form of privatization is the organized transformation of ownership of state enterprises. This is the area where progress has been the slowest. More important than the sale of state assets is their efficient future use, the social acceptability of the implied wealth redistribution, and the identification of a real owner with a real stake in the success of the firm.[61] In the long run, efficient firms will produce increased recurrent tax revenue both on wages and profits and will economize on all factors and inputs. As for the nonrecurrent income from the sale of assets, it should be treated as such. Unless the economy suffers from an excess of savings, it should thus be used to finance investment instead of current expenditure. Investment could be broadly defined to include the cost of institutional reforms, infrastructure, a firm-restructuring fund (although the relatively low purchase price may suffice, to avoid difficult industrial policy choices), or a business startup fund, and possibly the recapitalization of the banking system.

An issue actually linked to privatization is the recapitalization of the banking system. Although most enterprise debts were wiped out by the hyperinflation and inflationary correction of 1989–1990, they rapidly rebuilt themselves (at about the same pace as the monetary base, not so surprisingly). As 10%–20% of the banks' portfolios will most likely never be recovered, the banks have been encouraged to set up special departments to deal with this part of their portfolio and can subtract some preventive write-offs from their taxable income. The banks have also earned high profits in the high inflation and economic liberalization period. Recapitalization is thus not especially needed for the preservation of the liquidity of the system. Nevertheless, the persistence of dubious assets in the banks is seen by many as a cause for the persistence of high spreads between lending and borrowing rates and thus for the high real borrowing interest rates.[62]

Dealing with bad loans as well as with inter-enterprise debts poses serious problems of moral hazard and of credibility. Even limited to old enough loans and credibly done "once and for all," any external support can create financial room that can be misused again. A minimum condition for state assistance in recapitalization is that it be linked to action on the portfolio, such as privatization and/or restructuring of the bad debtors. Plans exist for a link with the "state enterprise pacts" that should soon clarify the fate of each state enterprise. There are actually already signs that enterprises are adapting to the new market and customer-oriented environment and that loss-making enterprises are reducing their losses. One form of recapitalization (in addition to the fiscal advantage of provisioning against bad loans) is the placement of treasury bonds in exchange for action taken on some nonperforming loans.[63] A very rough computation of the potential impact of such an operation is done in de Crombrugghe and Lipton (1992): the consolidated banking system portfolio reaches around 20% of GDP; thus the placement of about 2% of GDP of bonds (10% of the portfolio), would impose an interest burden of up to 0.5% of GDP on current budget expenditure (if inflation stays around 25%).

Overstatements have abounded, it seems, both on the potential cost of recapitalizing the banking system (after all, a few cautious bank closures, as already started by the NBP, may suffice), and on the potential revenue from asset sales in privatization. More important here is the clear statement of the objective of creating as soon as possible a large and integrated taxpaying, loan-repaying private sector, and credibly pursuing a noninflationary, no-bail-out economic policy.

5. CONCLUSIONS

This chapter has reviewed the first three years of the Polish stabilization program, studying its objectives, timing, and constraints. The main causes of the fluctuations of the budget have also been identified, noting that many observations are not limited to Poland. The transformation of the economy accounts for the largest part of the drop in revenue and the increase in expenditure. Stronger or faster reforms in expenditure and revenue could have reduced the strain, however.

The justification and the effect of the price adjustments may be relatively well known. A contribution of this chapter to the study of transformation processes is the identification of a second type of adjustments: relative wage adjustments. These adjustments are partially justified by the demand for new skills, by the reallocation of labor between sectors, and by incentives for better work. Nevertheless, in Poland, especially in 1991 (the second year of the reforms), the pressure on the budget, on prices, on average wages, and on unemployment took dangerous proportions, magnified by the widespread indexation mechanisms and the existence of insider market power in certain areas of the labor market. An additional justification for the tax on excessive wage increases can be found in the dangers of insider labor market power.

A related aspect that is also of concern is the low level of profits, which may weaken the signals for investment. Persistent inflation may also blur market signals, and the burden of the inflation tax may fall disproportionately on the nascent private sector.

As in many other stabilizing countries, luck was not always on the side of the reformers. The collapse of the Soviet Union imposed a hard supply shock to the Polish economy as a whole and a negative demand shock to some sectors geared to the Soviet market. This shock could have been anticipated better. Its costs should not have been shifted entirely to the state budget; enterprise profits and wages should have responded too.

On the expenditure side, except for a large cut in subsidies, most of the pressure comes from a lack of fundamental reform, leaving a preference for care over opportunities. Social expenditure, however, can partly be explained by the market-oriented shift from the provision of goods to the provision of income, and by the pressure on the safety net due to the economic shocks. Domestic and foreign debt service will soon add a burden to the budget.

On the revenue side, tax arrears should be monitored to avoid losses of credibility. Delays in tax reform have been especially costly. Base improvements came first in the corporate and personal income taxes. The turnover tax remained narrow-based for too long, and the VAT was unduly delayed. The loss for the budget is comparable to the trade shock. Moreover, the late extensions of the turnover tax brought a series of small price shocks that could have been absorbed by the "big bang" of January 1990.

The persistence of wage and price inflation maintained quite high nominal interest rates. Uncertainties around the fate of state firms, the future of inflation, and the strength of the private sector maintained large interest rate spreads in a still not-too-competitive banking sector. The unequal increases in consumer prices and producer prices favored service sector borrowers, while only part of this spread is due to a larger need to develop services than industry, the rest being due to administrative prices and external shocks.

The urgency of the completion of the reforms, their continuing interconnection, and the signs of adjustment already observed justify after the fact the chosen path of "shock therapy," or as Balcerowicz calls it, *szok kontrolowany*. Attention remains needed for the evolution of wages. Tax reform should be completed and expenditure reform initiated. The fragile recovery after more than two years of reform and the possibility of creating new economic opportunities for the population will not survive any weakening of the efforts to complete the stabilization and liberalization program initiated at the end of 1989.

Table 1
Polish Budget Summary
(Percent of GDP)

	1987	1988	1989	1990	1991 Cons.	1991 Cent.	1992 Final	1993 Budg.
Total revenue of which:	34.3	35.6	29.7	32.5	26.8	22.7	23.9	27.2
Turnover tax & tariffs	13.0	12.9	8.8	7.1	8.5	8.4	9.9	13.3
Profits, profit tax, div.	12.0	13.4	12.1	17.7	8.7	7.7	4.4	4.3
Wage & excess wage taxes	3.9	4.2	5.0	4.4	5.3	4.7	1.3	0.5
Personal income tax	*	*	*	*	*	*	5.5	6.8
Others (tax, non-tax)	5.4	5.1	3.8	3.3	4.3	2.0	2.8	2.3
							Prel.	
Total expenditure of which:	37.8	37.0	35.7	31.9	30.7	27.3	29.2	32.3
Investment	5.6	5.3	4.1	3.6	3.0	1.9	1.5	1.4
Subsidies	15.9	16.0	12.5	7.1	3.7	3.7	3.4	2.7
Transfers to social funds	1.5	1.5	2.3	3.3	4.7	4.7	7.1	7.9
Wage costs	4.2	4.0	6.0	5.7	7.2	6.5	7.8	8.3
Goods, services, interest	10.6	10.2	10.8	12.2	12.1	10.5	9.3	12.0
							Final	
State budget balance	−3.5	−1.4	−6.0	0.6	−3.9	−4.4	−5.3	−5.0
							Final	
Extra-budget. funds balance	2.7	1.4	−1.2	2.1	−0.5		0.2	0.3
Local governments balance	*	*	*	*	0.5		0.0	0.1
							Prel.	
General government (consolidated)								
Revenue	48.2	49.0	41.8	44.6	37.9		36.9	42.6
Expenditure	49.0	49.1	48.9	41.9	41.1		43.1	47.3
Balance	−0.8	−0.1	−7.1	2.7	−4.4		−6.3	−4.7
Memorandum items:								
GDP used in text (billion zlotys)	16.9[a]	29.6[a]	100[b]	607[ab]	930[c]		1,310[c]	1,594[d]
Alternative GDP (billion zlotys)	15.0[b]	24.4[b]	118[a]	592[e]	824[e]		1,145[d]	n.a.
Consumer Prices (Dec./Dec.)	174.0	740.0	350	160			144	132
Consumer Prices (Year/Year)	160.0	351.0	685	171			143	n.a.

See next page for table footnotes.

Cons.: Consolidated data of central and local governments. Local governments are included in central budget until 1990, separated since 1991.

1992: November 1992 (Prel.) and April 1993 (Final).

1993: Central Budget data.

*Negligible or not applicable.

n.a.: Not available.

Sources: Ministry of Finance, on a commitment basis, except debt service.
[a]GUS 1991.
[b]NBP March 1992.
[c]Ministry of Finance March 1992.
[d]Ministry of Finance 1993.
[e]GUS 1992.

Note: In this and following tables, totals may not add up due to rounding.

Table 2
General Government Finance 1988–1992
(Percent of GDP)

	1988	1989	1990	1991	1992	1993
1. General government finance	0.1	7.1	−2.6	4.4	5.1	4.7
Change in outstanding arrears	*	1.9	−0.3	0.9	−0.1	n.a
Domestic banks (net) of which:	*	5.0	−2.4	4.4	7.3	4.7
Central bank	*	n.a	n.a	2.9	2.7	n.a
Other domestic borrowing	*	0.5	0.1	0.0	0.5	0.4
Foreign financing (net)	*	−0.3	−0.7	−0.1	−0.2	−0.4
Other	0.1	0.0	0.7	−0.8	−2.5[a]	n.a
		1989	1990	1991	1992 I–XII	
2. Banking system borrowing data Govt. borrowing from						
domestic banks of which:	6.50	−2.88	4.43	7.82		
Central bank		4.49	−2.01	2.95	5.82	

[a]Outstanding dollar obligations integrated in the public debt.
*Negligible or not applicable.
n.a.: Not available.

Sources:
1. Author's estimate from budgetary data.
2. NBP Bulletin.

Table 3
Central Government Revenue 1987–1993
(Percent of GDP)

	1987	1988	1989	1990	1991 Cons.	1991 Cent.	1992 Prel.	1993 Budg.
Total revenue	34.3	35.6	29.7	32.5	26.8	22.7	23.9	27.2
of which								
Turnover tax	10.6	10.9	8.8	6.5	6.6	6.6	7.8	11.2
Profit tax	11.5	12.9	9.7	14.0	6.4	5.8	3.9	3.8
Wage tax	3.6	3.5	3.3	3.0	2.4	1.8	*	*
Personal income tax	*	*	*	*	*	*	5.5	6.8
Excess wage tax	0.3	0.7	1.7	1.4	2.9	2.9	1.3	0.5
Dywidenda	0.0	0.0	1.7	2.1	1.2	1.2	0.5	0.5
Foreign trade taxes	2.4	2.0	0.0	0.6	1.8	1.8	2.1	2.1
Other taxes	3.0	3.4	0.8	2.5	1.7	0.5	0.2	0.0
Total tax revenue	31.5	33.4	26.0	30.2	23.1	20.6	21.1	24.9
Privatization	*	*	*	*	0.2	0.2	0.5	0.6
Payments from profits	0.5	0.5	0.7	1.6	0.7	0.8	1.0	0.6
Others (non-tax)	2.2	1.7	3.0	0.7	2.9	1.1	1.3	1.1
Non-tax revenue (total)	2.7	2.2	3.7	2.4	3.7	2.1	2.8	2.3
Memorandum item								
Tax reliefs (new)	3.7	3.1	6.1	1.0	2.5	2.5	0.2	n.a.

Includes local governments until 1991 Cons.
*Negligible or not applicable.
n.a.: Not available.

Source: Ministry of Finance, budget for 1993.

Table 4
Central Budget Expenditure 1987–1992 (Percent of GDP)

	1987	1988	1989	1990	1991 Cons.	1991 Cent.	1992 Prel.	1993 Budg.
Total expenditure	37.8	37.0	35.7	31.9	30.3	27.3	29.2	32.3
Current expenditure	32.2	31.7	31.6	28.3	27.8	25.3	27.7	30.9
Public goods & services:								
Science & culture	0.6	0.8	0.7	0.6	n.a.	0.9	0.8	0.8
Education	3.6	3.4	4.3	4.7	n.a.	3.5	3.6	3.6
Health, sport, tourism	4.0	3.9	4.2	5.0	n.a.	4.7	4.8	5.0
Administration	0.8	0.7	0.8	0.9	1.2	0.7	0.7	0.9
Justice, police, defen.	3.9	3.6	3.3	3.6	3.1	3.1	3.4	3.6
Other current expenditure:								
Subsidies	15.9	16.0	12.5	7.1	n.a.	3.7	3.4	2.7
Social funds	1.5	1.5	2.3	3.3	4.7	4.7	7.1	7.9
Financial costs	0.1	0.1	1.3	2.0	n.a.	1.7	2.4	3.5
Other (residual)	1.8	1.7	2.0	1.2	n.a.	2.4	1.5	2.8
Capital expenditure investment & maint.	5.6	5.3	4.1	3.6	3.0	1.9	1.5	1.4
Memorandum items								
Salaries	3.0	3.0	4.3	4.1	5.4	4.9	5.8	6.3
Salaries & soc.sec cost	4.2	4.0	6.0	5.7	7.2	6.5	7.8	8.3

Unemployment support has been reclassified as transfer to social funds, and social assistance houses as health.
n.a.: Not available.

Sources: Ministry of Finance and GUS Rocznik 1991.

Table 5
Subsidies 1987–1992
(Percent of GDP)

	1987	1988	1989	1990	1991 Cent.	1992 Prel.	1993 Budg.
Total subsidies	15.9	16.0	12.5	7.1	3.7	3.4	2.2
To the population	10.0	10.0	8.2	3.8	2.3	2.4	1.6
Food	3.4	4.9	3.6	0.2	0.0	0.0	0.0
of which:							
Meat	0.8	1.4	0.1	0.0	0.0	*	*
Dairy	1.4	2.1	1.5	0.2	*	*	*
Cereals	0.9	0.9	0.5	0.0	0.0	*	*
Other consumer goods	0.7	0.4	0.2	0.1	0.1	*	*
of which coal	0.7	0.4	0.2	0.0	0.0	*	*
Transport	0.8	0.8	0.9	0.4	0.3	0.3	0.3
Housing	3.6	2.5	2.4	2.7	1.7	2.0	1.2
Medicines							
(imported)	0.3	0.5	0.1	0.0	0.0	*	*
Books	0.0	0.0	0.0	0.0	0.0	*	*
Private agric.							
inputs	1.0	0.9	0.9	0.2	0.0	0.0	0.0
Other subs.							
priv. agric.	0.1	0.1	0.1	0.1	0.1	0.1	0.1
To enterprises	5.9	6.0	4.3	3.3	1.4	0.9	0.9
Inputs and transport	1.0	1.1	3.2	1.5	0.5	0.1	0.0
of which:							
Coal	0.9	1.0	3.2	1.5	0.5	0.1	*
Transport	0.0	0.0	0.0	0.0	*	*	*
Foreign trade	2.5	2.2	0.2	0.0	0.0	*	*
Socialized agric.	0.6	0.5	0.2	0.1	0.0	n.a.	n.a.
Banks	*	1.2	*	*	*	*	*
Other enterprises	1.0	0.3	0.1	0.9	0.6	0.6	0.7
Other economic units	0.8	0.7	0.6	0.8	0.3	0.2	0.2
of which roads	0.4	0.3	0.3	0.3	0.0	n.a.	n.a.

*Negligible or not applicable.
n.a.: Not available.

Sources: Ministry of Finance; author's estimates for housing, adding part of the "rozliczenia z bankami."

Table 6
Wages and Social Benefits: Earners (P), Earnings (Y), Spending (E)

	1989			1990			1991			1992		
	P	Y	E	P	Y	E	P	Y[a]	E	P	Y[a]	E
Employees[b]	12.2	206	93	11.4	1,030	489	10.4	1,756	880	9.8	2,444	1,182
(real y/y)[c]		111	103		73	76		100	106		97	94
Retirees[d]	6.8	94	83	7.1	562	486	7.9	1,068	924	8.5	1,646	1,261
(real y/y)[c]		104	91		87	85		112	112		107	95
Unemployed	0.0			0.6			1.7			2.3		
Unemployed[e]										1.4	900	
Self-empl.[f]	5.0			5.3			5.7			n.a.		
Age > work[g]	3.8			3.9			4.0			n.a.		
Age < work[g]	11.4			11.3			11.3			n.a.		
Age = work[g]	21.9			22.0			22.1			n.a.		

P = Number of earners (or persons for age data) in millions.
Y = Net nominal earnings in 1000 zlotys per earner in the household.
E = Expenditure in 1000 zlotys per capita in the household.
[a]Per capita earnings 1991, 1992: employees 979, 1,360, retirees 945, 1,269 respectively.
[b]Annual average, Biuletyn 1993, 4, p. 23, and tables 7 and 11, Rocznik 1992, pp. 99, 190.
[c]Ratio of annual averages divided by the year to year consumer price index.
[d]Annual average, Biuletyn 1993, 4, p. 23, and table13, Rocznik 1992, p. 203.
[e]Unemployed earning benefits, author's estimate, and Biuletyn tables 9 and 13.
[f]Including individual farmers, end of year, Rocznik 1992, p. 96.
[g]End of year, Rocznik Statystyczny 1992, p. 42.

Sources: GUS, Biuletyn and Rocznik Statystyczny.

Table 7
Medium-Term Budget Speculations

	In trillion zlotys			In percent of GDP			
	1991	1992a	1992b	1991	1992a	1992b	MT
1. Budget summary							
GDP	930	1,310	1,200	100.0	100.0	100.0	
Central budget							
Revenue	218	308	324	23.4	23.5	27	27
Expenditure	249	430	384	26.8	32.8	32	28
Balance	−31	−122	−60	−3.3	−9.3	−5	−1
Local budgets							
Revenue	46		60	5.0		5	6
of which from central	13		12	1.4		1	1
Expenditure	44		60	4.8		5	6
Balance (cash)	+2		0	+0.2		0	0
Social funds							
Revenue	144		192	15.5		16	19
of which from central	45	116	72	4.8	8.9	6	5
Expenditure	148		192	15.9		16	18
Balance	−4		0	−0.5			+1
Deficit (Cash)	−41	−65	−60	−4.3	−5.0	−5	0
2. Revenue summary (central government)							
Total revenue	218	308	324	23.4	23.5	27	27
Turnover tax	62	86	108	6.7	6.6	9	10
Corp. income tax	60	72	72	6.4	5.5	6	6
Dywidenda	12	15		1.3	1.2		0
Popiwek	23	15		2.5	1.2		0
Wage/Personal tax	18	74	72	1.9	5.7	6	8
Customs duties	16	20	24	1.7	1.5	2	1
Privatization	4	4	4	0.4	0.3	0.3	
Profit transfer	7	5	6	0.8	0.4	0.5	0.2
Other/missing	17	17	38	1.9	1.3	3.2	1.8
3. Expenditure summary (central government)							
Total expenditure	249.0	430.0	384.0	26.80	32.80	32.0	28.0
Current expenditure	231.0			24.90			
Budgetary sphere		247.0			19.00		
Science	6.0	8.0	7.5	0.60	0.60	0.6	1.0
Education (base)	26.0	35.0	32.0	2.80	2.70	2.7	3.0
Education (high)	6.5	9.5	8.5	0.70	0.70	0.7	1.0
Health	37.0	55.0	48.0	3.90	4.20	4.0	1.0
Sport, culture, ...	3.0		4.0	0.30		0.3	0.5
Administration	6.3	9.5	8.5	0.68	0.73	0.7	0.6
Justice	3.2	6.0	6.0	0.30	0.50	0.5	0.4
Police	8.2	13.5	12.0	0.90	1.00	1.0	1.0
Defense	17.5	27.0	23.0	1.90	2.10	1.9	1.5
Social insur. & assist.	51.3	125.0	72.0	5.50	9.50	6.0	5.0
Subsidies	36.0	31.0	18.0	3.90	2.40	1.5	1.0
Gminas*	6.0		12.0	0.70		1.0	1.0
Financial expend.	22.4		36.0	2.40		3.0	5.0
of which foreign debt		18.0	15.0		1.40	1.3	
Capital expenditure	17.3		18.0	1.90		1.5	4.0
Others/missing	2.7	102.5	78.5	0.90	7.70	6.5	2.0

See next page for table footnotes.

*Local municipal governments.

Note: Totals may not add up due to rounding.

Sources:

1991: According to December 1991 revisions to 1991 budget law.

1992a: According to Ministry of Finance estimates. Revenue from Department of Financial Policy and Analysis (assuming unchanged policies), Expenditure according to various indirect sources, especially Gazeta Wyborcza, March 2, 1992.

1992b: According to author's estimates and recommendations, assuming GDP at 120, mainly because of the need to target a lower inflation for expenditure.

MT: Medium-term projections, based both on the specificity of the Polish starting point and on international comparisons.

Classification: Mostly according to Polish tradition, except that Social Assistance (Opieka Spoleczna: unemployment fund and social assistance houses) is added to Social Insurance (Ubezpieczenia Spoleczne) instead of being in budgetary sphere. For the medium-term projections, health insurance is included in social funds and social insurances.

Table 8
Government Debt Outstanding
(December 1990 and 1991)

	In trillion zlotys		In billion dollars	
	1990	1991	1990	1991
Total debt	532.9	658.2		
Domestic debt	69.6	126.4		
1. Central bank	5.9	25.3		
2. Commercial banks	58.0	86.0		
2a. in dollars	53.0	59.7	5.6	5.5
2b. treasury bills		5.4		
2c. other credits	5.0	20.9		
3. Other domestic debt	5.7	15.1		
3a. various bonds	0.1	0.8		
3b. advance sale of cars	4.6	3.3		
3c. arrears and others	1.0	11.0		
Foreign debt	463.3	531.7		
1. Convertible currencies	452.6	518.1	47.6	47.2
1a. Paris Club	311.4	345.4	32.7	31.5
1b. London Club	106.1	128.6	11.2	11.7
1c. Others	35.1	44.1	3.7	4.0
2. Other currencies	10.7	13.6		
Memorandum items:				
GDP (billion)	607.0	930.0		
Zlotys/Dollar (Dec. 31)	9,500.0	10,957.0		
Exports (conv. curr.)			10.9	12.8

The data are not corrected for the promised Paris club debt reduction. Exports including clearing transactions were 8.5, 12, and 14.6 billion dollars in 1989, 1990, and 1991 respectively (GUS Rocznik 1992, p. 366).

Sources: Ministry of Finance, March 1992, except exports: NBP Bulletin 1992.

Table 9
Budget Deficit and Inflation

	Budget Deficit in % of GDP	CPI Inflation (Dec/Dec)
Poland 1991	4.0	60.4
Poland 1992	7.0	45.0
Hungary 1989–1991	3.0	30.0
Greece 1989–1991	16.0	20.0
Portugal 1991	6.4	12.0
Italy 1989–1991	11.0	7.0
Belgium 1991	6.0	3.0

Sources: IFS, various issues; OECD country surveys.

Table 10
Alternative Measures of Seigniorage and Money Creation in Poland

	Percent of GDP			
	1989	1990	1991	1992
Central bank (Seigniorage)				
1. Annual increase in:				
Cash + compulsory				
reserves	n.a.	8.47	2.58	2.31
Cash only	10.1	5.82	2.17	2.05
2. Profits transferred				
to budget	n.a.	1.60	0.71	0.83
Banking system (Money creation and profits)				
1. Increase in broad				
money M2	17.28	16.90	9.30	8.61
2. Profit taxes	2.19	1.79	1.08	n.a.
Profits transferred				
to budget	1.08	1.74	0.75	n.a.
Profits	8.51	6.27	3.20	n.a.
	Previous Year = 100			
Real money				
Cash (Dec./Dec.)	63.33	107.58	88.53	96.59
M2 (Dec./Dec.)	39.27	139.89	104.15	109.08
	Trillion zlotys			
Memorandum items				
Nominal cash (Dec. 31)	12.80	48.10	68.3	85.70
Nominal M2 (Dec. 31)	26.40	129.00	215.5[a]	307.10
Nominal GDP	100.00	607.00	930.0	1,310.00
Inflation				
(Dec./Dec. index)	739.6	349.3	160.4	144.3
NBP gross foreign				
reserves ($bn)[b]	2.03	4.68	4.59	4.91

[a]M2 at end 1991 has been redefined as 196.5 for 1992 accounting standards.
[b]From NBP data in zlotys, converted at NBP end of year exchange rate.
n.a.: Not available.

Sources: NBP Bulletin, especially 4/91 and 13/92; GUS Bulletin 1993, no.2; GUS Rocznik 1991, p. 157; GUS Rocznik 1992, pp. 146, 149.

Table 11
Wage and Profit Dispersion Indicators

	1989	1990	1991	1992 (3Q)	1992
Wages (net, employment weighted) Average (thousand zlotys)					
20 industrial sectors	234	1,101	1,844	2,382	2,550
35 "material" sectors	210	1,024	1,817	2,343	2,485
Dispersion (coefficient of variation)					
20 industrial sectors, %	24.2	23.5	26.1	22.4	25.4
35 "material" sectors, % [a]	23.2	22.4	21.1	19.3	22.0
Profit/Sales (sales weighted) Coefficient of Variation					
20 industrial sectors	7.9	6.1	6.6	6.3	7.6
35 "material" sectors, %	9.2	7.2	6.8	6.3	6.9

Regression of 1991 relative sectorial wages

	Profit/Income (in %)	Empl./Firm (in 1,000 emp.)	Income/Firm (billion zlotys)	Rel. wage 89
20 industrial sectors on				
Coefficient	0.53	12.7	0.016	
t-statistic	2.4	7.5	4.3	
R2: 93%				
35 "material" sectors on				
Coefficient	0.57	−0.68	0.015	0.62
t-statistic	2.6	−1.0	2.4	5.3
R2: 75%				

[a]The lower coefficients are explained by the catchup of wages in material services on wages in industry.
empl: Employment.
rel. wage 89: Relative wage of the sector in 1989.
Sectors as in GUS Bulletin and "Wyniki finansowe przedsiebiorstw."
Profit/Sales = 100 if profit = 0, to compute coefficients of variation.
1992(3Q): first three quarters of 1992 only.

Table 12
Unemployment by Age and Experience

Unemployment by age group (percent of total unemployed)

	18–24	25–34	35–44	45–54
1992	34	30	24	9
1991	33	31	25	8

Unemployment by experience (percent of total unemployed)

	Entrants	(of which school-leavers)	Experienced	(of which Dismissed)
1992	22	(7)	78	(26)
1991		(10)		(23)

Unemployment by duration (percent of total unemployed)

	up to 3 months	3 to 12 months	more than 1 year
1992	17	38	45

All data are end of year situation at the unemployment offices.

Source: GUS, *Informacja o sytuacji spoleczno-gospodarczej kraju,* rok 1992.

Table 13
Private Sector Taxation

A) Tax revenue from the non-socialized sector 1987–1991 (percent of GDP)

	1987	1988	1989	1990	1991 Cons.	1991 Cent.
Total	2.24	2.37	2.46	2.08	1.60	1.09
Private & foreign firms	1.53	1.59	1.49	1.30	n.a.	0.55
Individuals	0.47	0.54	0.63	0.57	n.a.	0.53
Stamp duty	0.24	0.24	0.35	0.21	0.25	0.00

B) Sample of 21,368 large firms in 1991

	Percent of	Income	Taxes	Wages	Wage Tax
Profits by private & foreign firms	5.44	2.62	5.75	5.20	1.32
Idem + coop. & mixed ownership	27.40	10.52	23.73	22.98	7.87

Some of the stamp duty may be paid by socialized enterprises.
The local tax on fixed assets cannot be disaggregated for 1991.

A) Sources: Rocznik 1991, p. 148; Ministry of Finance, Rocznik 1992, p. 143.

B) Source: GUS, "Wyniki Finansowe Przedsiebiorstw I–IV kwartal 1991." Sample of firms with more than 20 employees (except in industry and construction, more than 50), reporting monthly on F-01 forms.

Table 14
Extra-Budgetary Funds 1987–1992
(Percent of GDP)

	1987	1988	1989	1990	1991	1992 Prel.	1993 Budg.
Revenue	16.9	16.6	16.9	17.9	15.7	19.3	21.4
of which from budget	3.0	3.2	4.8	5.8	4.7	7.1	7.9
Social Insurance Fund	10.1	9.1	9.7	9.5	12.0	14.6	16.3
of which from budget	0.7	0.7	1.3	1.5	2.4	4.0	4.6
Soc. Insur. Fund Farm.	0.9	0.9	1.1	1.4	1.6	1.8	2.0
of which from budget	0.7	0.7	1.0	1.2	1.5	1.7	1.9
Unemployment Fund	0.1	0.1	0.1	0.8	1.3	1.8	2.1
of which from budget	0.1	0.1	0.1	0.6	0.8	1.2	1.3
Science & Technology Fund	1.2	1.4	1.0	1.4	*	*	*
of which from budget	0.0	0.2	0.1	0.0	*	*	*
Export Devel. Fund	*	*	1.0	1.3	*	*	*
of which from budget	*	*	0.0	0.0	*	*	*
Foreign Debt Service Fund	1.2	1.2	1.0	1.6	*	*	*
of which from budget	0.0	0.0	0.9	1.5	*	*	*
Other funds	3.1	3.9	2.9	2.0	0.8	1.0	1.0
of which from budget	1.5	1.5	1.5	1.1	0.0	0.1	0.1
Expenditure	14.2	15.2	18.1	15.8	16.2	19.2	21.3
Social Insurance Fund	8.3	8.4	9.7	8.5	12.4	14.6	16.3
Soc. Insur. Fund Farm.	0.9	0.9	1.0	1.3	1.7	1.8	2.0
Unemployment Fund	0.1	0.1	0.1	0.6	1.4	1.9	2.1
Science & Technology Fund	0.9	1.4	1.0	1.1	*	*	*
Export Dev. Fund	*	*	0.9	1.0	*	*	*
Foreign Debt Service Fund	1.2	1.0	3.2	1.5	*	*	*
Other funds	2.8	3.5	2.2	1.9	0.8	0.9	0.9
Balance	2.7	1.4	−1.2	2.1	−0.5	0.1	0.1
Social Insurance Fund	1.9	0.7	−0.1	1.0	−0.4	−0.0	0.0
Soc. Insur. Fund Farm.	0.0	−0.0	0.1	0.1	−0.0	0.0	−0.0
Unemployment Fund	0.0	0.0	0.0	0.2	−0.1	−0.0	0.0
Science & Technology Fund	0.3	0.0	−0.1	0.3	*	*	*
Export Dev. Fund	*	*	0.1	0.3	*	*	*
Foreign Debt Service Fund	0.1	0.3	−2.1	0.1	*	*	*
Other funds	0.4	0.4	0.7	0.1	−0.0	0.1	−0.0
Extra-budgetary borrowing							
Bad debt restructuring	n.a.	n.a.	n.a.	n.a.	n.a.	n.a.	1.3

*Nonnexistent or in liquidation.
n.a.: Not available.

Source: Ministry of Finance.

Figure 1
Budgetary Revenue (R) and Expenditure (E) 1988–1991

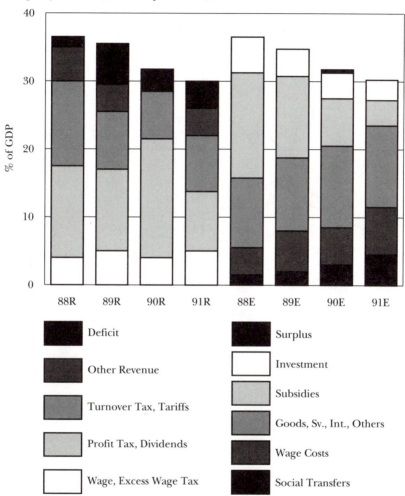

Source: Appendix: Revenue and Expenditure Tables.

Figure 2
Monetary destruction and stabilization 1989–1991

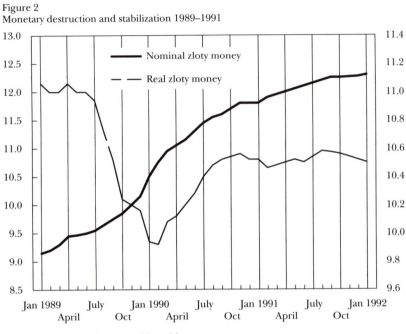

Both series expressed as natural logarithms.
Left scale nominal money.
Right scale real money, deflated by CPI, Dec. 1989 = 100.

Figure 3
Sectorial Gross Profits and Excess Wage Tax 1991

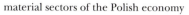

material sectors of the Polish economy

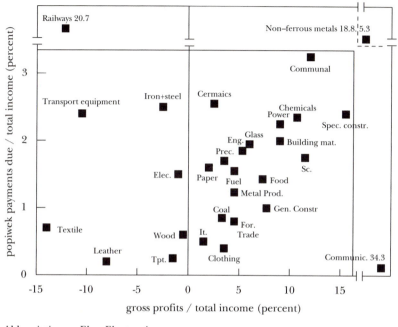

Abbreviations: Elec: Electronics
It: Internal trade
Prec: Precision instruments & apparatus
Sc: Services for construction
Tpt: Transport

Source: GUS, Monthly Bulletin, 1992:2.

Figure 4
Sectorial Gross Profits and Excess Wage Tax 1991

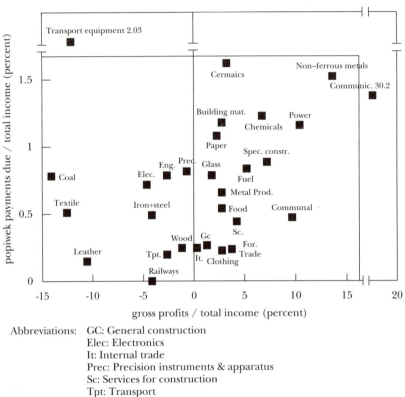

material sectors of the Polish economy

Abbreviations: GC: General construction
                  Elec: Electronics
                  It: Internal trade
                  Prec: Precision instruments & apparatus
                  Sc: Services for construction
                  Tpt: Transport

Source: GUS, Monthly Bulletin, 1993:2.

Figure 5
Real Gross Wages 1988–1991

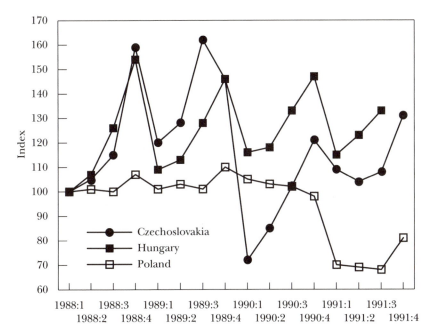

Gross wages deflated by domestic PPI.
Index = 100 for 1988:1.

Source: Poland: GUS Monthly Statistical Bulletin; Hungary: Monthly Statistical
Bulletin of the Central Statistical Office; Czechoslovakia: Ministry of
Labour.

Figure 6
Dollar Gross Wages 1988–1991

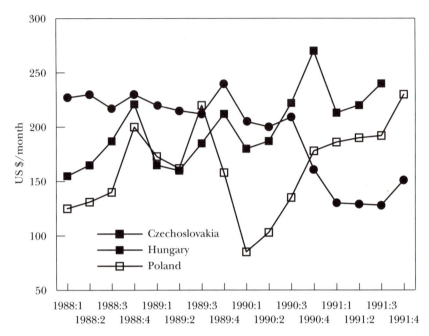

Gross average monthly wages divided by official dollar exchange rate.

Source: Poland: GUS Monthly Statistical Bulletin; Hungary: Monthly Statistical
         Bulletin of the Central Statistical Office; Czechoslovakia: Ministry of
         Labour.

Figure 7
Real and Dollar Net Wages, Poland 1987–1993

Net average quaterly wage, OECD–CCEET and GUS publications.
(1987–9:5 sectors, 90–3 plus Comm.Sv.; End of period official USD except 1992–1993).

NOTES

1. GDP for 1989 is set here at 100 trillion zlotys instead of 118. This choice does not affect the sign of the fluctuations of the described budgetary aggregates.

2. In January 1989, wages in the budgetary sphere were indexed to wages in the "six (material) sectors of the economy." Procurement prices to farmers were freed in April, squeezing farmers and putting pressures on subsidies; consumer food prices were then liberalized in August and subsidies frozen, but a wage price spiral then started.

3. The last communist prime minister was Rakowski. The first Solidarity prime minister was Mazowiecki (September 1989–December 1990). He was followed by Bielecki (January 1991–December 1991), Olszewski (January 1992-June 1992), Pawlak (June 1992) and Suchocka (June 1992–October 1993). Balcerowicz was finance minister from September 1989 until December 1992, then Lutkowski (January-February 1992), Olechowski (March–May 1992), and Osiatyński (July 1992–October 1993). Partial parliamentary elections took place in June 1989, presidential elections in November 1990, local elections earlier in 1990, free parliamentary elections in October 1991 and in September 1993.

4. Both the tax on excessive wage increases (*popiwek*) and the compulsory dividend (*dywidenda*) on the promoter's fund (*fundusz zalozycielski*) existed before 1990 at low rates and with payments limited to a fraction of profits (operating thus as a confiscation of profits by the state). In January 1990, rates were raised to a bracket of 200%–500% for the *popiwek* and to 32% for the *dywidenda*, and the limit was abolished to prevent wages from eating up alone the whole cash flow of enterprises whether profitable or not.

5. The only exception was a new tariff schedule that entered into force in August 1991, in preparation for the EC association agreement, raising 1%–1.5% of GDP in revenue.

6. GDP data for 1991, 1992, and 1993 in table 1 are those used in the original 1992 and 1993 budget drafts; final data are expected to be lower. Figure 1 is limited to 1991 because the separation of local budgets from the central budget in that year makes the graphic comparison of some items difficult for later years. Comparisons are possible in table 1 thanks to the existence of consolidated and central budget data for 1991.

7. Financial obligations cannot be summarized in one sentence. See specific paragraphs on the external debt and obligations in kind.

8. This is what de Crombrugghe and Lipton (1992) call the role of the budget—to ensure a specific allocation of goods in centrally planned economies.

9. State enterprises were not completely exempt from control: sanctions existed, such as a change of management or the refusal of wage demands. The degree of control varied across countries. In Poland, workers councils, unions, and the state often neutralized each other.

10. Depending on the elasticity of demand and supply, tax rates may nevertheless vary across goods and countries, precisely in order to minimize their distortional effect. Some taxes try also to "internalize" the externalities generated by the supply and demand of some goods. Nevertheless, the difficulty in computing and administering optimum rates and the risk of encouraging the formation of powerful lobbies often plead for relatively

uniform rates, except for some typical excises (e.g., on alcohol, tobacco, gasoline).

11. The belief in macroeconomic fine-tuning has weakened. Both its effectiveness and its theoretical foundations have been under strong attack in the last 25 years. The major central banks target a noninflationary growth environment. Budgetary policy also pursues objectives other than aggregate demand management, and many deficits have actually been ill-timed from a demand stabilization perspective.

12. At the time of writing (March 1993), I had not received 1992 data on the social funds. See tables 6 and 14 for some recent data.

13. The OECD survey on Poland, p.76, chart 13, also gives an interesting perspective on the social security costs. The ratio of benefits to wages and thus of earners to contributors leads to an explosion of the pension system.

14. The last communist government had created a three- to six-year broad tax exemption for new joint ventures; joint venture creation had been one of the most exploited loopholes. In 1991, this was finally abolished. Allowing the carry-over of losses over three years is a much more sensible measure to favor startups.

15. The wage tax was 20% of net wages, plus a social security contribution of 43% of net wages. The rate on gross wages (i.e., on wage cost) is given by $T = t/(1 + t)$ where T is the tax rate on gross wages and t is the tax surcharge on net wages. For 1991 this gives $T = 0.63/1.63 = 0.39$, close to 40%. In 1992, the rate T becomes $(0.2 + 1.2 * 0.45)/1 + (0.2 + 1.2 * 0.45) = 0.43$, with social security contributions as a surcharge on pre-income-tax wages.

16. In West European market economies, profit taxes raise sometimes as little revenue as half of what the wage and personal income taxes raise.

17. In 1989 and still in 1992, more than half of the turnover tax revenue came from excises on gasoline, alcohol, and tobacco. The base rate of the turnover tax was raised from 10% to 15% in 1989, yet revenue fell. The rate was raised again to 20% in 1990. Real gains in revenue came in 1992 only. In May 1992, children's clothing and most food items were finally introduced in the base at a 5% rate. In October 1992, a number of rates were raised above 20%.

18. In 1989, 20 industrial sectors accounted for 64% of all "material" sales (35 sectors); for the first three quarters of 1992, their share had fallen to 52%. This probably underestimates the trend, since nonmaterial services are growing as well and a part of the private services is not recorded. Partial liberalization often leads to lower tax revenue, as was also the case in China (Hussain and Stern 1992): profit and turnover tax can vanish with underpricing or underreporting of sales, which is the more tempting because some firms are subject to different taxes than others. Yet it seems that indirect taxes, especially the VAT, resist better than most other taxes.

19. This often does not require a law but simply a decision of the finance minister. Turnover tax broadening is thus very easy for a willing minister. A number of Eastern countries (e.g., Russia, Estonia) have even introduced the VAT in their initial package. Hungary had a VAT before 1989 but with numerous exemptions and zero-rated items.

20. Poland seems to have been very successful with the timing of tariffs. In 1990, the initial drastic trade liberalization had a major demonstration effect that forced the modernization of a number of local producers and retailers and offered numerous business opportunities to small entrepreneurs.

The new tariff structure boosted revenue and to some degree protection without returning to extreme distortions and without eliminating healthy competitive pressure. This may be one of the few exceptions to the disadvantages of "stop-and-go policies" and a mitigation of the "infant industry" protection argument. In the coming years, pressures for protection will come from foreign as well as domestic investors; it may be necessary to resist them, as well as to avoid export-hurting protection and to consider the cost and benefits of local-components rules that could favor local small- and medium-sized enterprises. The 1993 budget foresees a temporary surcharge of 10% on all imports as an emergency revenue-raising measure.

21. The Sejm finally passed the law on VAT and excises on November 28, 1992. The government optimistically counted on indirect taxes for 43% of its 1993 central budget.

22. A turnover tax increase could have reduced somewhat the extraordinary profits observed in 1990, and hence profit tax revenue. Lower extraordinary profits, however, could in turn have held down wage demands in 1991, with a positive impact on the budget. Anyway, the revenue from a broad turnover tax would have lasted much longer than extraordinary profits taxes.

23. Registration and licensing taxes should be better collected, e.g., by better assessing the underlying value of the transaction or activity. Alternatively, one could decide to lower these taxes and use them mostly as a way to collect information on transactions and activities.

24. Data from a Polish newspaper (*Rzeczpospolita*, March 10, 1992) discussing a World Bank report and investment data from OECD surveys and table 1 show the following: education at 3.8% of GDP is lower than Hungary (4%), Czechoslovakia (5.2%), and also Portugal (4.5%). Investment at 1.9% (or 3% including gminas or municipality) is lower than Hungary (3.6% in 1990) or Czechoslovakia (5%). Health expenditure at 4.5% of GDP is lower than in Czechoslovakia (5%) but higher than in Hungary and Portugal (less than 2%). Social benefits, at 15.5% of GDP, although lower than in Czechoslovakia (16.5%), are much higher than in Hungary (10%) or Portugal (9%), while those two last countries have maintained a lower unemployment rate during their transition (much below 10%).

25. The debate goes on even in OECD countries. Low initial compensations are suggested to stimulate search, higher compensations rely on the (private) insurance principle. Long-term low but not restricted assistance is suggested against poverty and marginalization, but this last is more a "rich country" problem and possibility.

26. In 1990, medicines went from an average 0.3% of GDP to almost 0.6% in the health budget, while social assistance housing (mainly for the elderly) jumped from less than 0.2% to 1.2%.

27. There is nevertheless a debate about targeting. Means testing may become distortionary and overdiscretionary. That is why low, broad-based benefits are sometimes advocated, family allowances based on number and age of children being an example.

28. Social benefits are often rights, not just budgetary decisions. In Poland, they can be well protected. Reversal of the constitutional tribunal's protection of old-law-based pensions and pre-budget-revision wages could not obtain the required two-thirds majority in Parliament in 1992 (payment in privatization vouchers is a compromise). It is worth asking how much state pensions should take high earnings into account unless there are also high

marginal tax rates. It may be more efficient to have relatively egalitarian state pensions with not-too-progressive tax rates, and numerous forms of private savings, preferably transferable from one place of employment to another rather than employer-dependent.

29. An excellent review of the present institutions has been prepared by the OECD in the framework of a labor market review of Poland.

30. The structural changes in expenditure have a higher potential for destabilizing the budget in the short run than do technical difficulties associated with new and more appropriate taxes. Hungary has had relatively few problems with the early introduction of value-added and personal income taxes. The government still collects more than 50% of GDP, far above Poland, but expenditure has exerted strong pressure in Hungary as well since 1991.

31. Investment and savings targets are discussed in de Crombrugghe and Lipton (1992). Public investment policies and prospects have been analyzed in a report of the World Bank resident mission in Warsaw.

32. Not to speak of a long tradition of ignoring the environment, which will eventually have to be reversed.

33. This is another reflection of the "producer-oriented" thinking under central planning. Rates of return and present value computations are more "consumer-oriented."

34. Table 7 also has alternative proposals for 1992, coming from an earlier draft of this paper. A key feature is that financial envelopes were calculated as percentages of GDP and assuming a GDP of 1,200 instead of 1,310 trillion zlotys. The method and the assumption of a low GDP reduce the aggregate demand pressures coming from the budget, which easily transform into inflation.

35. Financial planning is the art of simultaneously determining the acceptable rate of inflation, the rate of growth of the money supply, the rate of growth of the underlying foreign reserves, credit to the budget, to the state enterprises, and to the private sector. Recently, the main objective has been to reduce inflation and the constraints the demands of the budget deficit place on the banking system (due to the government's inability to close the gap between revenue and expenditure or to find nonmonetary sources of financing). The central bank has consistently maintained private sector credit targets to protect this sector from "crowding out" effects (and possibly also to avoid that high interest rate would select only very risky borrowers; see Stiglitz and Weiss 1981). Increases in real money demand and in real output (aggregate supply) can reduce inflation while also creating room for private and public borrowing (a virtuous circle usually requiring a virtuous government).

36. The advance sale of cars took 0.1% of GDP in the 1991 budget, and people can choose to import a duty-free car instead of waiting longer for a prepaid car. Credit guarantees for cooperatives were canceled for apartments not completed by March 1992 (reflected by a boom in new apartments statistics for that month!). A list of the outstanding obligations is hard to establish, and their cost is spread across various items of the budget, mainly "subsidies" (*dotacje*) and "settlements with the banks" (*rozliczenia z bankami*).

37. The sustainable debt depends also upon the rate of growth of GDP, and to a lesser extend of exports and tax revenue (de Crombrugghe and Lipton 1992). Some fear a debt/GDP ratio of 70% by 1994.

38. A third measure (not computed in table 10) is the potential interest saving for the government from having its debt held by the central bank rather

than by other creditors. The central bank indeed played an important role in absorbing treasury bills and bonds at auctions, especially at the end of 1991 and 1992. This third measure should also include the interest obtained by the central bank on foreign reserves. This third measure would not add much to the second one (profit transferred to the budget).

39. There is a public finance approach to equilibrium seigniorage, which suggests that a high inflation tax is appropriate in countries where the collection of other taxes is problematic. This is a second-best argument, the optimum being an efficient collection of the least distorting taxes. High reserve requirements also work as a tax and increase the spread between lending and borrowing interest rates; they were appropriate at the time they were imposed, and have been reduced since June 1992.

40. See De Broeck (1991) for a theoretical and empirical analysis of various strategies of government finance in the OECD area.

41. The present bonds are a one-year consumer price indexed-bond (a first issue of 1 trillion zlotys took place in June) and a three-year bond with a variable interest linked to the interest rate on three-month government bills (first issued in August 1992). The budget law anticipated raising between 10 trillion and 15 trillion zlotys; the actual financing from this source seems to have been around 7 trillion zlotys. Foreign banks could not take part in the bidding, as Poland is, understandably, still worried about the inflationary potential of speculative capital inflows.

42. This intersectoral difference in real interest rates (in terms of output prices) partly corresponds to differences in demand. The long-neglected service sector not surprisingly benefits from quickly rising prices and hence lower real interest rates.

43. When hyperinflation reaches 1985 Bolivian levels, a new set of relative prices, e.g., in dollars, may arise by itself.

44. Britain seems to have understood this argument very well. Just before the 1992 election, the Conservative government increased the budget deficit and then campaigned on the argument that a Labor government would spend and tax. Scared voters returned the Conservatives to power.

45. A more realistic description of the credibility game than the inflation-unemployment trade-off may be the following one. The government wanted the state firms to behave in a more market-oriented way than the firms actually wanted, and it threatened them with higher taxes and interest rates than it was actually willing to enforce. Today, it seems that the competition for production factors (including labor) and for customers from domestic and foreign firms may be putting more pressure on state enterprises than the still-to-be-tested bankruptcy threat. It will be interesting to see also what effect the "state enterprise pact" recently passed by the Sejm will have on the privatization process by involving the workers more than previous laws originally planned.

46. The figure is discussed further in the paragraphs on inter-industry relative wage adjustments.

47. After the revaluation of the "promoters' fund" in 1990, no further revaluations of the base took place. The rate was 32% of the base in 1990, 22% in 1991, and 10% in 1992.

48. In Hungary, bankruptcy proceedings have risen fast since the introduction of personal liability of managers who failed to declare bankruptcy when the legal conditions for it were reached by their firms.

49. A small upturn was also recorded at the end of 1990, but it went

together with the easing of wage and credit policies, a weakening of the trade balance, and a rise in inflation.

50. The strong macroeconomic performance of the CSFR is well known. It can nevertheless be asked how the relative wage pressures will be dealt with, once privatization advances and wage controls are lifted, and further trade readjustments are forced by the separation of the Czech and Slovak Republics. The transition of the CSFR from the highest to the lowest dollar wages is also interesting. It may be related to its different degree of dependence upon the former CMEA market (Rodrik 1992), or simply to its greater discipline after the devaluation of 1991. It may, in turn, explain the still limited need to start bankruptcies.

51. Boeri and Keese (1992) compare in more detail pre-reform low-paying jobs and high-paying jobs in Bulgaria, Romania, and the CSFR with low- and high-paying jobs in Austria, Germany, and Italy. The communist countries show lower wage differentials inside sectors and higher ones between sectors than the Western countries.

52. "Efficiency wage" theories suggest that the risk of becoming unemployed acts as a "disciplining" device on workers and reduces the cost of monitoring workers (Yellen 1984). Such theories contribute to the explanation of the existence of a natural or equilibrium rate of unemployment. They may thus explain part of the previously nonexistent unemployment in Eastern Europe. The "insider-outsider" approach may explain some additional unemployment and its persistence after economic shocks, up to the point where the threat of new entry (non-unionized firms, young people, increased bargaining power of the management in the presence of mass unemployment) becomes strong enough.

53. Data for the three first quarters of 1992 do not include the three bonus-months of the year. The first nine months showed a reduction in wage dispersion, and average wages for the year seem to show real wage moderation. Has the strength of the insiders weakened and competition increased?

54. On the basis of another data set, Boeri and Keese (1992) report lower coefficients of variation for Polish 1989 wages than in table 11. Nevertheless, the ranking of their coefficients of variation corresponds to the degree of liberalization attained: Hungary has the highest, Czechoslovakia the lowest. Their Eastern coefficients seem to be close to the highest Western ones.

55. The possibility for firms to set months of pay below the norm against months above the norm helped push wages up at the end of the year, especially in 1990, and made the start of the next year very hard unless the norm was raised.

56. It should be said that in countries with low inflation, indexation clauses work as a brake on wage demands, since there is no fear of losses due to unpredictable inflation. A luxury for rich and stable economies . . . ? But even then there may be external shocks that justify a departure from indexation, or the negotiation of nominal wage reductions.

57. Many industrial countries indeed have incentives for stages, first-job hiring, training, and other measures that would have to be considered given the high percentage of young people among the unemployed.

58. Tax policy may also offer some help. There may be some evidence that marginal labor income taxes are higher in "corporatist" economies (Gruber, Summers, and Vergara 1992), either to slow excessive wage increases

or pay the marginal workers out of the labor force (Sala-i-Martin 1992), but how desirable or affordable is a corporatist economy?

59. There is a choice between indexation on average wages and indexation on prices. Poland chose wages, which was cheap in 1990 and expensive in 1991. In the longer term, if still-needed price and tax adjustments are introduced and the Polish economy develops successfully, real wages will grow, and indexation on prices may prove less costly, while leaving room for maneuver for additional increases when possible.

60. A four percentage-point fall in profits, averaging 10%–15% of sales, reduces profits by about one-third and profit taxes by the same proportion. Profit taxes can thus fall from 10% or 12% of GDP to 6% or 8%. This is about what happened in 1991. It is not acceptable, however, that profits (and the budget) take the full burden of the faster economic depreciation of capital. Wages should take their share, since the reduction of capital reduces the productivity of a given labor.

61. A higher involvement of the workers in future profits could have helped reduce current wage demands. Delays can benefit pressure groups and rent-seekers while the firms deteriorate further. Privatization issues are developed in Lipton and Sachs (1990) with a focus on mass privatization, and in Bolton and Roland (1992) with more attention to workers' involvement and budget revenue.

62. Another reason may actually be the lack of collateral and notoriety, which is due to the smallness and newness of the private sector and of private wealth. The seigniorage tax (to cash and deposit issuers) is thus probably paid mostly by the private sector and benefits the government and state firms, correcting somewhat the impression of table 13.

63. In addition to action on the debtors, the loans could be securitized and sold. Anyway, banks should bear their fair share of the losses due to their lending behavior. The number of industrial firms reported in the NBP bulletin (9–10/1992) as having lost creditworthiness is around 25% of the total nationwide.

REFERENCES

Alesina. Alberto, and Allan Drazen. 1991. Why Are Stabilisations Delayed? American Economic Review (December).

Atkinson, Anthony B., and Joseph E. Stiglitz. 1980. *Lectures on Public Economics*. London: McGraw-Hill.

Balcerowicz, Leszek. 1992. *800 dni szok kontrolowany*. Warsaw: Polska Oficyna Wydawnicza "BGW."

Barro and Gordon. 1983. A Positive Theory of Monetary Policy in a Natural Rate Model. *Journal of Political Economy* 91, no. 4 (Aug.), pp. 589–610.

Berg, Andrew, and Olivier J. Blanchard. 1992. Stabilisation and Transition: Poland 1990–91. In *Transition in Eastern Europe*, ed. Olivier Blanchard, Kenneth Froot, and Jeffrey Sachs. National Bureau of Economic Research and University of Chicago Press.

Berg, Andrew, and Jeffrey Sachs. 1992. Structural Adjustment and International Trade in Eastern Europe: The Case of Poland. *Economic Policy* 14 (April), pp. 117–74.

Boeri, Tito, and Mark Keese. 1992. Labour Markets and the Transition in Central and Eastern Europe. *OECD Economic Studies* 18 (Spring), pp. 133–63.

Bolton, Patrick, and Gérard Roland. 1992. Privatisation Policies in Central and Eastern Europe. *Economic Policy* 15, pp. 275–310.

Bruno, Michael. 1992. Stabilization and Reform in Eastern Europe. mimeo, January.

Bruno, Michael, Guido Di Tella, Rudiger Dornbusch, and Stanley Fischer. 1988. *Inflation Stabilization*. Cambridge, MA: MIT Press.

Bruno, Michael, Stanley Fischer, Elhanan Helpman, and Oded Liviatan. 1991. *Lessons of Economic Stabilization and its Aftermath*. Cambridge, MA: MIT Press.

Bruno, Michael, and Jeffrey Sachs. 1985. *The Economics of Worldwide Stagflation*. Cambridge, MA: Harvard University Press.

Burgess, Robin, and Nicholas Stern. 1993. Taxation and Development. *Journal of Economic Literature* (forthcoming).

Calmfors, L., and J. Driffill. 1988. Bargaining Structure, Corporatism and Macroeconomic Performance. *Economic Policy*.

Calvo, Guillermo, and Fabrizio Coricelli. 1992. Stabilizing a Previously Centrally Planned Economy: Poland 1990. *Economic Policy* 14 (April), pp. 175–226.

Coricelli, Fabrizio, and Ana Revenga, eds. 1992. Wage Policy During the Transition to a Market Economy: Poland 1990–91. *World Bank Discussion Paper 158*, Washington, DC.

De Broeck, Mark. 1991. Essays on the Financial Structure of Government Debt and Government Debt Management. Unpublished Ph.D. Dissertation, Harvard University.

De Broeck, Mark, Alain de Crombrugghe, and Romuald Kudlinski. 1992. Budgetary Adjustment in Poland: Beyond Stabilization. In *Macroeconomic Stabilization and the Internationalization of the Polish Economy*, ed. Paul De Grauwe et al. The Leuven Institute for Central and East European Studies (forthcoming).

De Crombrugghe, Alain, and David Lipton. 1992. The Government Budget and the Economic Transformation of Poland. In *Transition in Eastern Europe*. See Berg and Blanchard 1992.

Gordon, Roger H. 1992. Fiscal Policy During the Transition in Eastern Europe. In *Transition in Eastern Europe*. See Berg and Blanchard 1992.

Gruber, Jonathan, Lawrence Summers, and Rodrigo Vergara. 1992. Taxation and the Structure of the Labour Market: The Case of Corporatism. NBER Working Paper 4063 (May).

Hussain, Athar, and Nicholas Stern. 1992. The Role of the State, Ownership and Taxation in Transitional Economies. Mimeo, CEPR and London School of Economics.

Kornai, János. 1990. *The Road to a Free Economy*. New York: W.W. Norton.

Krugman, Paul. 1988. Financing Versus Forgiving a Debt Overhang. *Journal of Development Economics* 29, pp. 253–68.

———. 1989. Market Based Debt Reduction Schemes. In *Analytical Issues in Debt*, ed. Frenkel, Dooley, and Wickham. Washington, DC: IMF.

Lipton, David, and Jeffrey Sachs. 1990. Privatization in Eastern Europe: The Case of Poland. *Brookings Papers on Economic Activity* 2, pp. 293–342.

———. 1990a. Creating a Market Economy in Eastern Europe: The Case of Poland. *Brookings Papers on Economic Activity* 1, pp. 75–148.

McKinnon, Ronald I. 1991. Financial Control in the Transition to a Market Economy. *Journal of Economic Perspectives* 5, no. 4, pp. 107–22.

OECD. 1988. *Economic Outlook*. Paris.
————. 1991. *The Role of Tax Reform in Central and Eastern European Countries*. Paris.
————. 1992. *Poland*. Economic Surveys Series.
————. 1992. *United States*. Economic Surveys Series.
————. 1992. *Progress in Structural Reform, An Overview*. Paris.
————. 1993. *Italy*. Economic Surveys Series.
Oudiz, Gilles, and Jeffrey Sachs. 1985. International Policy Coordination in Dynamic Macroeconomic Models. In *International Economic Policy Coordination*, ed. William H. Buiter and Richard C. Martson. Cambridge: CEPR and Cambridge University Press, pp. 274–319.
Persson, Torsten, and Lars E.O. Svensson. 1989. Why a Stubborn Conservative Would Run a Deficit: Policy with Time-Inconsistent Preferences. *Quarterly Journal of Economics* 104, no. 2 (May), pp. 325–46.
Rodrik, Daniel. 1992. Making Sense of the Soviet Trade Shock in Eastern Europe: A Framework and Some Estimates. NBER Working Paper 4112, June.
Rostowski, Jacek. 1993. The Inter-Enterprise Debt Explosion in the Former Soviet Union: Causes, Consequences, Cures. Forthcoming in *Soviet Studies*.
Sachs, Jeffrey. 1987. The Bolivian Hyperinflation and Stabilization. *American Economic Review* 77, no. 2 (May), pp. 279–83.
————. 1989. The Debt Overhang of Developing Countries. In *Debt, Growth and Stabilization: Essays in Honor of Carlos Diaz- Alejandro*, ed. de Macedo and Findlay.
Sala-i-Martin, Xavier. 1992. Transfers. NBER Working Paper 4186 (October).
Stiglitz, Joseph E., and Andrew Weiss. 1981. Credit Rationing in Markets With Imperfect Information. *American Economic Review* 71, no. 3.
Tanzi, Vittorio. 1991. Tax Reform and the Move to a Market Economy: Overview of the Issues. In OECD, *The Role of Tax Reform in Central and Eastern European Economies*. Paris.
Winiecki, Jan. 1992. Polish Transition Programme at Mid-1991: Stabilisation under Threat. In *Re-integration of Poland into the West European Economy*, ed. Kaczynski and Kawecka-Wyrzykowska. Warsaw: Foreign Trade Research Institute (IKC).
Yellen, Janet. 1984. Efficiency Wage Models of Unemployment. American Economic Review (May), pp. 200–205.
Other data sources:
GUS (Polish Central Statistical Office). Biuletyn Statystyczny 1989–1993 (4).
————. Informacja o Sytuacji Spoleczno-Gospodarczej kraju 1989–92.
————. Informacje Statystyczne: Handel Zagraniczny, 1990, 1991.
————. Materialy i Opracowania Statystyczne: Wyniki Finansowe Przedsiebiorstw I-IV kwartal 1990, I-III, I-IV kwartal 1991.
————. Rocznik Statystyczny 1991, 1992.
————. Roczniki Statystyczne: Handel Zagraniczny 1990, 1991.
URM (Urzad Rady Ministrow). Budgetary documents transmitted by the Council of Ministers to the Parliament, 1989–1992.
Rzeczpospolita and *Gazeta Wyborcza*, two Polish dailies.

5

Comments on de Crombrugghe

MAREK DABROWSKI

Fiscal crisis seems to be the main macroeconomic challenge threatening the prospective pro-market transformation in Central and Eastern Europe. One can distinguish two stages of such crisis in the history of postcommunist transformation: the initial fiscal crisis (IFC) at the very beginning of the transition process and the second (i.e., post-stabilization) fiscal crisis (SFC).

Concerning IFC, the starting point of individual countries in respect to the fiscal situation was not the same. In 1989, Poland suffered a huge budget deficit and near-hyperinflation. The same situation occurred later in Bulgaria and Albania, as well as in Russia, Ukraine, and other post-Soviet states. On the other hand, Czechoslovakia and the former GDR presented far more stable cases. Hungary also avoided very high inflation and the necessity of introducing "shock" stabilization therapy, but this country still has had chronic fiscal problems.

Among countries suffering IFC, one can distinguish two kind of policies. The first group of countries (Poland, Czechoslovakia, Hungary, and Slovenia) made serious fiscal and monetary adjustment, stopping further macroeconomic deterioration. This initial stage of fiscal reforms even showed a spectacular success in some countries. Price liberalization, i.e., removing most subsidies and tax exemptions, brought the budgets of these countries to relative equilibrium (Poland even achieved a significant budget surplus, due to hyperinflationary profits of state enterprises and banks in the first half of 1990). However, in the case of Poland it was only a temporary success; starting in 1991, the fiscal situation began to deteriorate very quickly. The second fiscal crisis (SFC) appeared.

Poland, Hungary, East Germany, and Slovakia suffer now and will continue to suffer important budget difficulties. Only the Czech Republic is in a better position, yet some of this country's problems (such as massive state enterprise bankruptcies and unemployment) may only be delayed in comparison with other countries in the region.

A significant budget deficit (between 5% and 8% of GDP) and limited possibilities for noninflationary financing (through domestic and foreign borrowing) still undermine price stability in most of the countries and seriously limit the prospects for sustainable growth. It is necessary to underline, however, that Central European countries suffering SFC are still in far more favorable position than the second group of countries (such as Russia, Ukraine and most other post-Soviet states, as well as Romania), which failed to make even the initial fiscal and monetary adjustment and entered on the high inflation (or hyperinflation) track. The latter group still tries to maintain the subsidization of many products, services, and enterprises, to avoid any adjustment in social programs, and to use monetary and fiscal policy as a tool for supporting the output level. Concerning this last policy target, i.e., counteracting the output decline, it is hard to see any success. As Alain de Crombrugghe underlines in his chapter, all countries across the region have suffered deep output declines, amounting in the case of industry to 20%–30% cumulatively.

Poland can be seen as a classic example of the above-mentioned problems. In the period from 1989 to 1992, this country suffered IFC, made successful initial fiscal and monetary adjustments connected with a radical and comprehensive transformation program (the so-called Balcerowicz program), and very quickly encountered SFC and tried to neutralize it. De Crombrugghe's chapter describes this process extensively and competently. The most interesting questions are connected with the root causes of SFC. To what extent was it influenced by objective factors common to all the countries in the region (such as decreasing profit margins of state-owned enterprises, consequences of the CMEA shock, and rising social safety net pressures), and to what extent was it the effect of specific policy mistakes made by the Polish authorities?

De Crombrugghe seems to be successful in specifying both kinds of reasons. Let me concentrate on the second one. The author underlines especially the role of the delayed tax reform (especially VAT) and of too slow a turnover tax adjustment in the unsatisfactory counteracting of the decline of other budget revenue (mainly from corporate income tax). I fully agree that this was a serious policy mistake. After initial success in pushing the stabilization and liberalization program forward in the beginning of 1990, the Polish government concentrated mainly on the current fiscal problem of minor importance rather than on quick implementation of the remaining longer-term-oriented fiscal reforms. The best political time for unpopular decisions (such as for an effective tax system) was lost, and later Poland entered a period of election campaigns and frequent changes of governments, which naturally slowed down tax reform.

Among other policy mistakes mentioned by de Crombrugghe, I would like to emphasize the following ones:

1. The general relaxation of monetary, fiscal, and income policies in the middle of 1990, prompted by a mistaken macroeconomic diagnosis (too early proclamation of a victory in the struggle with high inflation, attempts to reactivate the economy by using demand-type instruments, etc.) rather than by specific political pressure (which was rather weak at the moment). The set of decisions taken in early summer 1990 contributed both directly (increased spending in the budgetary sphere for industrial and agriculture policy purposes) and indirectly (rising wages in the material sphere, decreasing profitability of state enterprises, the necessity of increasing wages in the budgetary sphere, pensions and other benefits in tandem with wages, etc.) to the gradual worsening of the budget situation. The small fiscal reserves accumulated in the first half of 1990, which could have been used for other purposes (for example, a repayment of all government obligation to the banking system), were very quickly lost. The new inflationary pressure pressed the government and the NBP to implement the second stabilization package at the end of 1990. This overlapped with the CMEA shock in the beginning of 1991 and led to additional GDP losses.

2. The stop-go-stop macroeconomic policy and the lack of long-term fiscal programming, which has become the permanent weakness of Polish developments. The mistake from the middle of 1990 was repeated again in the second half of 1992, when Finance Minister Jerzy Osiatyński initiated a correction of the budget law of 1992 to increase the budget deficit originally planned by former Minister Andrzej Olechowski at a level of 5% of GDP. Fortunately, final fiscal results were closer to Olechowski's projection than to Osiatyński's correction. However, a lot of political time and energy was lost and necessary fiscal adjustment, especially in the social safety sphere, was delayed. Similar danger existed in the middle of 1993, when Suchocka's government made some pre-elections promises.

3. Errors in social policy, the area where the biggest policy mistakes were made at the end of 1989 and in 1990. Very "liberal" employment laws (e.g., too easy access to unemployment benefits), very high promises concerning revaluation of "old" pensions, and maintaining automatic indexation of

pensions, social benefits, and wages in the budgetary sphere
made the expenditure side growth of the budget very explosive. Excessive initial concessions in the social safety sphere
created very strong political constituencies trying to maintain
social "achievements." Subsequent attempts to withdraw or to
limit some social privileges (partly successful) needed a lot of
political energy and undermined seriously social support for
market-oriented reforms. The social legislation should also be
seen as a very important barrier to future fiscal adjustment.

All these policy mistakes in Poland can at least partly explain the
differences between the Polish and Czech situations. Additional explanation can be found in the sphere of income policy. I agree with de
Crombrugghe that postcommunist budgets are very sensitive to
changes in real wages (probably this statement is also valid in respect to
other countries, especially those with very wide systems of wage and
pension indexation). Polish wage policy seemed less restrictive and less
stable than it did in Czechoslovakia. In this context, it is necessary to
assess the role of the excess wage tax in Poland (the *popiwek*).

As de Crombrugghe mentioned in his chapter, the excess wage
tax played at least two roles in the transformation process. First, it
attempted to limit nominal wage increases (its macroeconomic role).
Second, it was to regulate the distribution of state enterprise value
added between wages and profits (its microeconomic function). I think
that there is a lot of statistical evidence that excess wage tax played a
rather secondary role as an instrument regulating the nominal wage
level. The latter changed mainly according to the fluctuation in the
monetary and fiscal policy (on the micro level, the credibility of hard
budget constraints played a crucial role here).

It is far more difficult to access the role of the *popiwek* as a
microeconomic tool. There is no doubt that it restricted the tendencies
of many employees' collectives to appropriate all the value added, and
instigated the aggressive behavior of trade unions. It is necessary to
say, however, that the above-mentioned microeconomic role of excess
wage tax started gradually to evaporate, especially after export
exemptions was introduced in the second half of 1992. The *popiwek*
probably also slowed down the process of wage adjustment in both
vertical and horizontal dimensions, negatively influencing the prospects of improving labor productivity.

Some other problems raised by de Crombrugghe in the last part
of his chapter, such as the links between output decline and fiscal
balances, or budget implications of the privatization process, need
further discussion and analysis. What concerns privatization is not

only the problem of weak tax discipline of the new private sectors but also wage behavior. Additionally, revenues from privatization, the costs of this process, and diminished revenue from excess wage and dividend taxes should be taken into consideration.

Concluding my comments, I should emphasize the following policy challenges that will influence the fiscal situation of Poland in the coming years:

1. rising social obligations, especially in attitudes toward pension programs;
2. the high cost of functioning and the low productivity of the budgetary sphere, which was not reformed in a market-oriented direction until now;
3. the potential financial crisis of the banking system;
4. the rising burden of servicing the foreign and domestic debt;
5. weak tax discipline and morality.

6

What is the Budget Reform in Czechoslovakia and the Czech Republic About?

VERA KAMENÍČKOVÁ
MILENA HORCICOVA
PAVEL ŠTĚPÁNEK
DRAHOMIRA VASKOVA

1. INTRODUCTION

Hungary and Poland had already begun their economic reforms when Czechoslovakia's November 1989 "Velvet Revolution" initiated far-reaching political, social, and economic changes. Although the time lag makes comparison of these countries more difficult, it enabled Czechoslovakia to learn both positive and negative lessons from its neighbors. A rapid start to economic reform with well-prepared, specific steps was what Czechoslovak reformers hoped to learn.

The then-named Czech and Slovak Federal Republic enjoyed certain advantages: relatively high economic stability and standard of living, high professional skill of the labor force, a negligible rate of inflation, and insignificant foreign indebtedness. Widely discussed, the reform program was basically finished in September 1990. The main principles of the economic reform consisted of price liberalization, foreign trade liberalization, internal convertibility of the currency, and privatization of state property. Macroeconomic stabilization policies, accompanied by restrictive fiscal and monetary policies, shaped the framework for the start of the economic reform; its feasibility was supported, however, by proposals for a social safety net.

In fact, economic reform started immediately after the events of 1989. A number of reform measures were adopted after the revolution, including restrictive budget proposals, the adjustment of the exchange rate toward a more realistic level, a discount rate increase, removal of negative turnover tax for foodstuffs, a rectification of some price deformations, and development of a classical two-tier banking system (i.e., separation of the central bank from the commercial banks).

The year 1991 was the beginning of the reform scenario implementation. All reform steps were enforced within the restrictive fiscal and monetary policies; in January, central price control was generally abolished—remaining effective only for the prices of about 15% of GDP. This level was lowered step by step so that at the end of the year prices of only 5% of GDP were still centrally regulated.

Together with price liberalization, the internal convertibility of the koruna was introduced, which meant free access to foreign exchange for legal subjects (mainly for corporations). Individuals could (and still can) change only a limited amount of Czechoslovak koruna. Together with foreign trade liberalization, the internal convertibility contributed to an opening of the economy, an increase in competition in the domestic market, the improvement of supply in the internal market, and export stimulation.

In February 1991, the first small privatization auctions started. During the course of the year, restitution programs began, although their magnitude was not comparable to other countries. The results of small privatization and restitution showed how economic reform was changing the daily life of Czechoslovak citizens. In this way, Czechoslovakia succeeded in "lowering" the comparative advantage of Poland and Hungary in the areas of small private business and household services.

Fiscal and monetary policies responded to the reform (fiscal policy will be dealt with later). Within the framework of monetary policy, the discount rate was increased at the beginning of the year, followed by rises in other interest rates. The move was a response to the price developments in 1991, but in the second half of the year, in connection with price stabilization, interest rates were lowered.

The Konsolidacni banka was founded, and took from commercial banks some of the "bad loans" (loans provided on a noncommercial basis in previous years) of enterprises. Together with a partial debt amortization of some state enterprises and strengthening of commercial bank capital, this step partially cleared commercial bank balances.

But the privatization issue was the main feature of 1992. It included first of all large-scale privatization, based on the coupon method, the use of which on such a large scale could place Czechoslovakia in the Guinness Book of World Records. However, bottlenecks in the reform process, especially the low adjustment of state enterprises, became evident.

The first wave of the coupon privatization was over by the end of 1992, and, at least in the sense that almost all coupon points issued nationwide were applied, it was a success. But the effective transfer of property rights by this method did not really occur. Rather, the whole year was marked by "pre-privatization agony" of state enterprises that took part in the first wave of the coupon privatization.

In 1992, the central bank abolished the nonmarket methods of commercial bank regulation—limits on credit volume, interest rate ceilings, and other methods. The importance in regulatory procedure was shifted to more market-oriented tools: minimum reserve ratios, refinancing credit, operational changes in discount rate, etc. The major change meant a shift in financing the deficit to the emission of treasury bills and state bonds. This step closed down the possibility of budget deficit direct credit from the central bank, which involved the danger of monetizing the governmental debt.

2. FISCAL FEDERALISM

Unlike in Hungary and Poland, the fiscal federalism issue became a crucial political, economic, and social concern in the former CSFR and a major complication of the transition process with heavy economic costs, both domestic and external. This period witnessed both extremes of possible fiscal federalism arrangements: an extremely centralized approach (up to 1989), and an extremely decentralized model in 1992, by which time economic processes in the federation were already beyond the limits of efficient central control.

The history of fiscal federalism between 1989 and 1992 had two dimensions, legal and quantitative. The first consisted of the power distribution among different levels of government (including the power to generate revenue and the power to use budget funds). The second was reflected in the amounts of funds channeled through different levels of the budgetary system. At any given time, the fiscal federalism issue was determined by both the constitutional issue (constitutional arrangements between the two national republics) and the specific phase of the transition process (or, more specifically, by its economic, social and—last but not least—political impacts).

Quantitatively, all developments of the past four years are reflected in table 1. The fiscal federalism of 1989 was based on the following principles:

- The major part of revenues flowed into the federal budget. The main sources of revenue were taxes and levies on enterprises (e.g., profit tax, payroll tax, tax on amortization). The principal criterion for revenue assignment followed the division of responsibility between the federation and the two republics over single enterprises (federal and republic enterprises). For example, the federation controlled such industries as mining, energy, machinery, and electronics. Other sources of income for the federal budget were a turnover tax and customs duties, which provided a stable and growing source of budget revenue. Tax sharing was not used, mainly because of potential troubles in the tax base assignment. Revenue from wage and (mainly cooperatives) non-state enterprises profit taxes belonged to the republic budgets.

- Public services and social transfers were largely financed by the republic and local budgets. The federal expenditures financed mainly federal functions and the federal economy (see above).
- Budgets of lower levels of government were strongly dependent on transfers from higher levels. Transfers from the federal budget covered about half of the expenditures of the republic budgets, including their transfers to the local budgets. The volume of federal transfers to republic budgets was determined separately for each republic. The specific subsidies were settled with the respective budgets at the end of each fiscal year; more remained at the discretion of the lower-level budgets. The lower levels of the budgetary system were given only restricted responsibilities and decision-making powers. All of that was reflected in the behavior of both republic and local budgets, which demonstrated unlimited "appetite" for subsidies and very little interest in their own revenue.

For a number of reasons (both economic and political), it was evident that fiscal federalism as applied in 1989 was not feasible. It was only federal in terms of constitutional law; its functioning was that of a unitary state. The economy under this model had suffered some structural distortions. The highly centralized system could afford the luxury of parallel jurisdiction at different levels of government. Moreover, all problems of fiscal federalism were multiplied by a considerable degree of inefficiency and by bad public sector management.

By the beginning of 1990, intensive discussions concerning the fiscal federalism issue had already started. The major requirement was to introduce a principle of "independence," a "self-sufficiency" of the respective budgets and a more equitable distribution of budget funds on a horizontal basis (between republics, but also within local authorities). Gradually, opinion strengthened in both national republics that the responsibilities of the federal government should be restricted to the minimum necessary for federal state functioning.

The design and composition of revenue distribution became a crucial point in the fiscal federalism debate. For political reasons, direct transfers between the federal and state budgets were ended because the 1991 budgetary system was to utilize a revenue-sharing approach.

More precisely (at least when speaking about the federal and republic levels), the revenue of certain taxes was assigned to the federal budget, that of others to the republics, with revenue from the remaining taxes shared between the federal and republic budgets. The shares applicable in 1991 and 1992 differed. These changes were motivated by a policy of alignment of the budget expenditure per capita level in both republics and also by that of revenue-sharing based on the republics' population ratio. This tendency was reflected by the ratio of total expenditure of the Czech and Slovak budgets (see table 2).

The total expenditure per capita in the Czech republic exceeded the Slovak one for the first time in the 1992 budget.

Turnover tax, profit taxes, and agricultural profit tax revenues were assigned to the sharing mechanism. The respective proportions are illustrated in table 3.

Despite frequent changes, the system of fiscal federalism adopted for 1991 and 1992 did not work. It suffered basically for two reasons:

1. The general political development, especially on the Slovak side, was simply oriented toward the split of the country (and even an efficient fiscal federalism arrangement could never have stopped that process).
2. It did not eliminate totally the nontransparency of flows of funds between the two national republics in a politically explosive situation.

3. BUDGET REFORM

The Czechoslovak economy until 1989 could be considered, with a certain exaggeration, as a big public sector, one with all the negative features connected with a public sector in any country. In the case of Czechoslovakia, however, these negative features were compounded by its size and all-encompassing character.

Postwar nationalization and development in the 1950s led to the state owning, with some small, insubstantial exceptions, everything. In contrast to Poland, Hungary, and the former GDR, practically all small businesses in manufacturing, agriculture, and handicrafts were liquidated in Czechoslovakia. At least in the initial period, everything was subordinated to the central authority, which outlawed almost all signs of independence in economic units. It was obvious that the position and functions of the budget underwent substantial changes.

Until 1989, the budget presented a tool of bulk redistribution from effective enterprises to less effective ones, from successful ones to less successful ones. The concentration of means in the hands of the central authority enabled considerable changes in the Czechoslovak economy to be implemented in a relatively short period of time, contributing to the imbalanced size structure of enterprises in the economy, which is to say the excessive weight of big firms. The direction of these changes was also motivated by the new role of the Czechoslovak economy among other CMEA countries—its conversion into "smithy and machine works" for the former CMEA economies.

The excessive redistribution influenced further economic proportions, too. The introduction of "free of charge" health care and education, the relatively wealthy social care system, and cheap housing—all these benefits were achieved because of the low wage level in Czechoslovakia. This led to comparative advantage in exports on one hand, but represented a drag because of the cost of services on the other, in lowering the level of "free of charge" and therefore on the volume of the budget as well.

Apart from the necessity of public sector limitation, the changes in 1989 unavoidably brought about a new approach to the budget itself. Gradual public sector restrictions were and are based on denationalization of state-owned enterprises, reduction of enterprise sector subsidies, and limitation on public consumption. None of these is easy or simple, because there is an adaptability barrier on the side of enterprises as well as on the side of the population. While the change of normative rules is relatively simple, the change in behavior of economic units demands a longer time period and, as might be predicted, comes only with difficulties.

The issue of whether a budget should or should not be of a restrictive nature was widely discussed. Under conditions of price liberalization, internal convertibility of the Czechoslovak koruna, and foreign trade liberalization, a tough fiscal policy accompanied by strict monetary policy was the only way to enable the economic reform to be launched. In spite of certain negative impacts of the restrictions on economic growth, it remained the only way to prevent the reform process from leading to an inflation spiral that would obviously make the reform implementation more difficult.

Nevertheless, the results of the economic reform in Czechoslovakia in 1990–1992, measured by macroeconomic aggregates, showed the legitimacy of this approach. This is so even if we take into account that the appraisal of these main macroeconomic aggregates— economic growth, inflation, unemployment, and foreign debt—is made in an economy that has had only little experience with inflation and unemployment. Moreover, it is an economy that in the long run had mainly shown a positive economic growth. It was and still is an economy where the priorities within these four tasks can be found with difficulty only because the level of fulfillment of the main tasks the economy and its citizens can bear is unknown.

Evaluating the reform process, it is evident that Czechoslovakia in 1992—after two years of transformation—had the lowest level of inflation and unemployment relative to other countries undergoing economic reform. Levels of these indicators are comparable with many developed countries. Moreover, the Czechoslovak economy exhibited signs that the lowest point of economic decline already has been reached in this period. Not even the level of foreign indebtedness forms a serious burden to further development.

The evaluation of the level of fiscal restriction itself is unambiguous. If the restriction is considered by the budget surplus solely, then the budget was restrictive in 1990 only. If the tax quota decrease is used, one can see that the decrease was not overwhelming. We are, however, convinced that for an economy in transition these synthetic indicators are insufficient.

As far as the enterprise subsidies are concerned, the development is unambiguous, although even here one can find moves in both directions. At least at the initial stage, there is the necessity of state involvement, for example, in the armament industry conversion, which operates against the restriction of state paternalism toward state enterprises. In this connection, the catastrophic state of the environment, at least in some parts of Czechoslovakia, should be remembered. Here the state intervention is and will be indispensable.

The shift from a situation where the state is responsible for the "felicity" of its citizens to one where the individual should rely on himself or herself must be gradual. The budget development has reflected this fact in the sense of increased transfers to citizens. Some new items (e.g., unemployment benefits supported by outlays for new job formation) appeared there; the amount of social benefits increased as well. The restriction of the excessive social system benefits viewed in light of economic feasibility plays an increasingly important role.

The decline in economic performance was evoked at the same time by the unsatisfactory structure of the Czechoslovak economy until 1989 and by the economic reform itself. It led to pressure for state intervention, which should at least partly compensate for this decline. The lack of experience and of theoretical knowledge of how to transform a planned economy to a market-oriented one is quite patent here. The question of how quickly state paternalism could be abolished marked the whole period of transformation and influenced the budget transformation and has been the subject of continuing discussions.

The budget transformation in Czechoslovakia was marked by discussions about federation arrangements from the very start. In other words, it was marked by a search for more viable relations between the federation on one side and the two republics on the other side. Many pages were written looking for answers to the question of who pays for whom and how much, and which ways will the transfers between republics be made.

In the period 1990–1992, the federation became weaker and weaker, especially under pressure from Slovak politicians. Budget development was heavily influenced by these movements. The increasing call for more and more independence for the Slovak Republic was reflected in restrictions of federal power, especially after the election in the middle of 1992, which led to the more obvious disintegration of the federal arrangement of Czechoslovakia. This process is still alive and need not be mentioned here. Czechs and Slovaks will have to wait for some time to learn the impact of this breakup on the economic and social processes in both republics.

Because of the federal arrangement of Czechoslovakia, and because the two republics acted as one, it is difficult to evaluate the budget and its changed position for the Czech Republic itself. Therefore, we describe the budget until 1992 for Czechoslovakia as a whole, but we must be aware of the different developments in the two republics even at that time.

The budget for 1993 was prepared as a budget for the independent Czech Republic for the first time. In the process of its preparation, some data for the Czech Republic for 1992 were additionally counted to enable the comparison with 1993.

We are aware that the comparison of some data is questionable, not only because the economy is undergoing a transformation process, but the budget itself has passed through substantial changes. These changes also affected the "value" of available statistical data. Moreover, the statistics themselves have been changing as well.

3.1. BUDGET CHANGES 1990–1992

The original budget for 1990 was in fact prepared by the old government. It included a deficit at the level of 5 billion korunas (Kcs). The way revenue and expenditure were planned in this initial budget suggested that the deficit would have been even greater. Therefore, at the beginning of 1990 it was agreed to use a provisional arrangement in the budget. In the course of the year a new budget was composed. It was already of a restrictive nature, a surplus as its outcome.

The main reform steps were prepared in 1990. The fiscal policy together with monetary policy tended to assure the maximum possible economic stability.

In the course of 1990 some budget management defects were removed. The negative turnover tax for foodstuffs was abolished in July. The introduction of state contributions compensated citizens for the increase in prices of basic foodstuffs. The impact of this policy was therefore neutral for people as well as for the budget. An election that took place at that time played a certain role in this procedure, too.

In 1990, in fact, the last central price accommodations were introduced. They aimed to draw prices nearer to their real values before the price liberalization took effect. Also these changes were reflected by the budget, as were the growing difficulties in mutual foreign trade with the former USSR and the other post-socialist countries.

Three devaluations of the Czechoslovak koruna took place in 1990. The first presented a response to the unrealistic exchange rate prior to 1990, although the last devaluation, which took place in December, was part of the preparation for the internal convertibility introduction. These devaluations influenced the level of state financial assets and liabilities.

The budget surplus in 1990 was higher than expected as a consequence of favorable development of major revenues, with the exception of turnover tax yield. The surplus amounted to 7.4 billion korunas, 1.5% of overall budget revenue.

The 1991 budget—the budget for the first year of the economic reform in Czechoslovakia—was also compiled as a restrictive and anti-inflationary one. The most important budget management measures comprised the unification of the turnover tax rates (the initial number of rates, exceeding 1,500%, was reduced to four rates—0%, 12%, 22%, and 32%), a decrease of the enterprise tax burden by 10 percentage points (to 55%), and introduction of an import surcharge to protect the balance of payments and the domestic market after internal convertibility.

The price liberalization led to a price increase of 25% in January 1991. This price jump, however, quickly disappeared in the course of the year and the price level stabilized. The budget reached a substantial surplus in the first half of the year due to the substantial increase of taxes paid by enterprises. There was a certain delay in the response of budgetary expenditures, but the response was then quite strong.

The reform steps adopted led at the beginning to an economic regression. A rather slow adjustment of enterprises to the new conditions played a certain role. Among other factors, traditional foreign trade disintegrated. The budget surplus was therefore partly used to value budget expenditure (for health care, education, and social services), and partly for demand restoration. Turnover tax rates were lowered by approximately 10 percentage points and, due to favorable balance of payments developments, the import surcharge was reduced as well.

The impact of the price increase on revenue diminished during the year. However, budget outlays showed the opposite effect: One could already see the weakness of the federation, because toward the end of the year both republics could have accommodated their expenditures to their revenues. This fact finally resulted in a budget deficit at the level of 17.5 billion korunas, i.e., 3.5% of budgetary revenue and 1.8% of GDP. Czechoslovakia learned some lessons from the Polish experience, where these events had taken place one year earlier.

The final budget deficit in 1991, as well as eventual deficits during subsequent years, could not have been further financed by direct central bank credit, as had been the case in previous years. The issues of treasury bills and state bonds were prepared to finance deficits.

Czechoslovakia re-entered the International Monetary Fund and World Bank in 1990. The budget draft for 1991 was therefore made in cooperation with experts from these institutions. Czechoslovakia received the first tranches of loans from these institutions in 1991. The use of these loans is bound, as in the case of any other country, to a set of agreed performance criteria. No relevant deviations from agreed criteria were found, and there was no need to change the agreed criteria.

As far as the state financial assets and liabilities are concerned, they were influenced by conversion of government claims in rubles to claims expressed in dollars, and also by reimbursement of exchange rate differences.

The budget for 1992 was burdened by the necessity of reimbursing the 1991 deficit. Nevertheless, it was drawn as a balanced budget, influenced by the basic reform steps previously adopted. Furthermore, the price liberalization was broadened, and there were some changes in relations between the state and the banking system—a solution of the Československá obchodní banka balance (the commercial bank that held external assets and liabilities of the CSFR and currently of the two independent republics).

In fact, the whole year was marked by discrepancies between actual budgetary revenues and expected ones. A great number of factors were involved—overestimated revenues, lower yield of turnover tax, savings ratio growth, the shift in demand of citizens toward goods with lower rates, increase in tax evasion, and growing intra-enterprise indebtedness. Tax arrears appeared for the first time.

The Czech government adopted a number of measures (including lower levels than projected of some expenditure) to prevent the budget from showing an excessive deficit. The Czech budget emerged with an apparently small deficit, while the Slovak budget reached a huge one.

In spite of a rather favorable budget deficit in 1992, the Czech Republic entered 1993 with a debt that did not derive from current budget management. The Czech budget "inherited" a proportionate part of the 9.5 billion-koruna federal budget deficit. The other part of the inherited deficit comes from the Czech Republic obligation, which followed from the solution of the Československá obchodní banka balance.

Budget development in 1993 will be fundamentally influenced by the tax reform put into effect in January, which represents a substantial intervention in the tax system. Apart from the most important innovation (the shift from turnover tax to the value-added tax—where the time for preparation was considerably short), almost all taxes were changed. Road and property taxes are completely new, while local budgets have been restructured.

With the end of the federation, the Czech budget took over some federal budget functions that have impact on the revenue and expenditure sides as well as on the debt.

3.1.1 State Budget Revenue Developments 1990–1992

Before 1989, state budget revenue heavily depended on levies paid by enterprises and on turnover tax; taxes paid by households represented only a small portion of the budget revenue. Those proportions were maintained during the whole analyzed period in spite of the fact that since 1990 a process of gradual reduction of the corporate tax burden had been initiated (at the same time, a more uniform tax approach to all types of corporate taxpayers was adopted). The weight of indirect taxation slightly increased.

In 1989, turnover tax yield was influenced by the existence of the negative turnover tax (which was by its substance a hidden retail price subsidy). It amounted to 49.1 billion korunas in 1989. The negative turnover tax on foodstuffs was abolished in July 1990; by that time, it had reached 34.6 billion korunas.

As seen in tables 5 and 6, the overall tax burden of households, measured primarily by the individual income tax, remained roughly the same during the whole period. The changes adopted in this period were oriented toward unification of the tax treatment of similar economic activities. Major changes were postponed until the tax reform scheduled for 1993.

At that time, small- and medium-sized entrepreneurs were given preferential treatment by lower tax rates, tax deferments, tax relief, and relatively high flat deductions of costs from the tax base.

The radical change in the share of the non-tax revenue was due mainly to additional revenue given to local budgets from various sources, representing a certain compensation for some of the adverse effects of privatization and restitution for formerly government-owned property (which led to a shift of a part of the revenue from local budgets to the central budget). The revenue that was lost was partly compensated for with money from the national property fund (a fund that concentrates privatization receipts) and by changes in the level of different local fees during the year.

The decline in the corporate income tax yield in 1992 reflected the decrease in economic activity in Czechoslovakia as a whole. This tendency was not reflected in the 1991 revenues because of the post-liberalization jump in January 1991, which resulted in an increase in profit tax revenue. A certain role was also played by the specific behavior of the still state-owned enterprises prior to their privatization: Most of the large state-owned companies had substantially shortened the time horizon of their decision-making processes and had concentrated essentially on their short-term position (for instance, preference was given to wage payments). The private sector is extremely dynamic, but it contributes to GDP only to a lesser extent. It has been developing basically in small- and medium-sized businesses where, as has already been stated, preferential tax treatment was applied. Therefore, the private sector dynamism has not yet been reflected in the state budget revenue.

3.1.2 State Budget Expenditure Developments 1990–1992

As relates to the budget expenditure especially since 1991, there was a relatively substantial decline of transfers to enterprises (see tables 7 and 8). The reduction of the non-investment part of those transfers was even sharper. In this sense, the state budget unambiguously played a restrictive role. That partly corresponded to the reduction of the tax burden on enterprises, even if the dynamics of both processes were not comparable. The taxation of profits was reduced between 1989 and 1992 by some 20 percentage points.

Besides the reduction of transfers to enterprises, a change of their structure was initiated. Before 1990, there were no fixed rules for corporate taxes. The corporate tax system was a nontransparent mixture of "aid" to enterprises in trouble and drawing-out of profits from profitable ones. Since 1990, the approach was gradually more and more oriented toward specifically targeted projects, especially in the area of the armament industry conversion, and also in the compensation for the negative effects of the price control in the remaining spheres of regulated prices (e.g., energy, urban transportation, rents).

The most important element of transfers to households is represented by social security benefits. They include the compensation benefits for negative turnover tax removal. Initially, that compensation was given in the form of general income support, while later only selected categories of households were eligible to receive it. In connection with the price developments, some adjustments of pensions and other social benefits for inflation were made.

A new item appeared in the form of unemployment benefits, which were especially abundant in Slovakia. Gradually, active employment policies (new job creation and retraining programs) with consequent budget expenditures became more important.

The development of transfers to households directly reflects the concern of the government to maintain the support of the population for economic transformation. Despite a relatively weak economic performance and a consequent shortfall in budget revenue, considerable budget funds were allocated to create a sufficient social security net to avoid an excessive decline in the living standard of low-income households. As a result of this policy, since 1989 there have been no major social conflicts, such as long and large-scale strikes, despite the decline in output and of real wages.

The most important part of the budget expenditure on public consumption is represented by education and health care outlays. It is necessary to remember that these services were and still are financed mainly from the budget. The role of the private sector is still only a marginal one.

Another cause of the expenditure increase is due to price developments, leading to an increase not only of material costs but also to an increase of wages, which were traditionally low in these sectors. Generally speaking, it is possible to say that the expenditure increase allowed for maintenance of the real level of those public services only.

By 1990, the first private schools had appeared, although they remain in a minority. Private schools obtain 90% of the subsidies allowed for public schools. Meanwhile, the main privatization thrust in the health care system is expected in 1993.

There were many changes in the expenditure structure in state administration. The whole analyzed period was marked by shifts of power from federal to republic authorities, resulting in the foundation of new ministries on the republic level, and new agencies were set up in accordance with the reform transition philosophy (anti-monopolistic agencies, labor offices, tax offices, and others).

A major decline of expenditure occurred in defense, mostly due to a change of the political climate in Europe. In 1990–1991, obligatory military service was shortened from two years to 18 months. By the middle of 1991, the last Soviet troops left Czechoslovak territory. On the other hand, a decline in military expenditure led to the decline of armament industry products and to armament industry conversion. The conversion issue was especially difficult in Slovakia, where the military industries were and still are more concentrated in comparison with the Czech Republic.

Many changes occurred in the internal security expenditure. The security system was adjusted and the function of the secret police was redefined. Internal security expenditure development could not have ignored the increase in crime, which partly resulted from the opening of borders and partly from the liberalization of the living conditions in Czechoslovakia.

Special attention should be paid to subsidies to agriculture. For a few decades, there was a tradition of agricultural production in large productive entities legally defined as agricultural cooperatives (created by force in the 1950s) or state farms. Food prices were heavily subsidized, and the final losses of the producers were compensated against the budget by a number of channels. Low prices in the past had led unavoidably to a relatively substantial overproduction and waste in food consumption.

Since 1989, especially after prices were freed in January 1991, food consumption has been reduced, and, consequently, so has production. This development had negative effects on producers. In addition, foreign trade liberalization led to an increase of imported food and food products.

The system of subsidies was shifted from a differentiated one to one involving a more uniform approach to all producers. In 1991, Market Intervention Funds were created in both republics, and in 1992 a federal one was added. Their main purpose is to stabilize prices of agricultural products. These funds make interventional purchases on domestic markets to guarantee prices of selected basic agricultural products and, on the other hand, contribute to the stability of basic food prices for consumers by occasional sales. They play a major role in foreign trade regulation and in eliminating the monopolistic practices of the food producers.

3.1.3 Budget Balance 1990–1992

Prior to 1989, the balance of budgetary activity and financing was entirely a formal issue. The state budget development in those years should be evaluated together with the monetary policies and the corporate finance developments, as there were many transfers among those sectors, open or hidden.

"Flexibility" in the enterprise tax system and in replacing budget transfers by administrative credit allocation made possible frequent changes in the financing of the budget expenditure according to immediate needs. Also, some typical budget expenditure (as, for example, financing of government credit abroad) was transferred to the banking system. By these means, it was almost always possible before 1989 to reach a balanced budget or a budget surplus every year. These moves in fact created no major difficulties in reaching the intended targets regardless of economic development. Balanced budgets or surpluses were by that time traditionally a major political goal.

Because of this, distortions of real budget development were enormous; the overall position of the government (including the state financial assets and liabilities) was distorted as well. Therefore, the development of the state financial assets and liabilities only partially reflected the budget results of the recent years. Another important factor was, for instance, administrative price changes (accounted for with the state budget) and other assets and accounting operations.

The deficit financing appropriate to a market economy only began in 1991. As we have already mentioned, the budget in 1990 showed an overall surplus of 7.1 billion korunas or 0.9% of GDP. (Note: the data on budget results are given according to the CSFR methodology, which corresponds to the decision-making process and differs from IMF statistics.) Of that, the central budget had a surplus (the federal by 4 billion korunas, the Czech by 200 million korunas, while the Slovak was in deficit by 400 million korunas). The surplus of local budgets was 3.3 billion korunas. The total budget surplus was used to increase the state financial reserves.

The year 1991 was a year of a budget deficit (altogether 10.4 billion korunas or 1.1% GDP), although the first half of the year showed a substantial surplus of 17.7 billion korunas. The separation of budget activities between the federal budget and the budgets of the two republics and the weak influence of the federal authorities on republic budget activities, and therefore on general budget activities as a whole, played a certain role in this process.

The total result of the general budget was a combination of the two national budget deficits, and the federal and local budget surpluses (the Czech deficit of 13.6 billion korunas, the Slovak deficit of

10.3 billion korunas, the federal surplus of 6.4 billion korunas and local budgets surplus of 7.1 billion korunas). The federal budget surplus was used as a compensation for the shortfall of some revenue of the republic budgets. By this operation, the Czech budget deficit was reduced to 9.9 billion korunas, the Slovak to 6 billion korunas. These final deficits of the republics were to be financed by issuing state bonds (prepared in 1992).

At the time of preparing this document, final data for 1992 were not yet available. The federal budget has recorded an estimated deficit of about 7 billion korunas. In addition, the federal government took the commitment to solve the issue of liquidity of the Československá obchodní banka. The federal budget participated in this cleanup operation because those liquidity problems were generated by old policies and decisions made on a non-market basis at the time when this bank was acting as an agent of the state.

The result of the Czech state budget is an estimated deficit of 1.7 billion korunas. The deficit in the Slovak Republic is estimated at 7.9 billion korunas. The surplus of the local budgets will represent, according to the latest data, 8.6 billion korunas.

All together, the total deficit of the Czechoslovak general budget for 1992 is 8 billion korunas, that is, 0.8% of GDP.

The net credit to government covers the deficit of the state budgets, including the local budgets, the development of the state financial assets and liabilities, and extrabudgetary funds (including local funds).

The net credit to government (see table 9) increased between 1990 and October 1992 from 5.9 billion korunas (1% of the domestic credit) to 40.5 billion korunas (4.8% of the domestic credit). Its development was very irregular during this period—by the end of 1990 it already represented 54.2 billion korunas and then it turned downward.

The development of net credit to government in this period was influenced by a number of factors that were not immediately connected with contemporary economic developments; rather, they were derived from the elimination of the distortions in the relationship between the government and the banking system in the previous years, and from distortions of the exchange rate.

A high increase of the net credit to government in 1990 was a result of state financial assets and liabilities operations. They concerned especially the takeover of the government credits abroad by the federal government, dealing with the impact of the major exchange rate changes in the economy, and the shift from the transferable ruble foreign trade financing with countries of the former CMEA area to hard currencies. In comparison with those operations, the result of current budgets played only a minor role.

In the following years, the net credit to government was reduced, particularly in connection with international institutions' loans to the government—the World Bank, EC, G-24, and others. A similar effect was generated by the conversion of transferable ruble assets to dollars. The opposite effect, i.e., an increase in the borrowing requirement, was caused by the current budget deficit in 1991.

In 1992, state bonds were issued for the first time, in the total amount of 13 billion korunas. The revenue of this issue was designed to finance state housing under construction. From February 1992, the three finance ministries issued treasury bills on a regular basis. The development of the net credit to the government in 1992 was no longer influenced by nonstandard operations; it therefore more accurately reflected current economic activities and the 1991 budget deficit.

In 1992, the state bank act went into effect, limiting budget deficit financing. Since February 1992, direct credit financing of the budget deficit has been prohibited by law, with one exception—a technical credit to cover the time lag between expenditure payments and revenue accrual is permitted, but it cannot exceed 5% of the current budgetary revenue.

The first year the state participated in the emerging Czechoslovak money and capital markets was 1992. There were all together 42 issuances of treasury bills by the three finance ministries that year. The treasury bill issuances ranged from 1 billion to 11 billion korunas; their maturity varied from 5 to 91 days. Most of the issues were placed through auctions, although nine were bought directly by the central bank at a fixed price. Compared with interest rates on interbank markets, the interest rates on treasury bills showed much more variation in the course of the year—above as well as below the market (those varied between 11.92% and 11.05%).

The federal and Czech treasury bills were placed without any problems; in both cases, the whole volume was sold. Some problems were recorded by the end of the year in Slovakia despite the relatively high interest rate applied. These problems were caused by a lack of resources in the Slovak commercial banks (due mainly to the lower savings rate in Slovakia) and by a lack of interest on the part of the Czech banks in investing in Slovakia. One auction in Slovakia had to be canceled.

Issues of treasury bills in Czechoslovakia were organized under conditions of a developing financial market. The number of partici-pants was restricted; in fact, mainly commercial banks and two insurance companies took part. A similar situation occurred when issuing the state bonds in the two republics. There were problems again only in Slovakia.

The Czech Republic issued state bonds at a nominal price of 8.7 billion korunas in two tranches (in May and August) with a maturity of two and three years. The interest rate was offered at 15%. The issue was successful; the selling price was for all the issues higher than the nominal one. The Slovak issue was divided into three tranches (in May, July, and September) with a maturity of five years. The interest rate was offered at 8%. Nevertheless, the whole issue was not sold. The revenue from these bond issues was used to finance state housing programs in both republics.

3.2 BUDGET CHANGES IN 1993

The first year of the independence of the Czech Republic was 1993, and thus its budget was prepared under entirely new conditions. Fundamentally influenced by the disintegration of the federation, it took over some federal budget functions as well as a proportionate part of the federal debt. It is also the year of the tax reform, which represents significant changes in the revenue as well as in the expenditure sides.

The tax reform in the Czech Republic means a formation of a completely new tax system, and an important shift toward institutions common in developed market economies. Almost all taxes were changed; moreover, all of it was done in a relatively short time.

Among other changes, the tax reform brought about a shift from direct financing of health care, social services, and unemployment benefits from the budget to financing by special funds, of which three were created.

In 1993, two of these funds—Social Care Fund and Employment Fund—still operate within the budget by special contributions paid by employers and employees, while the Health Care Fund is already separate from the state budget. The state budget will be involved in this fund through contributions on behalf of people who do not work for different reasons (women looking after small children, pensioners, jobless people, soldiers, and so on).

The goals of fiscal policy of the Czech Republic for 1993 are as follows:

- a stable economic development and minimal inflation through a balanced budget draft and other tools;
- maintenance of the social consensus by devoting as many means

as possible to compensate for adverse economic transformation impacts on citizens;
- continued decrease in the share of budget on GDP;
- renewed economic growth.

The fiscal policy was drawn on these macroeconomic background projections:

- Increase in GDP in the range of 1%–3%; the 1992 estimate is from −5% to −7%.
- Rate of inflation measured by CPI within 15%–17%; the 1992 estimate is 11%.
- A natural rate of unemployment in the range of 4%–5%; the rate of unemployment at the end of 1993 is estimated at 8%; the rate of unemployment at the end of 1992 reached 2.6%.
- A positive balance of payments; the surplus for 1992 is estimated for Czechoslovakia as a whole at $900 million, achieved mainly in the Czech Republic.

When preparing the draft of the budget for 1993 some data were adjusted to enable comparison between 1992 and 1993.

The estimated GDP of the Czech Republic for 1992 is 738.3 billion korunas and for 1993 870 billion korunas. The share of budget revenue in the GDP should decrease from 50% to 48.1%. This decrease is due to the overall tax burden decline.

The decrease in local budget revenue (see table 10) is due to the fact that these budgets were given additional revenues in 1992. They were partly compensated for revenue losses as a result of privatization and received some other additional revenues connected with their new functions. Local budgets also received the yield from state bonds for state housing under construction.

The revenue and expenditure composition changed as well. Local budget revenues consist of the yield from property tax, the yield from individual income tax, administrative and local fees, and revenue from sale and lease of local property. Earmarked subsidies include a contribution to state administration functions carried by local governments, compensation for local government social benefits that follow the law, and specific subsidies to ensure the standard level of education and health care services throughout the country. Local governments are obliged to make use of bank credit and bond issues.

In spite of several adjustments of data in table 11, they are not fully comparable. The tax reform brought about an increase in indirect tax share due to VAT introduction. By using VAT, the tax base was extended. There are two tax rates, 5% and 23%. Apart from

VAT, excises on fuel, tobacco products, spirits, beer, and wines belong among indirect taxes as well. Simultaneously, we can find a decrease in the corporate income tax rate, which is an aid in corporate sector development and a response to the previously high tax burden of enterprises.

The decrease of individual income tax share on the total is connected with the establishment of the Health Care Fund. Until 1992, contributions for health care were a part of both this tax and corporate taxes.

Within budget expenditures we can find a further increase of transfers to citizens. This reflects the social security benefit adjustment for inflation, amplification of the social safety net, an expected increase in unemployment, and some other aspects. Pensions and other social security benefits represent by far the most important item within transfers to citizens (60.3% and 21.8% respectively).

Decline of the share of transfers to enterprises on the whole corresponds to the continuing process of state paternalism limitation and the progress in privatization. On the other hand, growing outlays for private sector support are involved in these transfers. Among others, there is a subsidy to Ceskomoravská záruční a rozvojová banka (the Czech-Moravian Guarantee and Development Bank) and Exportní, garanční a pojišťovací společnost (the Institution for Export, Guarantees and Insurance). These two institutions aim first of all to provide the private sector with credit under more favorable conditions than do the other financial institutions and to guarantee and insure credit for exports.

In the 1993 budget, current public sector expenditures will increase. The reason was already mentioned—the most dynamic item is outlay connected with the establishment of the Health Care Fund. The substantial increase in the health care expenditure share in the total budget this year is mainly due to a one-time cost. The outlays for education were increased as well, but to a lesser extent. A part of this increase might be explained by the new system of financing health and social care, because organizations providing educational services will pay contributions to these funds for the first time in 1993.

The decline of public sector investment corresponds to the overall decrease in investment activity. Investments in capital formation used to be excessive in Czechoslovakia, so that a certain decline will not create a big burden, at least for a limited time. With the turning point in economic performance in 1992, it can be expected that there will be a stabilization in the growth of capital formation in the public sector. Meanwhile, assumption of a proportionate part of the former federal government loans (in 1992 partly financed from the federal financial assets) had its impact on the government loan increase.

The expected budget revenues in 1993 are marked by a number of risks. They follow partly from the not-yet-finalized arrangements between the Czech and Slovak Republics (mainly the split of assets and liabilities) and partly from the introduction of the new tax system (the risk from lower than expected revenue from new taxes and social security contributions).

Last but not least, there should be mentioned the mutual trade relations between the Czech Republic and the Slovak Republic after monetary union abolition. The monetary union survived only 38 days. The untimely end of the monetary union must be added to the risks of the 1993 budget development, as it will probably lead to a certain decline in economic activity, at least in the short run.

In 1993, a certain form of a bankruptcy law should go into effect, and at the first stage some budget revenue decline and pressure on budget expenditure might be expected.

4. ECONOMIC DEVELOPMENT IN 1990–1993: EVALUATION

All economies in transition have faced economic decline, price level increases, deepening unemployment, and an increase of foreign indebtedness in connection with economic reform. Czechoslovakia was not and probably could not be an exception to this rule. However, it is apparent that these negative impacts in Czechoslovakia have not been as severe as in some other Central and East European countries.

As detailed in tables 12, 13, and 14, economic growth in the period 1989–1992, measured by GDP, declined by 21% in real terms. While evaluating whether this decline was or was not excessive, one should be aware that an important part of the GDP before 1990 was either fed by artificial tools, and therefore consisted of a number of goods with no or very low demand, or that demand was generated because of lack of foreign goods. The share of inventories and unfinished capital formation was too high in comparison with developed market economies. From this point of view, a certain decline of GDP was desirable and formed a inherent part of the shift of enterprise interest from production toward sale of their products.

The economic performance decline was also marked by the fact that traditional foreign markets disintegrated during 1990 and 1991. In 1989, more than half of the Czechoslovak foreign trade was oriented to these traditional markets, while with market economies it was only 35%. The reorientation of foreign trade was apparently quick but not without pain, and the share of foreign trade with developed countries was already 60% in 1991 and has been growing since.

Real wage development has not contributed to inflation because of strict wage regulation throughout the analyzed period. On the other hand, it is obvious that continuing wage regulation could become a constraint on further economic development. Therefore the wage regulation for 1993 will be limited only to the public sector organizations.

Czechoslovakia demonstrated a negligible level of inflation until 1989 because, among other reasons, of central price regulation. At the end of the centrally planned period, latent and suppressed inflation was estimated to be less than 5% a year.

Price liberalization dismantled hidden price deformations. The eventual price increase reflected this fact as well as the learning process of producers and tradespeople in how to behave in a situation of radically reduced central price control. The difficulty of the learning process was again demonstrated at the beginning of 1993 with price rises after the VAT introduction.

As far as unemployment is concerned, its meaning is difficult to assess because Czechoslovakia had had full employment for a long period. Therefore, it is a new phenomenon in the country, and there is little experience with an unemployment policy (the initial unemployment policies were of a favorable but not of a stimulating nature) and little experience on the needs of unemployed people, too. Because the rise of unemployment started practically from zero, it might be considered high. Nevertheless, it still has not corresponded to the GDP decline.

Up to now, foreign indebtedness has not presented a serious constraint on economic development, because loans from the IMF and other international financial institutions and favorable balance of payments developments in the last two years have strengthened Czechoslovakia's foreign exchange reserves. The debt service is therefore manageable.

While on the side of economic growth it is believed that the lowest point has been reached already, and that the main factors of inflationary pressures have been dealt with successfully, on the side of unemployment and trade balance some "negative" tendencies can be expected. Impulses of these negative tendencies can be found in bringing to an end the first wave of large-scale privatization. The growth of the private sector will no doubt create new jobs, but at the same time the private sector has an inherent inclination to use the labor force effectively, which is not always the case in state-owned enterprises.

An increase in imports is to be expected due to the fact that the Czech Republic has already reached and passed the bottom of its economic decline. To a certain extent, the necessity to repay loans will act as a depressant. The expected revenue from tourism will operate in the opposite direction.

5. CONCLUSIONS

The budgets in Czechoslovakia and in the Czech Republic have undergone considerable changes. Their position in relation to economic activities has changed radically. The new tax system changed the revenue side, while the establishment of the three insurance funds changed the expenditure side of the budget as well.

In the future, the tax structure will have to be fine-tuned so that it is in accordance with the ongoing shift to market economy, so that it will be an aid and not a hindrance for the transformation process in the Czech Republic.

On the expenditure side of the budget, the separation of the two remaining insurance funds (Social Care and Employment Funds) is anticipated in 1994. The remaining parts of expenditure should also be changed step by step. By this we have in mind the shift from the so-called demand principle of spending ministries to their financing on the basis of integral medium-term programs. These programs should reflect the society's preferences for a certain period and should also contribute to more effective source allocation and to greater effectiveness of the public sector as a whole.

Through privatization and renewed real wage growth, and by the generally agreed tendency toward the lowering of tax quotas, a further restriction of the public sector in the Czech Republic might be expected. We believe that the Czech government will continue restrictive and anti-inflationary oriented budgets in the nearest future.

The last three-year evaluation of economic and social results suggests that the adopted principles of economic reform in the Czech Republic are basically the appropriate ones. Naturally, not everything went as it had been originally intended. Bearing in mind, however, the magnitude of what was to be done, such a development could not have been in any case expected.

Table 1
Structure of General Government Revenue and Expenditure
(in percentage of total)

	1989	1990	1991	1992
Total revenue	100.0	100.0	100.0	100.0
Federation	48.8	37.8	22.7	23.2
Czech Rep.	14.8	25.9	47.1	47.7
Slovak Rep	7.2	14.3	24.5	22.2
Local govt.	17.8	19.7	3.4	3.4
Others*	11.4	1.3	2.3	3.5
Total expenditure	100.0	100.0	100.0	100.0
Federation	27.3	33.0	21.7	21.3
Czech Rep.	20.9	21.3	31.2	33.3
Slovak Rep.	12.7	12.9	22.7	21.3
Local govt.	26.6	28.6	19.0	15.0
Others*	12.5	4.2	5.4	9.1

*Extra-budgetary funds, in 1989 funds of ministries.

Source: State budget documents 1989, 1990, 1991, 1992.

Table 2
Ratio of Total Expenditure of Czech and Slovak Budgets, 1989–1992

Year	State Budget of Czech Rep.	State Budget of Slovak Rep.
1989	1.78	1
1990	1.84	1
1991	1.91	1
1992	2.10	1

Source: State Budget Act of CSFR 1992, Federal Ministry of Finance 1991.

Table 3
Shared Revenue Ratios*

1991			1992		
Federal	Czech Rep.	Slovak Rep.	Federal	Czech Rep.	Slovak Rep.
35.0	40.0	25.0	35.0	41.5	23.5
	1.6	1.0		1.8	1.0

*These ratios represent the shares of the respective budgets of the "shared" revenues (turnover tax and profit tax revenues).

Source: State Budget Act of CSFR, Federal Ministry of Finance, 1992.

Table 4
Budget Revenue/GDP Ratio
(billion korunas)

	1989	1990	1991	1992*
(I) Budget revenue	415.4	463.1	505.5	540.0
(II) GDP	758.7	811.3	977.8	1,009.4
I as a % of II	54.7	57.0	51.6	53.5

*Estimates.

Source: Federal Ministry of Finance.

Table 5
Budget Revenue Development
(billion korunas)

	1989	1990	1991	1992
Total revenue	415.4	463.1	505.5	540.0
Tax revenue	377.3	422.8	477.1	467.0
direct taxes	293.3	304.6	342.3	325.0
from individuals	60.7	62.9	77.1	77.0
from corporations	232.7	241.7	265.2	248.0
indirect taxes	85.0	118.1	134.8	142.0
Non-tax revenue	37.1	40.3	28.5	73.0

*Estimates.

Source: Federal Ministry of Finance.

Table 6
Budget Revenue Development
(as % of total revenue)

	1989	1990	1991	1992*
Total revenue	100.0	100.0	100.0	100.0
Tax revenue	91.1	91.3	94.4	86.5
direct taxes	70.6	65.8	67.7	60.2
from individuals	14.6	13.6	15.2	14.3
from corporations	56.0	52.2	52.5	45.9
indirect taxes	20.5	25.5	26.7	26.3
Non-tax revenue	8.8	8.7	5.6	13.5

*Estimates.

Source: Federal Ministry of Finance.

Table 7
Budget Expenditure Development
(billion korunas)

	1989	1990	1991	1992*
Total expenditures	414.9	455.9	515.9	551.0
Transfers to enterprises	83.7	84.1	64.6	52.0
of which:				
investment	10.7	10.6	11.0	13.0
non-investment	73.0	73.5	53.6	39.0
Transfers to households	97.0	113.8	156.2	162.0
Public consumption	234.3	258.0	295.2	337.0
of which:				
investment	33.8	36.5	45.4	47.0
non-investment	200.5	221.5	249.7	290.0

*Estimates.

Source: Federal Ministry of Finance.

Table 8
Budget Expenditure Development
(as % of total)

	1989	1990	1991	1992*
Total expenditures	100.0	100.0	100.0	100.0
Transfers to enterprise	20.2	18.4	12.5	9.4
of which:				
investment	2.6	2.3	2.1	2.3
non-investment	17.6	16.1	10.4	7.1
Transfers to households	23.4	25.0	30.3	29.4
Public consumption	56.4	56.6	57.2	61.2
of which:				
investment	8.1	8.0	8.8	8.5
non-investment	48.3	48.6	48.4	52.7

*Estimates.

Source: Federal Ministry of Finance.

Table 9
Domestic Credit and Net Credit to Government
(billion korunas)

	1989	1990	1991	1992
(I) Domestic credit	583.6	640.2	749.1	847.0
(II) Net credit to govt.*	5.9	54.2	36.8	40.5
II as a % of I	1.0	8.5	4.9	4.8

*Including EC, WB, and G24 loans to government.

Source: Monetary Survey, SBCS.

Table 10
The Overall Budget of the Czech Republic
(billion korunas)

	1992*	1993
Revenue	369.5	416.7
of which:		
State budget	324.2	342.2
Local budget	45.3	41.0
Health insurance	33.5	
Expenditures	375.3	416.7
of which:		
State budget	309.1	305.2
Local budget	66.2	58.0
Health Insurance	53.5	
Surplus/Deficit	5.8	0

*Estimates adjusted for budget structure in 1993.

Source: Ministry of Finance.

Table 11
Structure of Budget Revenue and Expenditure
(billion korunas)

	1992*	Share %	1993	Share %
Total revenue	369.5	100.0	416.7	100.0
Tax revenue	296.6	80.3	247.4	59.4
indirect taxes & tarrifs	96.4	26.1	133.9	32.1
income taxes	131.6	35.7	104.9	25.2
individuals	48.8	13.2	19.0	4.6
corporations	82.8	22.4	85.9	20.6
other taxes	0.8	0.2	8.6	2.1
payroll tax	67.8	18.3	—	—
Nontax revenue	64.0	17.3	38.7	9.3
Social security contributions*	8.9**	2.4	97.1	23.3
Health insurance contributions	33.5	68.0		
Total expenditure	375.3	100.0	416.7	100.0
Transfers to households	106.6	28.4	122.8	29.5
Transfers to enterprises	37.5	9.9	35.7	8.6
Current exp. of public sector	175.3	46.6	206.5	49.6
Public sector investment	41.6	11.0	30.9	7.4
Government loans	2.9	0.8	7.3	1.7
Debt service	11.4	3.3	13.5	3.2
Deficit/Surplus	−5.8	−0		

*Only a limited number of people were obliged to pay these contributions in 1992.
**Estimates adjusted for budget structure in 1993.

Source: Ministry of Finance.

Table 12
Main Czechoslovak Economic Indicators

Memorandum items	1989	1990	1991	1992*
GDP				
in billion korunas, 1984 prices	732.9	719.8	611.4	576.0
indexed relative to previous year	—	98.2	84.9	94.2
GDP deflator (%)	—	108.9	141.9	109.6
CPI (%)	—	110.0	157.9	111.3
Gross foreign indebtedness ($US billion)	7.9	8.1	9.4	9.5
Unemployment (average level in %)	0	0.4	4.1	6.1
Real monthly wage in manufacturing in korunas, 1989 prices	3,335.0	3,116.0	2,316.0	2,449.0
indexed relative to previous year	—	93.4	74.3	105.7

*Estimates.

Source: Federal Statistical Office.

Table 13
Gross Domestic Product by Expenditure—Czechoslovakia
(billion korunas, 1984 prices)

	1989	1990	1991	1992*	1989–1992 (%)
GDP	732.9	719.8	611.4	576.0	−21.4
Private consumption	353.4	363.7	276.6	296.8	−16.0
Public consumption	167.8	165.8	137.2	130.9	−22.0
Investment	214.4	228.3	159.6	132.2	−38.3
of which:					
Fixed investment	205.7	211.1	144.0	140.7	−31.6
Change in stocks	8.7	17.2	15.6	—	−8.5
Net export	−2.8	−37.9	38.0	16.1	
of which:					
Export	258.0	236.4	225.1	234.0	
Import	260.8	274.3	187.1	217.9	

*Estimates.

Source: Federal Statistical Office.

Table 14
Gross Domestic Product by Expenditure—Czechoslovakia
(% of GDP, 1984 prices)

	1989	1990	1991	1992*
GDP	100.0	100.0	100.0	100.0
Private consumption	48.2	50.5	45.2	51.6
Public consumption	22.9	23.0	22.4	22.7
Investment	29.3	31.7	26.2	22.9
of which:				
Fixed investment	28.1	29.3	23.6	24.4
Change in stocks	1.2	2.4	2.6	−1.5
Net export	−0.4	−5.2	6.2	2.8

*Estimates.

Source: Federal Statistical Office.

7

Some Lessons from Fiscal Reform in Czechoslovakia: An Extended Comment on Kameníčková et al.

TESSA VAN DER WILLIGEN

Kameníčková et al.'s paper, "What is the Budget Reform in Czechoslovakia and the Czech Republic About?" presents a useful and comprehensive overview of fiscal developments in Czechoslovakia since the "Velvet Revolution" of 1989, and places them in the context of the overall Czechoslovak reform effort. In this chapter,[1] I present a few clarifications and attempt to draw some conclusions, focusing on the experience of the Czech and Slovak Federal Republic during the period 1989–1992.[2] The chapter is structured as follows: section 1 discusses some problems in measuring the government sector's influence on the economy; section 2 reviews the fiscal policy record, focusing on changes in the fiscal deficit; section 3 discusses the strategy of fiscal reform; and section 4 concludes.

1. CAVEAT EMPTOR: MEASURING THE GOVERNMENT'S INFLUENCE ON THE ECONOMY

Kameníčková et al. present fiscal data following the national methodology, which, as the paper itself notes, departs in certain important respects from international standards. I will discuss the most important of these deviations, which apply also to the successor republics. These caveats are crucial not only to an understanding of some of the numbers presented in Kameníčková et al., but also to an evaluation of fiscal data in official publications. Moreover, the issues are of relevance to economies in transition in general, and the following discussion may perhaps serve also as a general warning to users of these countries' fiscal data. Tables 1 and 2 show current estimates of the 1989–1992 Czechoslovak fiscal outturns according to the methodology of the IMF's Government Finance Statistics (IMF 1986) (with a few deviations noted below).[3]

General government in Czechoslovakia comprises:

- operations under the authority of the Ministries of Finance (through 1992, federal, Czech, and Slovak);

- the local authorities;
- a few small "extra-budgetary (or "state") funds";
- the National Property Funds (through 1992, federal, Czech, and Slovak), which are the recipients of privatization proceeds;[4]
- so-called subsidized (or contributory) organizations, which are agencies performing functions similar to those of budgetary agencies, but which keep their own revenues and receive transfers from the state budget;
- up to 1990, so-called funds of the ministries, which were essentially instruments of cross-subsidization between enterprises;
- from 1993 onward, in the successor republics, various social security and health funds.

In most of their chapter, Kameníčková et al. focus on the state budget, defined to include the budgets of the central and local governments. In so doing, however, they understate both the "size" of government, which can only be identified by also including all the other components listed above, and the extent to which it has shrunk over the last few years. In particular, large amounts of resources used to transit through the now defunct "funds of the ministries," so that focusing on the state budget alone understates the extent to which the government has scaled down its intervention into the economy. Partly offsetting this, there has been since 1990 a tendency to transform budgetary agencies into "subsidized organizations," and to assign to them some revenues that formerly accrued to the state budget; as a result, the state budget has shrunk artificially[5] Nor was the true size of the central state budget itself captured accurately in the national methodology prior to 1991: turnover tax revenue was recorded net of "negative turnover tax" (retail subsidies), and some netting out also took place between foreign trade levies and subsidies, so that both revenues and expenditures were understated. To the extent possible, the GFS methodology, as reflected in the attached tables, corrects for these various biases.

When it comes to the balance, rather than the size, of government, the central and local governments do indeed play the key role, as other components of government have traditionally stayed close to balance. But the reported state budget result does not accurately reflect the balance even of the central and local governments, and Kameníčková et al. tend to understate their deficit, for two main reasons.[6]

First, as in many other countries, various financing flows are recorded in the national methodology as revenue or expenditure. Thus:

- In local authorities, recorded budget revenues often include transfers from deposits accumulated in earlier years; thus, the sizable surpluses recorded by local authorities in successive years to some extent reflect a "recycling" of the same deposits, recorded as revenue each year and hence resulting in yearly surpluses.
- From 1992, the proceeds of certain bond issues earmarked to fund local government expenditure (particularly housing construction) are recorded as local government revenue.
- Amortization is recorded as expenditure (in practice, this has not yet become a major problem, because insignificant amounts of amortization have as yet fallen due).

Second, not all financial operations under the authority of the Ministries of Finance actually go through the state budget; expenditures outside the budget can be quite sizable—an estimated 2% of GDP in 1992, for instance. Thus:

- The Ministries of Finance have traditionally had accounts outside the budget, created as a result of past budgetary surpluses or through extra-budgetary operations, some of them going back to the 1950s. Some revenue accrues to these accounts, and they are sometimes used to fund sizable expenditures outside the budget. To take but two examples: in 1992, funds built up through a federal budget surplus of 1991 were used to provide subsidies to the railway, and funds from so-called state financial assets were used to extend loans. Neither operation went through the budget, and neither was considered to be deficit spending.
- From 1992 the proceeds of certain bond issues (notably those earmarked for the financing of Gabčíkovo dam) were spent outside the budget.

On two points of coverage, however, the national methodology scores high. First, proceeds from privatization are not counted as government revenue. While the correct treatment of privatization receipts in fiscal accounts is still a subject of controversy, there is agreement that at the very least such receipts should not be allowed to fund increased current expenditures. It can also be argued that the proceeds from privatization (the counterpart to a reduction in public assets) are really rather similar to the proceeds from borrowing (the counterpart to an increase in public debt) (see, e.g., Cheasty 1992), and should therefore be treated as financing. The Czechoslovak accounting treatment satisfies both these conditions, and goes even further in that it does not explicitly acknowledge any inflow of money from privatization. The National Property Funds (NPFs) are treated as entirely separate from the government, and their receipts, deposited with the banking system, implicitly increase the latitude for bank financing of the rest of government. But the indirect nature of these financing flows helps minimize the appearance of a financing bonanza and hence the temptation to allow the deficit to surge.[7]

Second, some extra-budgetary operations in an economy in transition are of a peculiar character, being aimed at correcting the arbitrary distribution of assets and liabilities that was inherited at the time the unitary "state" was dismembered into its component enterprise, bank, and government parts. Operations to clean up the banking system, in particular, typically do not represent a real transfer of resources, but merely a change in the name of the bank's debtor. Of course, excluding such operations from the fiscal accounts understates the increase in government debt, but including them overstates the flow of resources to government. As the starting level of government debt was largely an artifact anyway, excluding such operations from the fiscal accounts is the lesser of two evils. In Czechoslovakia, these operations have been carried out either by the NPFs or from the government's "state financial asset and liability" accounts, and they are included neither in the national presentation of fiscal results nor in those presented in the attached tables.

But even when the explicit revenues, expenditures, and overall balance of the general government have been identified, the resulting estimates still do not really capture the full role of government in the economy.

As a first step, government guarantees on credits to enterprises, which became a popular instrument in 1991, especially in Slovakia, need to be taken into account. The amounts of guarantees issued reached some 2% of GDP annually in 1991 and 1992, increasing the amount of resources allocated at government direction and—potentially—also increasing the government's debt.

In an even murkier area, there is the issue of "quasi-fiscal" operations—operations carried on the books of, typically, the banking system, that are really of the nature of government operations. In the Czechoslovak case, one such operation involved the foreign debt contracted by the foreign trade bank (Obchodni Bank) as the government's agent under the old regime. This debt was acknowledged to be a government responsibility—and indeed has now been formally taken over by the governments of the two successor republics—but interest on it was paid by means of transfers from the central bank. This correspondingly reduced the transfer of central bank profits to the government, so that this operation was at least implicitly captured in the government's bottom line. But there are also undoubtedly quasi-fiscal operations carried out by the commercial banks—notably lending to nonviable projects, which will eventually land on the books of the government and is thus a covert subsidy. There are no reliable estimates even of the stock of bad debt inherited from the past, let alone of the flow of bad loans being granted now. Given implicit or explicit public deposit insurance, this problem can never be entirely circumvented; however, the strengthening of bank supervision, of bank balance sheets, and of bank corporate governance through privatization all hold out hope that this will become less of an issue as time goes on.

2. THE FISCAL DEFICIT

As shown in table 2, general government revenue in Czechoslovakia is estimated to have fallen by almost 18 percentage points of GDP over the period 1989–1992. As the economy contracted by over 20% over the same period, the real fall in revenue was very much larger—close to 50% if deflated by the consumer price index. Nevertheless, the deficit was contained to 2% of GDP in 1991 and a little over 3% of GDP in 1992.

2.1 THE DEFICIT FROM A SHORT-TERM PERSPECTIVE

As argued by Kameníčková et al., tight fiscal policy was one of the cornerstones of the remarkably successful effort to rein in inflation after the devaluation, the CMEA terms of trade shock, and the price liberalization of early 1991; inflation was down to below 1% a month by July 1991. On the other hand, the fall in output was very large, and one must ask whether containing the fiscal deficit to 2% of GDP in the first year of reform did not amount to overkill.

The jury is still out on the issue of why output fell so much, and this chapter can only touch on some of the relevant considerations. Indications are that much (half to three-quarters) of the fall in output is traceable to the terms of trade shock and the collapse of exports to the former Soviet Union (see, e.g., Rodrik 1992). At the same time, domestic demand also fell, owing to the sudden loss of job security, real balance effects following the jump in prices, widening income distribution, a broadening in the array of savings instruments (stemming in part from privatization), the "limbo" status of enterprises prior to privatization, and—perhaps—restrictive monetary and fiscal policies.

Monetary policy *was* tight. To a large extent, relatively high interest rates were inevitable in the context of a fixed exchange rate policy, so that some contractionary effect on demand and output through this channel was inevitable. However, tight liquidity might have affected output also through another channel—by stifling production through a shortage of enterprise working capital (as argued by Calvo and Coricelli 1992 in the Polish case). As the banks were reluctant to lend in the prevailing highly uncertain environment, fiscal relaxation might have helped to alleviate such constraints by channeling liquidity directly to the enterprise sector (e.g., through a reduced profits tax take). There is no evidence, however, for this theory of the output decline: inventories rose on impact, firm managers are unanimous that the problem was in sales, and the emerging private sector appears to have had good access to credit. Instead, sector-level data suggest that tight liquidity was instrumental in stopping an unsustainable buildup of inventories and in forcing oligopolistic producers to charge realistic prices.

More conventionally, an easier fiscal policy might have helped by sustaining demand. Here, however, the critical question is whether additional demand stemming from fiscal relaxation would have fallen on domestically produced goods for which there was spare capacity. While production fell in all sectors (with, of course, the notable exception of the woefully underdeveloped services sector), it is still unclear how much—let alone which parts—of the resulting "spare capacity" would anyway have survived the radical change in the structure of prices. The fact that these answers continue to elude us even with the benefit of two years of hindsight goes a long way toward justifying the determination of Czechoslovak policy makers, at the outset of the reform program, to err on the side of caution.

2.2 THE DEFICIT FROM A MEDIUM-TERM PERSPECTIVE

Even in cases where a gradual fiscal adjustment path is financeable, the desirability of such a path depends on the level of public debt: the higher the debt, the less affordable are further increases in it. From this point of view, too, Czechoslovak fiscal policy can be counted a success. Czechoslovakia entered the reform period with virtually no acknowledged government debt, but this was merely a reflection of the planners' preferences as to how to channel financial flows through the accounts of different parts of the state. The results of these preferences were solidified at the Revolution, when one of the first priorities was to separate from the government those parts of the state that could and should function in a commercial fashion. As a result, a piecemeal re-evaluation of inherited stocks of assets and liabilities has been taking place over the course of the last three years.

In particular, since the end of 1989, the following main "stock adjustments" have taken place between the government (here taken to include the National Property Funds) and other parts of the former unitary state:

- The government has explicitly taken over debt associated with the devaluation losses of the banking system.
- The government (in this case, of the two successor republics) has taken over the foreign debt incurred by the foreign trade bank as its agent under the old regime; at the same time, it took over from the foreign trade bank a large amount of assets in nonconvertible currencies, but many of these are thought to be uncollectible, so that the true value of these assets is rather low.
- The National Property Funds have issued some 45 billion korunas in bonds, which have been used to recapitalize the banks and write down their bad loans.

On the positive side, the government's net debt was reduced by about 75 billion korunas that had been collected in proceeds from small and large privatization by the end of 1992.

As a result, and even though the cumulative fiscal deficits of 1990–1992 amounted to only 55 billion korunas, the acknowledged debt of the government (including the National Property Funds), net of its deposits with banks, had risen to some 170 billion korunas— about 17% of GDP—by the end of 1992. While this is still not a high figure, the adjustments consequent on the dismemberment of the state are not yet complete.

Even after the debt write-down already implemented, it is thought that a sizable stock of bad loans remains in the portfolios of the banks. Although the banks themselves have been provisioning against these loans, their capital remains weak, and they may not be able to withstand the enterprise bankruptcies that are expected to follow from the coming into full operation of bankruptcy laws in 1993. This is especially true of the Consolidation Bank, created in 1991 as a repository for 110 billion korunas in "loans for permanently revolving inventories," many of which were thought to be bad. Although the Consolidation Bank is funded by central bank refinancing and deposits from the savings banks, it is implicitly acknowledged that the government is responsible for its soundness. Sizable resources from the state—most likely from the NPFs—may be required to keep the Consolidation Bank afloat, and to mitigate the impact of bankruptcies on the other banks. On the other hand, conventional privatization is continuing alongside voucher privatization, and proceeds from this should go some way toward offsetting the bad debt problem.

Thus the true stock of the outstanding government net debt still cannot be evaluated. As was clear from the beginning, however, it is not negligible, and the government's success in limiting its further buildup through rapid fiscal adjustment will help to contain future interest burdens.

3. THE STRATEGY OF FISCAL REFORM

The sequencing of fiscal and other reforms in economies in transition has attracted considerable interest in recent years. Some, like McKinnon (1991), have argued that the risks of fiscal collapse under the old system are such that the tax system should be comprehensively overhauled right at the outset of reform. The Czechoslovak experience suggests instead that it is possible to contain the deficit during the initial stage of the transition period to new fiscal systems. This section examines how this was done. First, what declines in revenue can be expected, and what can be done to mitigate these declines? And second, what expenditure increases are unavoidable, and what can be done on the expenditure side to avoid an undue worsening of the fiscal position? Of course, any solutions under either of these headings must also make structural sense. Much of the detail required to answer these questions—insofar as they can be answered at present—can be found in Kameníčková et al.; I attempt below to distill the possible lessons.

3.1 REVENUE

It is by now a commonplace that the revenue systems of centrally planned economies are ill-suited to market economies and, by extension, to the transition. Early on, like other reforming economies, Czechoslovakia set itself the objective of overhauling its tax system entirely as soon as preparations could be completed. And indeed, on January 1, 1993, in both successor countries, turnover tax was replaced by a VAT and excise duties, the corporate profits tax was comprehensively modernized, a global personal income tax was introduced, and the payroll tax was replaced by employers' and employees' social security contributions. The new tax system has eliminated distortions inherent in the previous one, and, backed up by a strengthening of tax administration, should lead to improved compliance. However, all this has taken three years of preparation, and much had to be done already during these crucial first years of reform.

A necessary first task on the revenue side, as an integral part of the reform process, was to eliminate certain categories of revenues whose nature was inherently in contradiction with the workings of a market system: arbitrary confiscation of profits (6% of GDP in 1989; virtually eliminated in 1990), and levies that equalized the domestic and foreign prices of imports and exports (about 2% of GDP in 1989–1990; abolished in 1991). These two steps alone explain almost half of the decline in the revenue-to-GDP ratio between 1989 and 1992. In addition, turnover tax had to be comprehensively overhauled at the time of price liberalization, when its multitude of rates (which had been set as differences between administered wholesale and retail prices) was reduced to four, with special rates for items that would usually be subject to excises. However, this need not have been accompanied by a loss of revenue, and indeed the original overhaul was designed to be revenue-neutral. (It was only in mid-1991 that, under the pressure of the collapse of consumer demand, ad valorem turnover tax rates were reduced by about 10%; and it does appear that some revenue was lost through delays in adjusting specific tax rates in light of inflation.) Finally, with the commercialization of state enterprises came an urgent need to reduce the punitive burden of high statutory profits tax rates: in a process actually initiated under the old regime, these were unified and reduced from 75%–85% in 1989 to 55% in 1991–1992 (and further to 45% in 1993).

At the same time, the poor performance of some taxes is explained not so much by policy considerations, but by developments largely outside the government's control. In other countries, notably in Poland, such declines were particularly evident in profits tax (see, e.g., Berg and Blanchard 1992), but in Czechoslovakia it was turnover tax and payroll tax that bore the brunt of the transition. These two taxes provide a useful case study of the various reasons why revenues may fall in the transition; they fall broadly into three groups: changes in the structure of the economy, arrears, and evasion and avoidance.

Changes in the structure of the economy played a major role.[8] Turnover tax was a tax on consumption, and consumption fell more steeply than GDP. In addition, with the drop in incomes, the pattern of consumption probably shifted toward items subject to lower tax rates. Payroll tax was a tax on employment, which (surprisingly, as these features were inherited from the communist regime) treated the services sector and the self-employed more favorably than the rest of the economy; these, of course, were the sectors that expanded during the transition. The services sector was subject to a lower rate of payroll tax (20% compared with the standard rate of 50%). The self-employed and their employees—almost nonexistent under the previous regime— were essentially subject to a type of payroll tax (notionally earmarked to finance social security), the level of which they were free to choose, depending on the level of benefits they wished to assure themselves. Not surprisingly, most chose to pay minimal amounts.

By contrast, changes in the structure of incomes, which played havoc with corporate profits taxes in neighboring countries, do not appear to have had the same effect in Czechoslovakia. As in Poland in 1990 (see, e.g., Schaffer 1992), there was a surge in profits tax receipts in 1991, the year of the price jump, as inventories of lower-priced goods were fed into the production of new higher-priced output. Taxation of these paper profits is estimated to have contributed about three percentage points of GDP to revenue; and the lesson here is that policy makers should not allow themselves to believe that this initial revenue boom is permanent.[9]

In 1992, however, profits tax collections in relation to GDP were still slightly higher than they were in 1989, despite the rate reductions that had taken place in the meantime. The resilience of profits distinguishes Czechoslovakia from most of the other economies in transition: if anything, the structure of incomes shifted toward profits and away from wages—yet another reason why payroll tax declined. Real wages fell by no less than 22% between 1990 and 1992, and, although employment fell less steeply than output, real unit labor costs nevertheless fell by 11% over the same period.[10] The trends, however, point in a potentially dangerous direction: in a partial recouping of very large falls in 1991, product wages and unit labor costs in industry rose 8%–10% in 1992, with wages in other sectors growing faster. Unless significant labor-shedding takes place, wage rises may well erode profitability in the near future, the more so as wage regulation was abolished in 1993. Dangerous as this would be from the point of view of investment and growth, it is not, however, obvious that it would by itself have direct adverse fiscal consequences. Largely because of continuing high social security contribution rates,[11] the tax burden on a koruna spent on labor costs is now very similar to the taxes (45%) on a koruna of profits.[12]

A second cause of revenue shortfalls, tax arrears, appears to have been particularly important in turnover tax and, especially, payroll tax. Interestingly, these two taxes are those that enterprises must pay whether they make profits or not, and are thus also the revenue categories where one would expect a problem of tax arrears to first manifest itself.

Evasion and avoidance are undoubtedly on the increase in all taxes, and indeed it is likely that even profits tax has been affected by them, as profits have shifted into the less easily taxed private sector. But the mark of avoidance and evasion is again especially evident in turnover and payroll tax. The phenomenon of increased evasion seems inevitable during the period when tax administration is attempting to catch up with taxpayers' growing interest in minimizing their tax payments. Avoidance, however, can be attacked more directly by closing loopholes in outdated laws (though, of course, this may merely turn some avoidance into evasion). Examples of such loopholes abound in the old turnover and payroll tax laws. Take, for instance, the absence of rules in the turnover tax law regulating "transfer pricing" between related firms or individuals. One of these related agents, registered as a remitter of turnover tax, would sell goods cheaply to a second agent outside the "ring" of turnover tax remitters. As turnover tax is charged only once, when a good leaves the "ring," it is charged on this artificially low price, and the second agent profits. In payroll tax, it was the preferential treatment of the self-employed that created a giant loophole. Many thousands of employees appear to have connived with their employers to convert themselves into self-employed contractors. This problem does not seem to have been fully resolved—and thus seems to have turned from avoidance into evasion—even after the employment law and commercial code were amended in 1992 to define clearly what constituted employment and self-employment.

The government took action in two areas to mitigate the fall in revenue. The personal income tax system was peculiarly unsuited to market conditions. First, there was virtually no provision for taxation of the incomes of the self-employed. A so-called citizen's income tax was introduced in late 1990 to remedy this, but, with a one-year lag in collections, revenues were not forthcoming immediately. Second, the taxation of wage incomes was geared to a very uniform distribution of income, with a standard rate of 20% applied at all levels. In 1992, a marginal rate of 30% was introduced for wages above 10,000 korunas a month (roughly 2.5 times the average wage).[13]

In the area of taxes on international trade, the government took a number of revenue-enhancing actions. One of these—the expansion of coverage of customs duties, which had previously been imposed selectively—was aimed at reducing distortions and raising revenue. The fiscal impact of the others—the imposition of a temporary surcharge on imports of consumer goods, and a restructuring of customs duties, which slightly raised the previously very low average rate—was incidental, their main focus being the balance of payments.

3.2 EXPENDITURE

Total expenditures are estimated to have fallen by no less than 17 percentage points of GDP between 1989 and 1992, and by close to half in real terms. This is a remarkable achievement. Because far more, and far smaller, decisions are involved in making expenditures than in putting in place the tax framework, it is more difficult to give a full account of this achievement. However, the government's expenditure philosophy is clear, and is clearly reflected in the data in table 2.

First, the social safety net had to be strengthened. In late 1989, unemployment benefits were introduced, just ahead of the appearance of sizable unemployment. In 1990, the removal of food subsidies was fully compensated by the introduction of "general income support," income supplements initially given to everyone, and augmented in 1991 in the case of children and pensioners to compensate for the removal of energy subsidies. And pensions were adjusted for inflation, though not fully (the lowest pensions being raised more than the higher ones); economy-wide wage restraint was again helpful here, as it dampened expectations. Perhaps because the public mentality had as yet changed little, some of the measures taken early on in the reform period still bore the mark of the old regime, which had left behind an almost totally untargeted system of social benefits. Universal "general income support" was peculiarly wasteful, and unemployment benefits were initially generous, in duration (12 months), in amount (there was no ceiling), and in the eligibility requirements (which were broad enough to include people who had not previously been employed, as well as those who turned down successive job offers).

Soon, however, the system of social benefits began to be tailored to a situation where some people's needs were greater than others. From the beginning of the reform period, universal child benefits remained constant in nominal terms, despite inflation. General income support was abolished for the employed and self-employed in 1992; the duration of unemployment benefits was shortened to six months, a ceiling was imposed, and eligibility requirements were tightened. In addition, an attempt was made to make the right to a pension dependent on actual termination of employment, as several hundred thousand people were receiving both a pension and a wage. The attempt, however, failed in Parliament, and in a compromise the rate of wage tax for working pensioners was raised (until this too was struck down by the Constitutional Court in late 1992). Finally, as a crucial counterpart to better targeting, the delivery system for social assistance, the benefit of last resort, was strengthened.

Second, consumption expenditures had to be held down as much as possible, and key investment expenditures had to be protected in light of great infrastructural needs. In the event, the former fell by 28% in real terms—reflecting wage restraint, cuts in government employment, and across-the-board savings enforced through improvements in expenditure control—and the latter by close to 40%.

There is no doubt, however, that the tremendous cut in government expenditure was mainly concentrated in subsidies. First to go, in 1990, were the arbitrary cross-subsidies—left to the discretion of a "branch" ministry—that were the counterpart to confiscatory levies on profits. Then came the turn of most retail subsidies, with full or partial compensation in the form of income support: food subsidies, in mid-1990, and most energy subsidies, on what came to be known as Black Wednesday, May 1, 1991. Among energy subsidies, only subsidies for heating were not fully eliminated; the problem here was the absence of metering devices in individual dwellings or even apartment blocks—a classic problem bequeathed by regimes uninterested in making people pay for what they used. Also in early 1991, with price and trade liberalization, foreign trade subsidies were eliminated. By 1992, only the most politically sensitive subsidies survived: the heating subsidies; subsidies to agriculture (much reduced from their previous levels, and now targeted specifically at producer price stabilization and restructuring); those to transport (also significantly reduced, as tariffs had been gradually raised); and those to housing (subsidies to low-interest loans and to rents, the latter substantially reduced during 1992).

4. SUMMARY AND CONCLUSIONS

This chapter has argued that, once account is taken—quantitatively and qualitatively—of various reasons why the most commonly reported fiscal indicators for Czechoslovakia are misleading, Czechoslovak fiscal policy over 1990–1992 can still be counted a success. It contributed to rapid stabilization and kept the increase in government debt—the true level of which is still highly uncertain—to a minimum. The Czechoslovak authorities broadly foresaw a large decline in revenue, stemming partly from necessary policy changes—the elimination of taxes that were inconsistent with a market system, and a reduction in excessively high profits tax rates—and partly from changes in the structure of the economy, from an increase in tax arrears, and from an increase in evasion and avoidance.

On the revenue side, the government acted where it could, most notably on personal income taxes—which had been geared to a system where most incomes were wages and where wages were rather uniform. But a tremendous effort was required on the expenditure side, and this despite the fact that, with the drop in incomes, social safety net spending inevitably increased. Some targeting of social benefits, considerable restraint in consumption expenditure (with an improvement in expenditure control), cuts in investment, and—especially—the elimination and reduction of a host of subsidies were the key factors that allowed the deficit to be kept to a minimum.

Table 1
Czech and Slovak Federal Republic: Fiscal Operations 1989–1992*

	1989	1990	1991 Prel.	1992 Est.
		(billion korunas)		
Revenue	527.9	501.9	516.5	532.5
Profits tax	83.2	100.3	134.3	117.9
Other levies on profits	46.6	0.1	—	—
Personal income tax	52.5	54.7	60.0	77.7
Turnover tax	134.6	147.8	123.6	125.8
Payroll tax**	114.3	118.2	106.6	107.3
Foreign trade levies	13.4	19.3	—	—
Customs duties***	0.5	6.5	11.5	17.6
Other	82.8	55.0	80.5	86.4
Expenditure	548.2	504.8	535.7	565.7
Consumption expenditure	191.1	201.9	238.5	265.2
Interest	0.2	1.7	4.6	11.2
Transfers to households	103.0	111.3	157.7	165.5
Current transfers to enterprises	189.5	133.2	75.0	52.5
Capital expenditure	12.5	16.9	40.9	52.5
Capital transfers to enterprises	46.4	39.0	12.8	17.4
Net lending	5.4	0.7	6.2	1.4
Balance	−20.3	−2.9	−19.2	−33.2
Memorandum items		(in %)		
Real GDP growth	—	−0.4	−15.9	−6.0
Consumer price inflation (year average)	1.4	10.8	57.9	11.0

*Data include central and local governments (both budgetary and off-budget operations), subsidized organizations, and extra-budgetary funds (except National Property Funds; in addition, only transfers to the Fund for Market Regulation in Agriculture are included). Data do not include "stock adjustments"—book transactions, primarily with the banking system, that adjusted the stock positions of different parts of the state upon dismemberment.

**Includes social security contributions paid by the self-employed.

***Includes import surcharge.

Sources: Data provided by the Czechoslovak authorities, and IMF staff estimates.

Table 2
Czech and Slovak Federal Republic: Fiscal Operations 1989–1992*

	1989	1990	1991	1992
	(% of GDP)			
Revenue	69.5	61.2	52.8	52.0
Profits tax	11.0	12.2	13.7	11.5
Other levies on profits	6.1	0.0	0.0	0.0
Personal income tax	6.9	6.7	6.1	7.6
Turnover tax	17.7	18.0	12.6	12.3
Payroll tax**	15.0	14.4	10.9	10.5
Foreign trade levies	1.8	2.4	0.0	0.0
Customs duties***	0.1	0.8	1.2	1.7
Other	10.9	6.7	8.2	8.4
Expenditure	72.2	61.6	54.8	55.2
Consumption expenditure	25.2	24.6	24.4	25.9
Interest	0.0	0.2	0.5	1.1
Transfers to households	13.6	13.6	16.1	16.2
Current transfers to enterprises	25.0	16.2	7.7	5.1
Capital expenditure	1.6	2.1	4.2	5.1
Capital transfers to enterprises	6.1	4.8	1.3	1.7
Net lending	0.7	0.1	0.6	0.1
Balance	−2.7	−0.4	−2.0	−3.2

*Data include central and local governments (both budgetary and off-budget operations), subsidized organizations, and extra-budgetary funds (except National Property Funds; in addition, only transfers to the Fund for Market Regulation in Agriculture are included). Data do not include "stock adjustments"—book transactions, primarily with the banking system, that adjusted the stock positions of different parts of the state upon dismemberment.
**Includes social security contributions paid by the self-employed.
***Includes import surcharge.

Sources: Data provided by the Czechoslovak authorities, and IMF staff estimates.

NOTES

1. The views expressed here are those of the author and do not necessarily reflect those of the International Monetary Fund. I am greatly indebted to Miroslav Havel, Bohdan Hejduk, Pavel Štěpánek, Bibiana Jílková, Tomas Spurný, L'ubomír Klimo, and their staffs, all of whom have spent countless hours educating me. I am also grateful to participants in the conference on Public Finance Reform in East Central Europe and to Peter Doyle, George Kopits, Leslie Lipschitz, Roman Skarzynski, and Emmanuel Zervoudakis for insightful comments. None of these is responsible for any errors that remain.

2. The discussion in this chapter applies also, *mutatis mutandis*, to the Czech and Slovak Republics, following the division of Czechoslovakia.

3. Data for 1989–1990 are based on final consolidated reports by the Federal Ministry of Finance for the IMF's Government Financial Statistics Yearbook (GFSY). Data for 1991 are based on the preliminary consolidated GFSY report by the Federal Ministry of Finance, and data for 1992 are IMF staff estimates based on individual—sometimes incomplete—revenue and expenditure reports for the different components of general government.

4. For reasons given below, these are not included in tables 1 and 2.

5. No budget is presented for subsidized organizations, and data for them become available only with a long lag. As data for 1991 and 1992 are not yet final, it is conceivable that some of the apparent shrinkage in the size of government over 1990–1992 reflects inadequate capture of subsidized organizations.

6. There is also a timing issue. There has traditionally been a "complementary period," lasting well into a particular fiscal year, when operations can still be booked to the previous fiscal year. Adjustment to a cash basis, however, does not typically change the reported results very much.

7. Although the bulk of NPF transactions are in the nature of financing, they undoubtedly include some true revenues and expenditures; however, it has not proved possible to identify these, and they are not included in tables 1 and 2.

8. It is of course difficult to distinguish between the effect of changes in the structure of the economy and the effect of increased evasion, as the latter may also distort the data from which the structure of the economy is inferred.

9. It might in principle be preferable to introduce inflation adjustment into the profits tax prior to the price jump, perhaps temporarily imposing a surcharge on profits tax to offset the loss of revenue; this would, however, require considerable sophistication in tax administration.

10. All wage and productivity data quoted refer to industrial enterprises with more than 25 employees.

11. In the Czech Republic in 1993, employers' social security contributions are payable at 36% of wages (26.5% of total labor costs, defined as wages plus employers' social security contributions), employees' social security contributions at 13.5% of wages (10% of labor costs), and personal income tax in the lowest bracket at 15% of wages net of employees' social security contributions (9.5% of labor costs); the marginal tax burden in the lowest income tax bracket is thus 46% of labor costs. Similar relations hold true in Slovakia, where social security contribution rates are slightly different (38% and 12% respectively).

12. Prior to the 1993 tax reform, the tax burden on profits (55% in

1991–1992) was somewhat higher than the standard tax burden on wages (47%), and substantially higher than the tax burden on wages in sectors subject to preferential rates of payroll tax; a shift from profits to wages would thus have had a direct negative impact on revenues.

13. A third change to the personal income tax system is discussed elsewhere, as it was a partial substitute for a politically difficult improvement in the targeting of the social safety net.

REFERENCES

Berg, Andrew, and Olivier Blanchard. 1992. Stabilization and Transition: Poland 1990–91. Paper presented at the Conference on Transition in Eastern Europe, National Bureau for Economic Research, Cambridge, Massachusetts, February.

Calvo, Guillermo, and Fabrizio Coricelli. 1992. Stabilizing a Previously Centrally Planned Economy: Poland 1990. *Economic Policy* 14, pp. 175–226.

Cheasty, Adrienne. 1992. Financing Fiscal Deficits. In *Fiscal Policies in Economies in Transition*, ed. Vito Tanzi. Washington, DC: International Monetary Fund.

International Monetary Fund. 1986. *A Manual on Government Finance Statistics*. Washington, DC.

———. 1992. *Government Finance Statistics Yearbook*. Washington, DC.

McKinnon, Ronald. 1991. *The Order of Economic Liberalization*. Baltimore: Johns Hopkins University Press.

Rodrik, Daniel. 1992. Making Sense of the Soviet Trade Shock in Eastern Europe: A Framework and Some Estimates. Paper presented at the Conference on the Macroeconomic Situation in Eastern Europe, International Monetary Fund and World Bank, Washington, DC, June.

Schaffer, Mark. 1992. *The Enterprise Sector and Fiscal Performance in Poland 1990–91*. London: Center for Economic Performance Working Paper, no. 280.

8

The Lessons From
Fiscal Reform in Democratic Spain

PHILIPPE BACCHETTA

1. INTRODUCTION

After almost 40 years of dictatorship under Franco, Spain took the
road towards democracy in 1975. After two years of political transition,
the first general democratic elections in 1977 produced a center-right
government. Since the 1982 elections, however, the Socialist Party has
ruled the country. An important political objective under democracy
has been European integration. In particular, Spain entered the
European Community (EC) in January 1986 and the Exchange Rate
Mechanism of the European Monetary System in June 1989. Another
important change within Spain has been the process of decentralization, with the delegation of political power to regions (*Comunidades
Autónomas*).

In addition to political changes, Spain has experienced important
economic ones. In the 1940s and 1950s, Spain was an autarkic and
highly regulated economy. After an IMF-led stabilization plan in 1959,
the country opened up slightly and a number of liberalizing measures
were implemented. In the early 1970s, the need for further reform
and restructuring was patent, but no change was undertaken until
Franco's death. Since 1975, however, Spain has followed a process of
catching up with other European countries and has deeply modernized its economy.[1]

Most of the changes started with the Moncloa agreements in
October 1977. After Franco's death, the Spanish economy was in
particularly bad shape (in the summer of 1977, the inflation rate was
45%) and required substantial adjustment. A political consensus led to
a set of agreements that dealt with monetary, fiscal, exchange rate, and
income policies. Thus, the early years of democracy led to many
reforms. The pace of reform, however, slowed down in 1979–1982
under a weak center-right government, recovering speed in 1982 after
the Socialists came into power with an absolute political majority.

A particular element of change since 1975 has been the reform of
the public sector. Under dictatorship, the state was highly interventionist but had a small budget. This situation has drastically changed in the

last 15 years, as the interventionist aspect of the government has declined and the state budget has exploded. One of the main objectives throughout the reform period has been catching up with respect to other European countries.

In the 19th century, the size of the Spanish state budget was already smaller than in other European countries (see Comín 1989a). In the 20th century, the role of the public sector has significantly increased, but the state budget did not grow until the early 1960s. The regulatory aspects of the state developed primarily, especially during the first two decades of Franco's dictatorship; regulations introduced in most sectors of the economy created numerous distortions and led to inefficient rent-seeking activities. In the latter part of Franco's era, starting in 1959, the tendency towards less regulation and a larger state budget began. Moreover, although several state-owned firms were created under Franco's regime, they represented only a small share of the economy. For example, in 1975 their gross value added was less than 6% of GDP, and they accounted for less than 4% of total employment (see Myro 1989).

The increase in the general government budget is documented in figure 1. In the first ten years of the transition, from 1975 to 1985, the increase in expenditure was dramatic. From 25% of GDP, it rose to about 43%. This ratio has stabilized somewhat in recent years, being at 45% in 1991. The increase in revenue has also been strong, from 25% of GDP in 1975 to 39% in 1991. While an increase in the state budget is a common feature of most OECD countries over this period, the growth experienced by Spain has been much stronger.[2] Comparatively speaking, the size of the Spanish government in the early 1990s is in general smaller than other EC countries, but is somewhat larger than non-EC OECD countries.

It can be observed from figure 1 that the increase in expenditure has exceeded the one in revenue. This contrasts with the 1959–1975 period, where the government budget was usually in surplus. In other words, democracy in Spain has coincided with the appearance of budget deficits (reaching 7% of GDP in 1985). These deficits have led to a sharp increase in public debt, documented in figure 2.

This chapter deals only with the government budget and does not consider other aspects of the public sector, such as its regulatory role, public sector firms, or the economic impact of the government.[3] Furthermore, this chapter can only give an overview of the main issues; a detailed analysis would require a full book.[4] Finally, it should be mentioned that detailed analyses of the public sector in Spain are scarce, and several of the issues examined in this paper have not received the attention they deserve.

2. REVENUE

The increase in government revenue has been substantial over the last two decades. Table 1 shows that all major revenue items are larger in the 1990s than they were in the 1970s (in proportion to GDP).[5] This increase is explained by several factors, including a tax reform in 1977. A reform was needed for at least three reasons. First, the tax system had to be simplified and made more compatible with those of other countries. Second, revenue had to be increased to finance the desired increase in expenditure. Third, taxes had to be modified to face the changing structure of the Spanish economy.[6]

This section first describes the 1977 reform and then examines the main items of revenue: personal income tax, corporate taxes, indirect taxes, and social security contributions.

2.1 THE GENERAL PROCESS OF TAX REFORM

Spanish government revenue programs in the 1960s and 1970s were characterized by complexity, inefficiency, and unfairness. The need for reform became obvious in the early 1970s, and proposals for a more modern tax system were elaborated in 1973 and 1975. Nevertheless, no legal change was adopted until 1977, after the first general elections. In October 1977, all political parties represented in Parliament asked for the reform through the Moncloa agreements. The main reason why no reform took place before democracy was the lack of political support; as the most privileged were those who benefited greatly from the old tax system, a drastic change was difficult to introduce. Moreover, the authorities were particularly weak at the end of the Franco regime (the prime minister was assassinated in December 1973, while Franco himself was in poor health).

The three main elements of the new tax system were an integrated personal income tax, a corporate tax on profits, and a value-added tax (VAT). These sources of revenue were complemented by a tax on net wealth, a tax on property transfers, and excise taxes. The design of the new tax system was inspired by existing or proposed systems in other OECD countries and by potential future harmonization with EC countries.

The tax reform, however, did not take place overnight and has been a gradual process. A few steps were taken in 1977, such as temporary surtaxes on corporate profits, high-bracket personal incomes, and luxury goods. Moreover, several measures were taken to restructure the Ministry of Finance, with an improvement in inspection and data processing. However, the new personal income and corporate tax systems were not introduced until 1979, the VAT not until 1986. Furthermore, social security and regional state finance were not really considered by the reform.

2.2 DIRECT TAXES

The most dramatic increase in fiscal revenue comes from direct taxes, which have practically trebled in proportion to GDP. From 4.4% in 1975, they rose to 11.8% in 1991. The major element of this growth in income comes from the personal income tax. Yet although the increase has been spectacular, it should be noticed that direct taxes are still lower than the EC average.

2.2.1 Personal Income Tax

Before the tax reform, there was no integrated personal income tax to speak of. Various sources of income were taxed separately, and only a few individuals were taxed on their (usually underestimated) general income. Moreover, while tax rates were generally high, exemptions were numerous and monitoring was almost nonexistent. In particular, high incomes faced a small tax burden.

This antiquated system gave way to a more modern one introduced in 1979. Revenue increased substantially—growing 90% in real terms from 1979 to 1980 and continuing to increase afterwards.[7] The increase was immediate, as most of the tax was paid through withholding at the source. However, the number of individuals filing tax forms increased much less (15% from 1979 to 1980),[8] with most of this increase caused by individuals asking for tax refunds.

While the situation has improved over the years, tax evasion is still pervasive and many individuals in Spain have never filed a tax form. It was recently estimated that in 1987, 41% of potential taxpayers did not declare their income and that 43% of income was evaded (Lagares et al. 1990). Given that this evasion comes mostly from entrepreneurs and independent workers, wage earners bear a large burden of the tax.[9] The problem of tax evasion has received more attention in recent years, in particular with the creation of a tax collection agency (Agencia Tributaria).

In addition to this unequal treatment of taxpayers, the personal tax presents several other undesirable aspects. First, there is a large number of tax rates (initially 28 marginal rates; this number went up to 34 before being reduced to 14 in 1988). Second, capital income is simply added to other sources in the computation of the tax rate, while measures taken to alleviate the problem of double taxation are limited (e.g., only 10% of dividends can be deducted). Consequently, capital income is often taxed at a very high marginal rate (the top marginal rate was 56% in 1992). Third, no automatic correction for inflation was introduced in the new tax system. Although corrections have been made on several occasions, the progressivity of the tax system has increased over the years.[10] This is particularly distorting for capital income. Furthermore, no adjustment for inflation has been introduced for capital gains. Finally, one can mention the strong incentive to be a homeowner, given the partial deductibility of the mortgage interest burden (there is no equivalent deduction for rents).

The personal tax system has been in a constant state of flux since 1979. Tax rates, the number of tax brackets, deductions, the treatment of capital losses, and the taxation of nonresidents have changed several times, and continue to do so. For example, for 1992 the government announced a reduction in tax rates. In mid-1992, however, this reduction was postponed until 1993.

2.2.2 Taxes on Corporate Profits and Other Direct Taxes

Compared to the personal income tax, the corporate tax system was functioning relatively well in the 1970s, and thus the increase in corporate profit tax revenues has been much smaller. The tax rate on corporate profits has traditionally been small (35%) and was not affected by the tax reform. The tax treatment of foreign-owned subsidiaries in Spain is attractive, while the taxation of potential foreign investment by Spanish multinationals is high (see González-Páramo 1992).

The increase in revenue can be attributed mainly to an increase in firms' profits. The main changes introduced by the reform have been a 15% investment tax credit and a lump-sum subsidy for job creation. Moreover, an extraordinary tax on profits was introduced in 1977.

The other direct taxes are on property, and they are of a much smaller magnitude (5.5% of total revenues in 1990). The main elements are a tax on property transfers, a tax on net wealth, and a tax on real estate. While the structure of these taxes changed, the revenue they generated represented less of an increase than did other taxes.

2.3 INDIRECT TAXES

The introduction of the VAT was approved in 1977, but only became effective in 1986, when Spain joined the EC.[11] The design of the system adopted was basically the one dictated by the various EC directives on that issue. Initially, however, the number of tax rates was discretionary, so four were chosen: 0%, 6%, 12%, and 33%. These rates were modified in the early 1990s in harmonization with other EC countries (the 33% rate was eliminated, while the main rate rose to 15% from 12%). It is useful to notice that the timing of each modification of tax rates was influenced by the impact on prices; higher tax rates were introduced only when inflationary pressures were not too strong.

The system preceding the VAT was complex and particularly distortionary. It included a turnover tax on firms (cascade tax), a tax on luxury goods, excise taxes, and state monopolies. The transition to a new tax system such as the VAT is usually costly, as it requires a greater control from the tax authorities and might represent an additional administrative burden for firms. However, this transition was particularly smooth in Spain, because postponement of its introduction gave the authorities time to restructure and to inform firms.

Officials had hoped that the VAT would increase revenues, but most of the increase from indirect taxation occurred before the VAT system was introduced. Additionally, the degree of tax evasion seems to be higher than in other EC countries.[12]

2.4 SOCIAL SECURITY CONTRIBUTIONS

This source of revenue increased from 10% to 13%, but was not subject to reform at the beginning of the transition process.[13] Thus, most of the increase can be attributed to the increase in economic activity and occurred in the 1970s. The magnitude of this source of revenues is in line with the EC average, which in turn is higher than the OECD average. However, as with the personal income tax, these contributions are disproportionately paid by wage earners. Consequently, the quantity of social security paid by workers is among the highest in EC countries, especially the share paid by the employer. Empirical studies show that this factor might be partially responsible for the high Spanish unemployment (see, e.g., Lamo and Dolado 1991).

A reform of the social security system took place in 1985, but affected mainly the benefits side (see below). On the revenue side, it broadened the tax base and slightly reduced the rate. These changes did not have much impact on total revenues.

3. EXPENDITURE

As mentioned in the introduction, the increase in expenditure has been even more spectacular than the one for revenue. This increase continued a process initiated in the late 1950s: the ratio of expenditure to GDP increased from 13% in 1958 to 25% in 1975. Table 2 presents the evolution of the various components of expenditure since 1970. In the first ten years of the transition, the proportion of total expenditure to GDP almost doubled. On the other hand, the increase since 1985 has been modest. Generally speaking, the changes that occurred in Spain in the 1970s and 1980s are similar to those that occurred in other OECD countries one or two decades earlier. While expenditure included mainly traditional public goods until the late 1950s, there has since been a shift towards functions associated with the welfare state.

The initial increase in expenditure in the mid-1970s came from public consumption, capital transfers, social security benefits, and subsidies.[14] These items stabilized in the mid-1980s (subsidies and capital transfers even declined), but two other items started to increase at that time: public investment and interest payments.

There seems to be no systematic plan for restructuring or increasing expenditure. On the contrary, it seems that the authorities have been rather passive, and a major task has been to limit the growth in expenditure due to transfers. This growth was caused by a series of factors, such as the increase in deficits of public sector firms, massive unemployment, and the duplication of expenditure through decentralization.

3.1 PUBLIC CONSUMPTION

Current consumption has experienced a progressive increase from 9.2% of GDP in 1975 to 15.6% in 1991, although it is still below the OECD average. Most of the increase in consumption came from an increase in personnel (the increase in wages was moderate). This includes an increase in the administration at all levels of government and in the education system. Until recently, the health care system did not experience a major increase in total resources, either in current expenditure or investment.

3.2 TRANSFERS TO HOUSEHOLDS

The increase in social security benefits between 1975 and 1985 comes from three factors. First, the number of recipients increased, for demographic and business cycle reasons. Second, the amount of pensions per recipient increased more rapidly than GDP. Third, the extent of fraud increased, especially in disability pensions, which grew at an 8.5% annual rate. Social security benefits in the late 1980s were higher than the OECD average.

In 1985, the social security system underwent a comprehensive reform. The eligibility requirements were raised and measures were taken that decreased pensions per capita. These measures stabilized the proportion of social security benefits to GDP. Nevertheless, the social security system remained in deficit; in 1990, the difference between benefits and revenues represented 1.6% of GDP.

Unemployment benefits increased from 0.5% of GDP in 1975 to 2.9% in 1985. This was caused both by an increase in unemployment and an increase in benefits per unemployed. A 1980 reform of the system, combined with the decline in unemployment in the late 1980s, led to reduced growth in such expenditure.[15]

3.3 SUBSIDIES AND TRANSFERS TO FIRMS

An important feature of the Spanish economy early in the reform process was the magnitude of government transfers to firms. These transfers more than doubled between 1975 and 1985, reaching more than 5% of GDP. They benefited mainly firms in restructuring sectors (e.g., the steel industry) and public firms with large deficits.

A progressive process of privatization, as well as the improvement of economic conditions with an increase in firms' profits, led to a decline in this type of expenditure in the late 1980s.

3.4 PUBLIC INVESTMENT

Until the 1980s, public investment had been particularly low compared with other countries; some areas of public investment even experienced a decline between 1975 and 1981. This implied a very weak infrastructure system, especially for transportation and communications (see Viñals et al. 1990). The need for improvements led to a significant increase in investment in the late 1980s, in contrast with the reductions experienced by most other OECD countries. However, the level of the public capital stock is still low and requires further efforts.

4. DEFICIT FINANCING

A major feature of democratic Spain is the appearance of large budget deficits, which reached 7% of GDP in 1985. A consequence of repeated deficits has been the explosion of public debt. From about 13% of GDP, it went up to 45% in 1991 (see figure 2). Most of the increase occurred between 1979 and 1987.

Nevertheless, a significant proportion of the deficits was monetized, without which the debt increase would have been much more dramatic. In the late 1970s, Spain experienced very high inflation rates (up to 25%); in the 1980s, the inflation rate decreased, but total seigniorage remained at high levels because of increased implicit taxation on financial intermediation. In 1984, two restrictions were introduced in the banking sector: high reserve requirements (up to 20% of total deposits) and compulsory investment coefficients for low interest-rate treasury notes (up to 10% of total investment). The amount of seigniorage actually increased in the 1980s.[16] According to Repullo (1991), seigniorage revenues were 2.3% of GDP in 1990, against 1.6% in 1980.

The implicit taxation of the financial sector is being reduced through the process of financial integration into the European Community. Investment requirements were progressively eliminated until January 1993, while reserve requirements experienced a sharp reduction in March 1990.[17] The decline in implicit taxation, combined with a potential decline in the inflation rate caused by the process of monetary integration, will significantly reduce seigniorage revenues. This decline may represent more than 1% of GDP, or more than 5% of tax revenues.

While a significant proportion (more than 90%) of the deficit was financed by the Banco de España in the 1970s, its financing started to rely on short-term securities marketed in the early 1980s. Treasury notes (*Pagarés del Tesoro*) were introduced in 1981, treasury bills (*Letras del Tesoro*) in 1987; these two instruments represented about half the debt in 1990. The proportion of short-term debt actually increased in the late 1980s. In 1990, the average maturity was 1.4 years, against 2.6 years in 1986 (see González-Páramo et al. 1991). While the share of the debt held by nonresidents is rapidly increasing, most of it is still held by residents. In 1990, only 3.9% of the debt was held by nonresidents (see OECD 1992a); this proportion reached almost 15% in early 1993.

Given the large increase in debt in the 1980s, interest payments sharply increased, up to 3.5% of GDP in 1990. Nevertheless, the cost of servicing the debt is relatively low as it implies an average interest rate of 8% (compared to 15% for the interbank market rate). The reason for this low cost of the debt is that treasury notes yield only 5.5% (at least in the late 1980s). Some of these notes are held by banks through the compulsory coefficient of investment, and are thus included in the computation of seigniorage. The rest is voluntarily held by the public, as it represents an investment for tax-evaded income due to its anonymity.

While there is a presumption that the increase in the public debt caused a crowding out effect and an increase in domestic interest rates, there is no clear empirical evidence on this issue.[18]

5. THE PROCESS OF DECENTRALIZATION

The democratization of Spain was accompanied by a rapid process of decentralization. In 1978, regional governments (*Comunidades Autónomas*) were created, with a degree of autonomy depending upon the regions.[19] The autonomy of local authorities has increased substantially as far as expenditure is concerned. For example, some regions have almost full autonomy for education and health care. In 1990, expenditure by local governments represented 40% of total expenditure (excluding transfers). A negative aspect of the decentralization process has been the duplication of expenditure.

On the other hand, the possibility of raising taxes has heretofore been limited (except for the Basque country and Navarre). For example, local governments can raise a surtax on personal income and a tax on wealth. In 1990, local taxes represented only 13% of total taxes.

The other source of revenue for regional governments comes from transfers from the central government, specifically: i) automatic transfers, proportional to the central government tax revenues;[20] ii) transfers through the Fondo de compensación interteritorial (FCI) to finance new infrastructure; and iii) transfers tied to specific uses.

A disturbing trend among local governments has been the recent tendency to run increasing deficits. In 1991, the sum of regional deficits amounted to more than 1.5% of GDP. Moreover, local government accounted for 15% of total debt.[21] This development reduces the control of the central government on fiscal policies. In 1992, negotiations between the central administration and regional governments were undertaken to reduce the amount of overspending.

6. BUDGETARY PROCESS AND FISCAL POLICY

The central government has only limited control over fiscal decisions. First, regional governments and most public sector firms take autonomous decisions. Second, the central government seems to have great difficulty in controlling its expenditure.

The budget is first proposed by the minister of the economy and finance to the government. At this stage, expenditures are often revised upwards. The budget is then presented to the Parliament, where it is usually approved. However, additional credits are granted during the year, especially when revenue increases more than expected (these practices were reduced in the early 1990s). In the 1980s, these credits represented around 15% of the proposed budget. Furthermore, unused credits can be used in other categories of expenditure or in other years.

Two serious problems related to the budgeting process should be mentioned. First, the actual budget deficit always exceeds the proposed one.[22] This systematic bias (possibly explained by excessive optimism) undermines the credibility of the central government, especially when restrictive policies are subsequently announced. Another problem is that the share of automatic expenditure seems to be larger than in other countries, which makes a restrictive policy all the more difficult.

Although reform of the monitoring process for expenditure was planned in 1977, no change occurred until 1983. Moreover, the effort in this direction (an attempt to introduce program budgeting) seems to be totally insufficient (see Zapico 1988), especially given the substantial increase in expenditure. The background of the administration personnel and the incentive scheme are often inadequate for an efficient application of the budget. Thorough changes are still needed to reduce the highly bureaucratic nature of public administration and to improve the quality of its services and the efficiency of its management.

One of the most undesirable features of the lack of control over expenditure is the misuse of fiscal policy as a macroeconomic stabilizing instrument. Even though the budget deficit declined in the late 1980s, fiscal policy has actually been procyclical.[23] One of the main reasons for this development has been the strong increase in expenditure because the economy was booming and tax revenue was high. The evolution of the fiscal deficit has therefore exacerbated the business cycle, conflicting with the economic objectives of the government. To reduce inflation, the authorities had to rely heavily on monetary policy, with high interest rates leading to an overvalued currency and a large current account deficit.[24] The procyclical fiscal stance is likely to continue through the early 1990s, as the government is applying a more restrictive policy (the Plan de Convergencia) as the Spanish economy is entering a phase of very slow growth.[25]

7. CONCLUSIONS FROM THE SPANISH EXPERIENCE

Since 1977, the public sector in Spain has gradually but dramatically modified. While some of the changes followed a conscious process of reform, several items of the budget developed autonomously. Nevertheless, the long-run objective of catching up and harmonizing with other EC countries has remained an important focal point and has guided many decisions regarding change.

In some sense, the reform of the Spanish public sector can be judged highly successful. First, the tax reform has permitted implementation of a modern tax system, increasing the amount of revenue with little social resistance. Second, the size of the public sector and in particular the size of the public debt have remained at reasonable levels compared to the EC average and, contrary to the situation in other countries, do not represent a problem in the medium run. Moreover, while large government deficits were experienced in the mid-1980s, the primary deficit has been sharply reduced in the past few years.

Such an optimistic evaluation, however, ignores numerous short-comings that are becoming more apparent every day. The main problems are the following:

- Tax evasion is still pervasive, both for direct and indirect taxes. Too little effort has been devoted to reducing this problem, possibly because of a lack of political will and certainly a lack of resources (e.g., inspectors) in this area. An improvement in this direction should diminish the distortions created by the tax system, allowing for a reduction in tax rates.
- The monitoring of expenditure is insufficient. Moreover, both the quality of services of the public sector and its cost-efficiency are particularly low. This is especially true for social security (disability pensions, unemployment benefits, health care, etc.).
- Fiscal policy is misused as a macroeconomic stabilization instru-ment. In the late 1980s and early 1990s, the fiscal stance has been procyclical, thereby exacerbating the business cycle.
- The process of decentralization has led to a duplication of expenditure and to irresponsible fiscal behavior by regional authorities. This problem has intensified the two previous flaws mentioned.

Most of these problems could be foreseen early in the reform but were not addressed. While this passive behavior might partially be explained by the so-called Latin character, a deeper analysis is required. The laxity might be explained either by political or by economic factors. First, it might be that the political cost of being "tougher" was too high, given the enormous changes required. For example, doubling the tax burden in a few years might have been politically unacceptable.

From a more strictly economic point of view, the passivity of the authorities might simply be explained by high transition costs, espe-cially of human capital. For an efficient public sector, important investment in skilled labor is needed. But this is costly. First, a quantitative change in the administration entails the hiring of new skilled personnel, which is in short supply and faces high demand from the private sector. Second, a qualitative change in the existing administration is also needed. It should be remembered that the role of the state in the economy was drastically modified during the reform, with less intervention and a larger budget. Consequently, the function of public administrators has shifted from regulators to managers. Such a change for existing personnel might be even more costly than new hiring.

If either the political or economic costs of being "tougher" are high, the laxity might be optimal in the transition. Moreover, it should disappear over time. Thus, if these views are correct, the above problems should be reduced over time. The bad news is that there might be less political consensus in the future as the Socialist Party lost its absolute majority in 1993. This political evolution will make the reforms more difficult to implement in the future.

The above discussion suggests that a global evaluation of the timing of the reform is a difficult task.[26] One can talk of excessive gradualism in areas such as tax reform and of lack of reform in other areas. Leaving aside transition costs and neglecting political considerations, a more rapid pace of reform would have been desirable. On the other hand, it might be argued that gradualism allowed the Socialist Party to maintain its absolute majority and to successfully implement other reforms (see, e.g., Dewatripont and Roland 1992 on the virtues of gradualism when political factors are taken into account). Moreover, the numerous distortions existing in the economy might justify a gradual approach, as the cost of restructuring the private sector is higher. For example, Bacchetta and Dellas (1993) examine this issue in the context of trade policy and show that gradual reform might be optimal when capital markets are imperfect or when bankruptcy costs are high. In the context of public sector reform, allowing tax evasion by firms gives them more liquidity to restructure and reduces unemployment (and unemployment benefits). While a better result might be reached through an efficient tax system that includes tax breaks, the setting up of such a system is costly.

Finally, an important issue related to policy timing is the path of budget deficits. While the standard literature on political economy can easily explain the debt increase under democracy, the actual time path of its increase is more difficult to justify by using simple two-party models. A simpler explanation is that the cost of increasing tax revenue far exceeds the cost of increasing expenditure. Thus, if an increase in the size of government is desired, it is optimal to have a temporary deficit. Nevertheless, this explanation deserves further analysis, given that public expenditure also increased under Franco between 1958 and 1975 (from 13% to 25% of GDP), without leading to deficit.

While a 15-year horizon seems to be enough to evaluate a reform, a longer time span is desirable. This is especially so when the reform has been gradual. Thus, a longer horizon will allow us to determine whether Spain has implemented a very gradual or an incomplete reform of its public sector. Nevertheless, at this stage, and although several problems remain, the overall assessment of the Spanish fiscal reform is rather positive. It is not clear, however, that other reforming countries can easily replicate the Spanish experience, as they are likely to face conditions that are much less favorable. The pre-reform conditions in Spain were especially good, as both the level of expenditure and debt were at very low levels. It is much easier to increase expenditure than to decrease it, and any adjustment is less costly if the debt burden is low. In addition, the absolute majority of the government in power since reform made implementation much easier. It is unlikely that other countries, in particular East European countries, will experience such favorable conditions. The Spanish experience therefore shows that they have a difficult road ahead.

Table 1
Revenues, 1970–1991
(Percent of GDP)

	1970	1975	1980	1985	1990	1991
Total revenue	22.9	24.8	30.7	35.2	38.6	39.4
Total tax revenue	19.3	21.4	26.9	30.9	34.6	34.8
Taxes on income, profits, &						
capital gains	3.5	4.4	6.8	8.2	11.7	11.8
Individuals*	2.8	3.6	6.0	7.1	7.5	—
Corporate*	1.0	1.1	1.2	1.6	3.0	—
Taxes on goods & services	7.9	6.8	6.9	9.7	10.0	9.9
Taxes on production, sale,						
transfer, etc.	6.0	4.7	5.2	7.9	9.4	9.5
Customs & import duties	2.0	2.1	1.6	1.8	0.6	0.4
Social security contributions	7.9	10.3	13.2	13.0	12.9	13.1

*Computed from "Contabilidad Nacional de España" (base 1970), INE. Statistical Appendix, Banco de España, annual reports, 1987–1992. Given the difference in data sources, the sum of individual and corporate taxes does not correspond exactly to the line "Taxes on income, profits, & capital gains."

Source: "Actuación económica y financiera de las AA.PP. 1984 and 1991" (IGAE).

Table 2
Public Expenditure, 1970–1991
(Percent of GDP)

	1970	1975	1980	1985	1990	1991
Total expenditure	22.5	25.0	33.6	42.6	43.2	45.1
Public current consumption	8.5	9.2	13.4	14.6	15.1	15.6
Wages and salaries	6.7	7.2	9.8	10.5	10.9	11.3
Goods and services	1.4	1.6	2.9	3.1	3.2	3.3
Fixed capital consumption	0.4	0.4	0.9	1.0	1.0	1.0
Transfers	11.3	13.4	18.2	24.2	23.1	24.1
Transfers to households	7.6	9.3	12.2	14.3	14.5	15.3
Subsidies and capital						
transfers	1.9	2.1	3.7	4.7	3.5	3.2
Interest payments	0.6	0.5	0.7	3.4	3.5	3.2
Other current transfers	1.2	1.2	1.5	1.6	1.5	1.5
Gross investment	2.7	2.7	1.9	3.7	4.9	5.2

Source: "Actuación económica y financiera de las AA.PP. 1984 and 1991" (IGAE).

Figure 1
Government Revenue and Expenditure, 1970–1991
(% GDP)

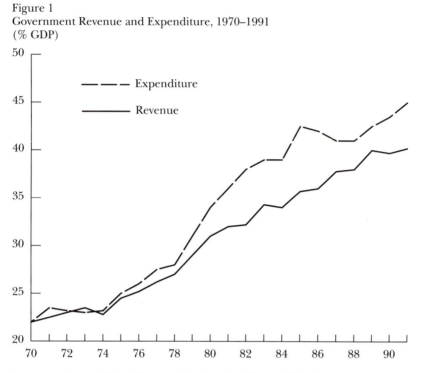

Source: "Contabilidad Nacional de España" (base 1970), Instituto Nacional
           de Estadistica. *Actuación económica y financiera de las Administraciones
           Publicas, 1991,* Intervención General de la Administración del Estado
           (IGAE).

Figure 2
Government Debt 1975–1991
(% GDP)

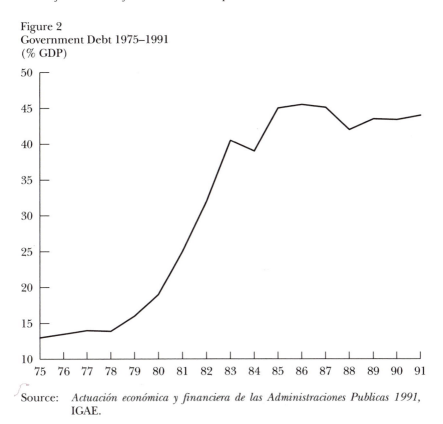

Source: *Actuación económica y financiera de las Administraciones Publicas 1991*, IGAE.

NOTES

This chapter benefited from comments by Val Koromzay and participants at the Institute for EastWest Studies conference on "Public Finance Reform in the Transitional Countries of East Central Europe" in Prague. I am grateful to Maite Pastor for research assistance.

1. See Lopez-Claros (1988) and Viñals et al. (1990) for a general analysis of the evolution of the Spanish economy in the last decades.

2. See Oxley and Martin (1991) for a recent analysis of the evolution of the public sector in OECD countries.

3. It was already mentioned that government intervention declined in the democracy. The relative size of public sector firms increased (it represented about 8% of GDP in 1985), but to a lesser extent than the budget.

4. General analyses of the evolution of the Spanish public sector can be found in various issues of *Papeles de Economía Española*, in several chapters in Albi (1990), and in Comín (1989a, 1989b), Fuentes Quintana (1991), González-Páramo (1992), and OECD (1989).

5. These increases are larger than the average increases experienced by OECD countries. See OECD (1992b) for a comparison.

6. An important structural change was the opening up of the economy. This has been a continuous process, beginning with the integration of goods markets and followed by the liberalization of capital movements in more recent years (for an analysis of this latter issue, see Bacchetta 1992).

7. See González-Páramo et al. (1987) for more details.

8. Nevertheless, this number previously increased by 169% between 1977 and 1979.

9. In 1983, the proportion of tax fraud for dependent workers was estimated to be 37%, while it was 75% for other individuals.

10. For example, the marginal tax rate for the "average" worker was 17% in 1979, 33% in 1986, and 27% in 1991 (see OECD 1989 and 1991). A major part of the increase in personal income tax revenue can be attributed to inflation.

11. See Carbajo (1991) for more details.

12. The EC Commission formally complained about it, as the contribution of EC members is proportional to their VAT revenues.

13. Reform of the social security system was part of the Moncloa agreements in 1977, but only organizational changes were undertaken.

14. The increase in transfers is partly explained by the strong recessions suffered by Spain from the two oil shocks.

15. Another reform took place in 1992.

16. Most of the increase came in 1989–1990, where the difference between the return on compulsory investment and market interest rates increased substantially.

17. See Bacchetta and Caminal (1992b) for an analysis of the impact of these reductions. The reduction of reserve requirements did not decrease revenues initially, as it was accompanied by the introduction of low interest (6%) Banco de España certificates of deposits. The certificates are being eliminated progressively until the year 2000. Reserve requirements were reduced further in 1992, to reach 3.5% of total deposits.

18. Ballabriga and Sebastián (1993), for example, find no relationship between government deficits and interest rates.

19. For example, the Basque country and, to a lesser extent, Catalonia got more autonomy than other regions.

20. The proportional factors are based on several factors such as population, per capita income, relative poverty level, etc.

21. Local authorities are allowed to raise debt in domestic currency, as long as the cost of debt servicing is less than 25% of revenue.

22. For example, the 1992 budget projected a deficit below 2%. In reality, this deficit will turn out to be more than 4% of GDP despite additional tax increases and expenditure reductions. It should be mentioned that in the late 1980s the Ministry of the Economy and Finance projected a zero deficit for 1992.

23. See González-Páramo et al. (1991) for estimates of the fiscal stance.

24. The overvaluation of the peseta was partially corrected in the fall of 1992, with two devaluations with respect to the Deutsche Mark.

25. It seems, however, that fiscal policy will be much less restrictive than presented by the government. See González-Páramo (1992).

26. A specific area where the timing might have been optimal is the temporary increase in implicit taxation of financial intermediaries. Such an increase can also be observed in other South European countries and was shown (theoretically) to be optimal before a liberalization of capital movements (see Bacchetta and Caminal 1992a).

REFERENCES

In English

Bacchetta, Ph. 1992. Abolishing Capital Controls in Spain: A Challenge for the Nineties. In *Economic Integration and Financial Liberalization: Prospects for Southern Europe*, ed. H. Gibson and E. Tsakalotos. London: Macmillan Press, pp. 173–94.

Bacchetta, Ph., and R. Caminal. 1992a. Optimal Seigniorage and Financial Liberalization. *Journal of International Money and Finance* 11, pp. 518–31.

————. 1992b. Reducing the Implicit Taxation on the Spanish Banking Sector: Who Gains and Who Loses. *ESADE Working Paper*, no. 88.

Bacchetta, Ph., and H. Dellas. 1993. Firm Restructuring and the Optimal Speed of Trade Reform. Mimeo.

Carbajo, D. 1991. The Spanish Experience with VAT. In OECD, *The Role of Tax Reform in Central and Eastern European Economies*. Paris.

Dewatripont, M., and G. Roland. 1992. The Virtues of Gradualism and Legitimacy in the Transition to a Market Economy. *Economic Journal* 102, no. 411, pp. 291–300.

González-Páramo, J.M., J.M. Roldán, and M. Sebastián. 1991. Issues on Fiscal Policy in Spain. Banco de España, *Documento de trabajo*, no. 9121.

Lopez-Claros, A. 1988. The Search for Efficiency in the Adjustment Process: Spain in the 1980s. IMF Occasional Paper no. 57.

OECD. 1989. *Economic Survey: Spain*. Paris.

————. 1991. *The Tax/Benefit Position of Production Workers*. Paris.

————. 1992a. *Economic Survey: Spain*. Paris.

————. 1992b. *Revenue Statistics of OECD Member Countries, 1965-1991*. Paris.

Oxley, H., and J.P. Martin. 1991. Controlling Government Spending and Deficits: Trends in the 1980's. *OECD Economic Studies* 17.

Repullo, R. 1991. Financing Budget Deficits by Seigniorage and Implicit Taxation: The Cases of Spain and Portugal. *CEMFI Documento de Trabajo*, no. 9105.

Viñals, J. et al. 1990. Spain and the EEC 1992 Shock. In *Unity with Diversity in the European Economy*, ed. C. Bliss and J. Braga de Macedo. New York: Cambridge University Press.

IN SPANISH

Albi, E., ed. 1990. *La Hacienda Pública en la Democracia*. Barcelona: Ariel Economía.

Ballabriga, F., and M. Sebastián. 1993. Deficit público y tipos de interés en la economía española: ¿existe evidencia de causalidad?. *Revista Española de Economía* (forthcoming).

Comín, F. 1989a. Las administraciones públicas. Ch. 9 in *España, economía*, ed. J.L. García Delgado. Madrid: Espasa-Calpe.

———. 1989b. Reforma tributaria y política fiscal. Ch. 23 in *España, economía. See* Comín 1989a.

Fuentes Quintana, E. 1991. La hacienda pública de la democracia española frente al proceso de integración europea. *Papeles de Economía Española*, no. 48, pp. 2–34.

———. 1989. Tres decenios de la economía española en perspectiva. In *España, economía. See* Comín 1989a.

González-Páramo, J.M. 1992. El papel del sector público español en el proceso de integración económica en Europa. Working paper, Universidad Complutense de Madrid.

González-Páramo, J.M., J.A. Rodríguez Ondarza, and J.J. Rubio Guerrero. 1987. El impuesto sobre la renta de las personas físicas: notas para un balance. *Papeles de Economía Española*, no. 30–31, pp. 108–37.

Lagares, M. et al. 1990. Fraude en el IRPF (1979–1987). Instituto de Estudios Fiscales, mimeo.

Lamo, A.R., and J.J. Dolado. 1991. Un modelo de mercado de trabajo y la restricción de oferta en la economía española. *Working Paper No. 9116*, Banco de España.

Myro, R. 1989. Las empresas públicas. Ch. 10 in *España, economía. See* Comín 1989a.

Zapico Goñi, E. 1988. La modernización del gasto público. *Papeles de Economía Española*, no. 37, pp. 465–81.

9

Comments on Bacchetta

VAL KOROMZAY

This very useful chapter by Philippe Bacchetta documents the modernization of tax and expenditure systems in Spain from 1977—following the re-establishment of democratic government after the demise of the Franco regime—to the present. In assessing the relevance of the Spanish experience for the countries of Central and Eastern Europe, I cannot but agree with the final conclusion of the author that whatever difficulties Spain has encountered in fiscal reform, those facing the countries of Central and Eastern Europe are substantially greater. In the case of Spain, the challenge was to move towards a "European" concept of the role of government and to establish tax and expenditure patterns consistent with it. In practice, this entailed a doubling of the size of government in proportion to GDP, over a period when GDP itself was growing relatively strongly. In the economies of Central and Eastern Europe, the challenge is to shrink the share of government at a time when GDP itself is falling sharply. If fiscal reform in Spain can be seen as a gradual process of rationalizing tax and budget arrangements in the context of a steady increase in the "social property rights" of Spanish citizens, in Central and Eastern Europe a similar rationalization of fiscal structures has to be linked to a *reduction* in the social income aspirations of the population. This is far more difficult task.

Bacchetta argues that because of the social and political difficulties of implementing fiscal reform, the Spanish approach that combined gradualism and a certain laxity in implementation was at least inevitable and perhaps even optimal in a broader perspective. I can go along with this up to a point—in a democratic system, a government cannot easily take or enforce measures whose consequence is that it is voted out of office. And clearly it takes time to develop the administrative capacities to run a fiscal system efficiently: there is no scope for a "big bang" approach to fiscal reform. But overall, I would emphasize that the countries of Central and Eastern Europe will need to be substantially more ambitious than Spain has been in terms of the speed of implementing reforms and the strength of the measures. From this perspective, there are five aspects of the Spanish experience documented in Bacchetta's chapter that seem to me to offer important cautionary examples.

First, the problem of tax evasion. Bacchetta cites evidence that as much as 43% of personal income goes unreported for tax purposes in Spain. He argues that some tolerance of tax evasion may be necessary to sustain political support for reform. A similar argument may be advanced in Central and Eastern Europe with even greater force: tax evasion by private citizens stimulates the development of the private sector. But I am not confident that tax morality is something that can be enforced "in the future." Habits of tax evasion, once established, are likely to become more and more deeply entrenched. Indeed, if tax evasion is not tackled energetically from the beginning, the legitimacy of taxation itself comes into question as people lose confidence in the fairness of the process. "Why should I pay taxes when others don't?"

Second, the issue of decentralization. Bacchetta has emphasized that the process of moving from a highly centralized system under Franco to one where there is substantial regional autonomy in fiscal matters has entailed increased budget expenditures through functional duplication, and some loss of control over fiscal policy. This is not a sufficient argument against decentralization—it could well be outweighed (quite aside from political considerations) by the advantages of having governments "closer to the people." I do think, however, that two cautionary remarks are in order. First, the power to tax and the decision to spend need to be united—to a substantial extent—within each level of government. The pleasure that local or regional governments derive from spending money needs to be counterbalanced by the pain they feel when they have to impose the taxes to pay for it. Second, effective limitations need to be imposed on the capacity of regional or local governments to borrow. Without such limitations, overall fiscal control is almost impossible to sustain.

Third, the question of seigniorage. It may be inevitable, during the transition phase, that some part of the budget is financed through implicit taxes on financial intermediation (this is not quite the formal definition of seigniorage, but I share Bacchetta's preference for viewing the matter in this light). But these implicit taxes are very expensive. They show up, one way or another, in a widened wedge between borrowing and lending rates in the economy as a whole and thus directly impinge on savings and investment. Furthermore, since these taxes are, at least up to a point, highly elastic with respect to the inflation rate, reliance on them makes disinflation that much more difficult to achieve.

Fourth, the problem of credibility. Bacchetta notes that in Spain, budget deficit out-turns are consistently worse than projected. This is a bad habit to get into, not least because it weakens discipline within the government and the Parliament. Obviously, in conditions of transition, projection errors—perhaps large ones—may be inevitable, and mid-course corrections are difficult. But once the habit of solving budget problems by wishing them away becomes entrenched, real solutions become almost impossible to find.

Fifth and finally, the issue of allowable deficits. As noted in Bacchetta's chapter, Spain started out from a position of very low public debt. The debt-to-GDP ratio exploded during the early 1980s, but has broadly stabilized since then—at around 45%, a moderate level by OECD standards. From this perspective (and I believe that the debt ratio is the key indicator for assessing the sustainability of budget deficits), Spain could afford to let expenditures run ahead of tax revenues to the extent that this in fact occurred. I am much less optimistic about the "room for maneuver" in the countries of Central and Eastern Europe—though there are clearly differences between them. The essential point is that, in all these countries, governments have massive contingent liabilities in the form of obligations to restructure banks and state enterprises; and all except the Czech Republic also have substantial recorded debt. I doubt if privatization receipts will compensate to any significant extent. Given these conditions, the scope for running sustainable budget deficits strikes me as very limited indeed.

To sum up, I would argue that while the reform task in Central and Eastern Europe is more difficult than that faced by Spain, these reforms will have to be undertaken with greater speed, and greater rigor.

About the Authors

Philippe Bacchetta, adjunct professor at the Autonomous University of Barcelona, specializes in problems of public finance in Europe, particularly regarding the Spanish economy.

Fabrizio Coricelli is an economist with the World Bank.

Marek Dabrowski, former Deputy Finance Minister of Poland, is currently Chairman of the Board of the Center for Social and Economic Research in Warsaw.

Alain de Crombrugghe, professor at the University of Namur in Belgium, has examined the economic transition in Poland for the OECD and has assisted Jeffrey Sachs and the Polish Ministries of Finance and of Privatization. He has concentrated his writings on the government budget and the economic transformation in Poland.

Milena Horcicova is Deputy Director of the Financial Policy Department in the Ministry of Finance of the Czech Republic.

Vera Kameníčková is a senior official at the Financial Policy Department in the Ministry of Finance of the Czech Republic.

Val Koromzay is Head of the Central and Eastern Europe Department of the Organization for Economic Cooperation and Development.

Kálmán Mizsei, Pew Economist-in-Residence at the Institute for EastWest Studies, has written extensively on structural reforms in postcommunist economies, in particular stabilization policies in Hungary and Poland during the transition to a market economy.

Jacek Rostowski is a professor at the University of London. He has been an advisor to the Polish government and the Russian government of Yegor Gaidar.

András Semjén is the Head of the Incomes and Social Policy Section at the Institute of Economic Policy and Planning in Budapest.

Pavel Štěpánek is Director of the Financial Policy Department in the Ministry of Finance of the Czech Republic.

Tessa van der Willigen, an economist at the International Monetary Fund and desk officer for the Czech and Slovak Federal Republic from 1990 until the January 1993 split, is currently concentrating on Slovakia. She has written on stabilization and structural reform in Czechoslovakia.

Drahomira Vaskova is an official at the Financial Policy Department in the Ministry of Finance of the Czech Republic.